ADVANCE READER COPY

UNCORRECTED PROOF

The text in this file is subject to minor changes before the official publication date.

Scheduled Release: January 7, 2026

Contact hello@modernherocollective.com for questions or feedback.

LEEWAY

Emerging Through the Modern Hero's Journey

THE MODERN HERO SERIES
BOOK 1

LEE MALCHER

COPYRIGHT AND PERMISSIONS

IMPORTANT DISCLAIMERS:

This book contains personal stories and experiences drawn from the author's life and work. To protect the privacy of individuals, certain names, identifying details, and circumstances have been changed or composited. Some dialogue has been reconstructed from memory and reflects the spirit rather than verbatim accuracy of conversations. Any resemblance to actual persons in these altered accounts is coincidental.

This book is not a substitute for professional advice.

This work is intended to be a philosophical, psychological, and spiritual guide for personal growth, self-reflection, and life direction. The theories and practices discussed—including Jungian concepts, the hero's journey framework, and references to altered states of consciousness and emotional integration—are drawn from the author's personal experience, research, and interpretations of various spiritual and psychological traditions. The information, anecdotes, and exercises provided are for educational and exploratory purposes only. They are not intended as, and should not be considered, medical, psychological, financial, or legal advice.

Always consult a qualified medical or mental health professional before making any significant changes to your physical or mental health regimen, especially if you have known medical conditions or are struggling with severe trauma, depression, or anxiety. The reader assumes full responsibility for their physical and emotional well-being while applying the concepts presented in this book.

THANKS

To everyone who has played a part, big or small, in my emergence—Thank you. This journey is richer because of you.

— Lee

"Deep in the human unconscious is a pervasive need for a logical universe that makes sense. But the real universe is always one step beyond logic."

- Frank Herbert, (Dune)

CONTENTS

ACKNOWLEDGMENTS

This book began as an idea planted by my close friend, Fletch, and grew through the steady support of my wife. But its roots run further back, woven through a lifetime of experiences and shaped by an amazing ensemble of people.

To my parents, whose unconditional love set the highest benchmark and provided a foundation of belonging that sustained me through every challenge. To my brothers, whose silent camaraderie and shared journey have been a constant source of strength.

To my two best men, whose humble insights and enduring friendship, built through shared adventures, have significantly impacted my path and whose banter has kept me grounded.

To my uncle, Andrew, who opened the door to the world of personal growth. And to Chris Kawaja, whose timely nudge helped me walk through it.

To Michael Mervosh and Josef Beraha of the Hero's Journey Foundation, and to the men's groups I've been involved with—all of whom have provided unguarded havens for genuine self-reflection, challenging growth, and valuable connection with fellow travelers and wise elders.

To the mentors and guides I've met along the way and the many therapists, facilitators, and participants in my retreat experiences whose wisdom and shared vulnerability have lit my path.

Even to past relationships and experiences that, though sometimes painful, inadvertently guided me to confront my ego, embrace my demons, and ultimately understand the nature of authentic connection and love.

Finally, to my wife, whose brilliant mind, unwavering belief in me, and boundless love continue to light my way as we journey side by side. This book would not exist without your support, insights, and patience.

DEFINITIONS

lee /liː/ *noun*

- A sheltered space, a place of calm amidst the swirling winds of life: *in the lee of the boulder.*
- A clearing, an opening within a protective barrier from the elements.
- In nautical terms, the side sheltered or protected from the wind.

way /weɪ/ *noun*

- A path, route, or direction for traveling from one place to another.
- A method, manner, or means for doing something.
- A journey or progress through life.

leeway /ˈliːweɪ/ *noun*

- Extra space needed to adjust course when forces push you sideways.

classic hero /ˈklæsɪk ˈhɪroʊ/ *noun*

- A being of exceptional strength and courage, often possessing divine connections or extraordinary abilities.
- Example: Superman, with his otherworldly powers.

modern hero /ˈmɒdərn ˈhɪroʊ/ *noun*

- An individual whose primary journey centers on overcoming internal struggles, confronting personal flaws, and striving for self-understanding.
- Example: You, navigating life's complexities and striving to become a better version of yourself.

PREFACE

At some point, every one of us stands at a crossroads. We feel the weight of expectations pressing down, the stubborn pull of old patterns, the whispering voice of fear. We sense there's something more—something more real, something more alive—but the path forward is shrouded in uncertainty. I've stood at that crossroads more times than I care to count.

And for the last five years, I've carried what I can only describe as a nagging calling to write this book—a persistent, almost overwhelming urge that created genuine anxiety as I felt time constantly running against me. This restlessness was particularly challenging while juggling a demanding professional career and other responsibilities, especially since writing wasn't something I'd ever done before. The irony isn't lost on me that a book exploring the Hero's Journey and internal conflict was itself born from my own internal struggle with a calling I both yearned to answer and found reasons to postpone.

This nagging feeling—this sense of something incomplete, something waiting to be expressed—is exactly what we'll explore together in these pages. My resistance to writing this book mirrored the very "refusal of the call" stage I describe in the Hero's Journey, later. The tension between knowing I needed to write this and finding countless practical reasons why I couldn't or shouldn't, became its own kind of threshold crossing.

It was during this internal tug-of-war that I found myself drawn to the wisdom of ancient seafaring traditions, searching for a metaphor that could capture both the challenge and the opportunity of navigating life's uncertainties.

Throughout history, sailors embarking on perilous journeys across vast, unpredictable oceans have relied on a crucial concept called leeway. When powerful storms, winds, and currents threatened to push them off course, these seafarers sought the sheltered side of an island (a "lee") where winds calm and waters settle. This protected space allowed them to pause and reassess while maintaining enough room to maneuver their "way" back on course toward their destination. This dual wisdom of finding shelter while maintaining adaptability became known as leeway. Just as sailors navigate treacherous waters toward distant shores, our human journey toward growth and potential demands both: sheltered spaces for rest and reflection, and just enough margin to adjust as we navigate life's unpredictable currents.

Through my own struggles and growth, I've come to recognize three essential elements that support personal transformation—what I've come to call LeeWay: finding shelter for much-needed respite and deep reflection, creating space to adjust course amid life's unpredictable currents, and gathering support from fellow travelers. These three things together form the foundation for navigating life with resilience, authenticity, balance, and purpose. When we honor our need for sanctuary while maintaining the ability to maneuver, and surround ourselves with the right support, we can engage with life's challenges and opportunities. Through this balanced approach, we emerge as modern heroes—not in a single moment of triumph, but through a lifelong practice of courageous and conscious living. LeeWay doesn't eliminate life's storms; it provides the wisdom to sail through them while staying true to your authentic course.

In that spirit of vulnerability, I really have to address something that's been keeping me up at night: the title of this book. When I realized the connection between "leeway" and my own name, an internal battle erupted between my ego and my deeper self. Would naming a book about ego transcendence after myself seem a bit hypocritical? Would readers see it as self-promotion?

But the thing is, this agonizing internal conflict perfectly exemplifies the central theme of this book: the ongoing dance between ego and soul that defines our journey toward self-actualization. The very fact that I questioned my motivations and wrestled with this decision—that's the essence of the modern Hero's Journey.

The classic hero possesses exceptional strength and courage, often with divine connections. The modern hero, though, must overcome internal struggles, confront flaws, and strive for self-understanding. They navigate loneliness, use introspection for growth, and recognize when to reach for connection as challenges overwhelm.

"Leeway: Emerging Through the Modern Hero's Journey" is the book I wish I had as a young man beginning my own journey. It swings between deep reflection and my admittedly humble attempts at British humor— and heads up, it occasionally wanders through strange anecdotes and metaphorical rabbit holes that reveal unexpected insights. Throughout these pages, you'll witness my struggles with ego, my moments of both insight and blindness, my successes and failures.

I've come to understand that growth is an unstoppable force, encoded into the very nature of the universe. I've also come to understand that resistance to this force can often lead to our most significant conflicts. By combining perspectives from psychology, drawing on the foundational work of thinkers like Carl Jung and Abraham Maslow, the universal narratives found in mythology through the lens of Joseph Campbell, and insights from science and spirituality, this understanding creates a purpose-driven approach to life. When combined with the ongoing prac- tice of the Hero's Journey, it's designed to activate and realize true human potential, transcending the limits imposed by conventional beliefs.

My journey was shaped by an ensemble of mentors—from my parents who set the benchmark for love, to my wife Brooke who showed me true love's boundless horizons. The Hero's Journey Foundation provided an unguarded haven, while even my past relationships inadvertently guided me to confront my ego and embrace my demons.

One final thing: In this book, I try not to present myself as a guru or sage with all the answers, but as a fellow traveler instead—still failing and still learning, but has mapped some of the territory ahead. I offer my expe- riences as we navigate this collective journey together. This book is an invitation to pause, find wisdom in shared stories, and to create space for powerful transformation.

I'd be lying if I said the self I was five years ago when I began this project is the same self writing these final words. Some of the views and perspectives shared here have probably shifted—subtly, perhaps, but shifted nonetheless. If you spot these evolutions, I hope you'll see them not as flaws, but as evidence of the book's central premise: the Hero's Journey is an unending spiral of continuous becoming, where today's certainty gives way to tomorrow's deeper insight. We're all always emerging.

So, whether you're at a crossroads now or sensing one approaching on your horizon, my hope is that somewhere in these pages, you'll find a spark—a flicker of awareness from which growth naturally unfolds. Think of this as your roadmap of inspiration and encouragement, ready whenever you choose to take that heroic next step into the unknown.

GROWTH & EVOLUTION

From Stardust to Self-Discovery

THE HERO'S JOURNEY

You've Been On It This Whole Time (You Just Didn't Know It)

The makeshift tent of Roy Bell's traveling boxing show barely contained the potent cocktail of stale beer, sweat, and sawdust that hung in the air. There I stood, a skinny 18-year-old English lad with flowing locks, my bony shoulders draped in a neon yellow satin robe, checkered Vans on my feet, facing a furious Indigenous fighter whose eyes carried generations of righteous anger. This was no professional arena—just a weathered tarp stretched over poles, a worn canvas mat laid on top of sawdust, and a *Fight Club*-style circle of spectators serving as the only boundary between combatants. The crowd pressed in close enough to feel their breath, becoming living ropes that contained the action. This traveling sideshow, one of Australia's last remaining tent boxing outfits, had been touring the Australian circuit since the 1920s—a bizarre carnival tradition where seasoned street brawlers took on local challengers for cash and glory. One thing's for sure, this really wasn't the adventure I'd imagined when I'd fled my mundane existence back home.

Just months earlier, I'd been trapped in fluorescent-lit purgatory, selling questionable infomercial products on late-night TV. Each morning I'd knot my tie with a growing sense of dread, watching it transform from an innocent workplace accessory into what felt increasingly like a ceremonial noose for my dreams.

At 18 years old, wasn't life supposed to be an adventure rather than a sentence?

While mates shared tales of gap-year explorations and university escapades, I tracked sales figures and memorized scripts about abs-of-steel gadgets that probably belonged in a tombola of questionable inventions. So I hatched my escape plan, squirreling away every pound I could spare, building a financial runway alongside my courage. When I finally had enough for a one-way ticket to Australia, I leapt without a safety net—joining my childhood best mate, Danny, who was already carving his path through that sun-drenched continent. Little did I know that my desperate bid for freedom would lead me into experiences that would completely dismantle and rebuild who I was.

This carnival adventure began when Danny burst through the door of our shared apartment in a small Australian outback town one sweltering afternoon. "Pack your bags, Lee—NOW!" he announced with a mischievous glint in his eye. "I've found us a ride east, but there's a twist—you're going to have to fight along the way. And he's outside waiting, so we need to move!"

"Are you having a laugh?" I sighed, already scrambling for my belongings, wondering what he'd gotten us into this time. My fighting "experience" consisted of a few schoolyard scuffles and one or two scraps in this outback town—the kind of fights outsiders inevitably face—nothing remotely close to the blood-and-sawdust world of prizefighting.

With a churning mixture of terror and exhilaration, I quickly stuffed my life into a backpack and followed Danny outside—only to stop in my tracks at the sight waiting for us. "You're joking," I muttered, but Danny was already throwing his bag up. With no other option, I climbed aboard what can only be described as a Mad Max vehicle made from scrapyard bits and bobs that never quite made it to the final cut. I'm honestly not exaggerating here—this wasn't just some beaten-up old campervan—it was literally a weird mash-up of **three** different vehicles fused together: a white truck cab fused to a separate middle section added for extra passenger space, with a massive metal shipping container strapped to the flatbed behind it. The whole thing looked like it had been assembled during an apocalypse by someone with access to a welding torch, three entirely different vehicles, and a disregard for what a vehicle should actually look like. Inside, rickety bunks were hammered together from scrap metal, topped with worn mattresses where springs poked through like metallic weeds. Threadbare blankets were our only protection from the jumble of boxing tent equipment and installation gear haphazardly thrown into every available space. The rattling alone suggested it was held together by nothing more substantial than luck and stubbornness. Behind the wheel sat Michael, a towering figure with hands like weathered shovels and a face that suggested he'd seen every hardship the outback could conjure and found them all mildly amusing. As we prepared to depart, I watched with a mixture of fascination and horror as he casually hot-wired the ignition—no keys necessary for this particular ride. This ramshackle contraption made perfect sense when I learned that Michael's family, Roy Bell's troupe, had been traveling the Australian circuit since the 1920s—generations of making do with whatever would get them to the next town.

There was the 'Young Moree Mauler' with knuckles that never seemed to heal—partly because he was always picking and biting at the scabs; 'Fugzi' who we'd literally just picked up from the juvenile detention center, gap-toothed grin and all, though it never quite reached his wary eyes; and then there was another lad who said absolutely nothing, just sat in the corner watching us with a stillness that was somehow more unnerving than all the scabs and suspicious grins combined.

For endless days we traveled, our bodies packed into cramped quarters of the shipping container that offered little respite from the heat or each other. The makeshift bunks felt like premature coffins, the truck's rusted door secured by nothing more than a frayed rope tied to a screwdriver wedged in the latch—our improvised lock against the vast, unknown Australian night. Picture that for a security system—or a death trap!

When we reached the fairground, we transformed the empty spaces into arenas of contained violence. The Big Top Boxing ring was bare-bones —more reminiscent of an underground setup like the one in *Fight Club* than a professional venue. In exchange for our labor erecting this temple of testosterone (yeah, I know how that sounds), we received basic accommodation, simple meals, and the promise of a cut from our fight earnings. Around the weathered mat, spectators gathered in rings of increasing bloodlust, many openly hoping to see the skinny English lad take a proper beating. Charming crowd, really.

The carnival's reputation drew rough men from every corner—miners with fists shaped by years of breaking stone, farmhands whose muscles had been shaped in daily battle with the unforgiving land. I quickly realized my role in this theater of masculinity—I was the sacrificial lamb, the appetizer before the main course of "real" fights.

When showtime arrived, mustard-yellow banners promising "Nobody Barred" and "Cash Prizes" fluttered in the evening breeze as Michael, our ringleader, worked crowds into frenzies with practiced showmanship, flashing those gold teeth whenever he grinned. We fighters stood on elevated platforms like exotic animals, instructed to pose menacingly to entice potential challengers. Learning that Danny hailed from Yorkshire, Michael—never one to miss a marketing trick—rebranded him as "The Son of the Yorkshire Ripper" fresh off the boat and hungry for Australian blood. A bit dramatic and controversial, but effective, I'll give him that.

After awkward sparring sessions clearly revealed me as the weak link in our troupe, Michael wasted no time casting me in my role—the opening warm-up act. Think court jester, but with boxing gloves. I was bait, thrown in to whet the appetite of the crowd and draw them in for the "real" fights to come. And my first exhibition match? A cruel twist of fate pitted me against Danny, my brother-in-arms and only ally in this strange new world. Brilliant.

So there I stood, face to face with my best mate, both of us encircled by a ring of eager strangers beneath the canvas tent's dim lights. We'd shared everything from schoolboy antics to the last scraps of food in our backpacks, and now we were supposed to punch each other senseless for the entertainment of drunk strangers. Life has a wicked sense of humor sometimes.

A few hundred pairs of eyes watched in the dusky twilight, their collective hunger for violence almost tangible in the air. The crowd's restlessness grew with each passing second, the murmurs swelling into a low growl of impatience. Sweat trickled down my spine, though it wasn't from the heat.

Danny caught my gaze, a silent conversation passing between us. With the subtlest movement, he signaled for me to throw the first punch—a courtesy I hadn't expected. I hesitated, my gloves suddenly feeling like lead weights. Was this some psychological tactic? A way to get me to expose myself?

The crowd's growl transformed into jeers. Someone shouted for action. Beer splashed near the edge of our makeshift ring.

I watched as Danny's face transformed before me. His expression suddenly shifted from encouragement to resignation, his head dipping in reluctance, his face falling, and his eyes closing momentarily.

The next thing I knew? His fist cracked my jaw like a bloody sledgehammer.

The impact sent me stumbling backward, my brain registering both pain and surprise. Had we traveled halfway around the world together for this? To become adversaries in a dusty ring? The crowd roared its approval as I steadied myself, tasting blood on my lip. I locked eyes with Danny, seeing a flash of apology before his fighter's instinct took over again. Right then, I understood—in this world, friendship had to take a backseat to survival.

For three punishing rounds, we traded blows, each impact testing the very foundation of our friendship. Doubts flooded my mind between gasps for breath: Was there some hidden resentment fueling Danny's attacks? Had he been waiting all these years for a legitimate excuse to rearrange my face?

Just paranoid thoughts, I told myself—the desperate rationalizations of an insecure 19-year-old kid getting the shit knocked out of him by his best mate, the one with actual fighting experience. Danny, meanwhile, was clearly enjoying the chance to unleash the pent-up annoyance built up from sharing every minute on the road together for the last few months. Seems he figured out a more physical alternative to the silent treatment. Fantastic.

The paranoia clung to me like the sweat on my back. Three rounds of punishment had left me with one burning question: Would our friendship survive the bell?

When the final bell rang, we paused briefly to catch our breath. Then, bloodied and exhausted, we embraced, discovering a newfound level of respect and connection that hadn't existed before. Our friendship hadn't broken under pressure; instead, it had turned into something stronger through our shared experience of fear, doubt, surrender, and courage. This unique bond between Danny and me remains unshakable to this day.

While my fight with Danny tested the bonds of friendship, my bouts against the Indigenous fighters connected me to Australia's complex racial history in ways I never anticipated.

Their fury felt fueled by something more than just the immediate fight —a response to generations of oppression and pain. I later learned about the tent's complicated history, where Indigenous boxers were often under-paid or not paid at all, exhibited as "darkies" for the entertainment of white crowds. For many, it was simply a way to make ends meet when other opportunities were scarce. Yet in a strange way, these tents were also rare spaces where races mixed and Indigenous Australians could find moments of empowerment through their skill and strength. How fitting that I, a pasty English kid, would face three Indigenous fighters nightly for a week! Talk about karma, eh?

Each of those fights was character-building hell—three minutes that stretched into small eternities of pain and determination. I sometimes wondered if being spared the fights with members of the audience was a blessing or a curse, as my Indigenous opponents seemed to take an awful lot of pleasure in demonstrating their prowess against me. Can't say I blamed them. Yet despite the humbling I was taking, something unex-pected happened: I discovered depths of resilience I never knew I possessed. The crowd, initially hoping to see me take a beating, began to cheer my stubborn refusal to stay down. Bloodied but never broken, I earned their grudging respect.

The boxing tent changed me in ways no university course ever could. Look, there's something brutally honest about getting punched in the face repeatedly—it strips away bullshit and shows you exactly who you are. I learned that resilience and perseverance mean getting back up round after round, when that little voice in your head is getting louder and louder, begging you to stay down and give up. That ring taught me humility without crushing my spirit and the importance of keeping your wits about you always. But most of all, amid all that controlled volatility, I discovered the potential for connection through conflict.

After our prizefighting stint, Danny and I saved enough to leave the carnival behind and found ourselves in a little surf town paradise where, after some much-needed R&R, we decided to go our separate ways for a time. While I instinctively clung to the familiar comfort of our friendship, Danny recognized what I couldn't yet see—that true growth required us to create independent paths. That separation, painful as it was, forced me to face my deepest fears about standing alone in the world.

For two more years, I continued my adventures down under, immersing myself in the laid-back coastal lifestyle, forming bonds that would last a lifetime. This period of sun-soaked discovery took on new life when two of my oldest other friends joined me for eight unforgettable months.

So that's how I went from selling quirky gadgets on late-night TV to getting my arse handed to me in the Australian Outback—and somehow finding myself in the process.

And I know what you're thinking—what does any of this have to do with your life? Fair question. But here's what I discovered years later that changed everything for me: that story wasn't actually unique at all. It turns out my adventure, and most other similar adventures, actually follow an ancient pattern—one that appears in stories spanning every culture, era, and continent on Earth. This same pattern has been recognized by shamans teaching initiates, mythologists studying legends, and psychologists mapping human development too. From Odysseus to Luke Skywalker, from Buddha to Batman, this universal pattern reveals how ordinary people have been transforming through extraordinary challenges for millennia.

Without knowing it, I'd lived through the world's most fundamental narrative—the same story humans have been telling around fires since language began. And it all revolves around a question as old as storytelling itself: What transforms an ordinary person into a hero?

WHAT IS A HERO?

When we hear the word "hero," what images flash through our minds? Caped crusaders leaping tall buildings? Mythic warriors with divine gifts? These archetypes have certainly shaped our collective imagination. But I've come to understand that there's something more complex—and far more attainable—at the heart of heroism.

The classic hero, with superhuman strength and otherworldly powers, makes for captivating stories. But this vision of heroism can feel really distant from our everyday experiences, leaving us as passive spectators rather than active participants in our own heroic becoming.

I remember watching superhero movies as a kid, feeling that familiar mix of awe and, if I'm honest, a twinge of discouragement. How could an ordinary kid like me ever measure up to such extraordinary standards? Those heroes never seemed to doubt themselves or struggle with the mundane challenges that filled my days. Their heroism felt like a different species of experience altogether.

As I've grown older, and after weathering my fair share of life's storms (spoiler: there were more than a few)—from those boxing matches in the Australian outback to corporate boardrooms, from relationships that shattered me to connections that healed me—I've come to understand heroism very differently. To me, the modern hero isn't defined by superpowers or special bloodlines, but by something far greater—their willingness to take on the messy work of becoming fully human.

The modern hero faces battles that rarely make headlines: confronting inner fears and insecurities, navigating feelings of disconnection, questioning inherited values, and summoning the courage to live authentically even when it would be easier to conform. The modern hero's challenges aren't against supervillains but against the subtle but powerful forces of doubt, inertia, and fear that keep us small.

The journey of the modern hero centers on overcoming internal struggles, confronting personal flaws, and striving for self-understanding. It involves navigating periods of loneliness and making use of solitude for growth. Here's what took me years to learn: true heroism often means acknowledging when we can't do it alone—when we need to reach out, be vulnerable, and ask for help. That's been the hardest part for me. Maybe it is for you too.

I see this modern heroism playing out in the parent who breaks generational patterns of trauma; in the professional who risks financial security to pursue more meaningful work; in the friend who faces their addiction and begins the vulnerable work of recovery. I see it in small acts of courage that never make the evening news but slowly transform lives and communities.

The modern hero might possess flaws, limitations, and imperfections —but it's exactly these qualities that make them heroic. Their heroism lies in their ability to learn, grow, and persevere through challenges while remaining deeply human. They remind us that growth isn't about becoming superhuman but about becoming more fully who we already are.

When I look back at my own stumbling journey, I don't see a straight line to success—but more like a spiral of continuous becoming. Each challenge wasn't just an obstacle to overcome but an invitation to evolve. Each failure wasn't just a setback but a lesson in humility and resilience.

In this day and age where we're all scrolling endlessly between dopamine hits, where we curate perfect travel photos while feeling strangely absent from our own experiences, many of us encounter a nagging emptiness. We mistake this inner restlessness for a problem to solve, a void to fill with external validation or the next superficial fix. But what if this discomfort isn't something broken? What if it's actually a call toward something greater? What if everything we really seek already dwells within us—not waiting to be purchased or accomplished, but to be discovered, understood, and lived out? Whether we dream of being caped vigilantes saving the day or wanderlusting vagabonds exploring distant shores, this universal yearning for something more isn't a flaw—it's the first whisper of purpose, an invitation to uncover the richer life waiting just beneath the surface of our distracted days.

That's the essence of the modern hero—not perfection but progress, not conquest but transformation, not isolation but connection. The Hero's Journey isn't reserved for the chosen few with extraordinary powers; it's the birthright of every person willing to engage with life's biggest questions and challenges.

Remember that sailor's wisdom from the beginning of this book? Just as they seek lee—a sheltered space where winds calm—and maintain leeway to adjust course, modern heroes need protected spaces for renewal, flexibility amid life's currents, and support from fellow travelers. This trinity of shelter, space, and support forms the foundation for navigating life with resilience and authenticity. When we honor all three aspects, we can face life's challenges not as threats to be avoided, but as opportunities for growth, emerging as heroes through an ongoing practice of conscious, courageous living.

You—yes, you—reading these words right now, navigating your own complex life with all its joys and sorrows, possibilities and limits, are already on a Hero's Journey. The everyday person who faces fears, seeks moments of self-reflection, and strives to become a better version of themselves is a modern hero whose journey inspires us all.

The question isn't whether you can become a hero—it's whether you'll recognize the heroic journey you're already on and engage with it deliberately, with courage and an open heart. But unlike those cinematic heroes who reach a final victory, the modern hero understands that each triumph simply opens the door to the next adventure. There is no final destination —only continuous cycles of growth.

That's where the Hero's Journey comes in—a roadmap for growth, a guide through the trials that shape us into the heroes we're meant to be.

So brace yourself as we explore the modern Hero's Journey together. I promise fewer punches than my outback odyssey...or at least I hope so! But like my time in that sweaty tent, this journey will challenge you, change you, and reveal the hero waiting within.

WHAT IS THE HERO'S JOURNEY?

Years after my Australian adventure, I discovered Joseph Campbell's work on the "monomyth" and the *Hero's Journey*. It instantly resonated with me —like that moment when someone finally names something you've felt your whole life but could never quite put into words. You know what I mean?

You see, the Hero's Journey is this pattern that just shows up everywhere—*Star Wars*, *The Matrix*, your cousin's gap year in Thailand. Campbell spotted something that cultures have been telling stories about forever: regular people becoming heroes not because they suddenly develop superpowers, but because they actually show up for the messy business of growing. They hear some kind of call (usually when life's comfortable but boring), face their demons (literal or metaphorical), and come back different. Simple formula, absolute nightmare to live through.

Looking at my outback boxing experience through this lens, I can see now how I was unknowingly following this ancient template. I left my ordinary world of office boredom, crossed the threshold into the unknown (quite literally in that Mad Max contraption), faced trials in the boxing ring that tested more than just my physical strength, and eventually returned transformed.

What makes Campbell's framework so valuable for us modern heroes isn't its structured neatness but its practical truth. The Hero's Journey describes the universal human experience of breaking free from inherited limitations to discover something more authentic. It maps how transformation actually works—not just what changes, but how that change unfolds.

This journey isn't about becoming some idealized, perfect version of yourself. It's about stripping away what isn't really you to reveal the authentic Self beneath. The discomfort, struggles, and moments of despair aren't detours—they're essential parts of the path.

Understanding this journey provides context for our challenges and reassurance that difficulties serve a purpose. When you recognize where you are on this path, even the darkest moments gain meaning as necessary stops on your journey.

So let's explore the stages and steps of this journey that connects us to heroes across time and cultures, not because we seek to battle dragons or save kingdoms, but because we seek to live with authenticity, purpose, and courage in our modern world.

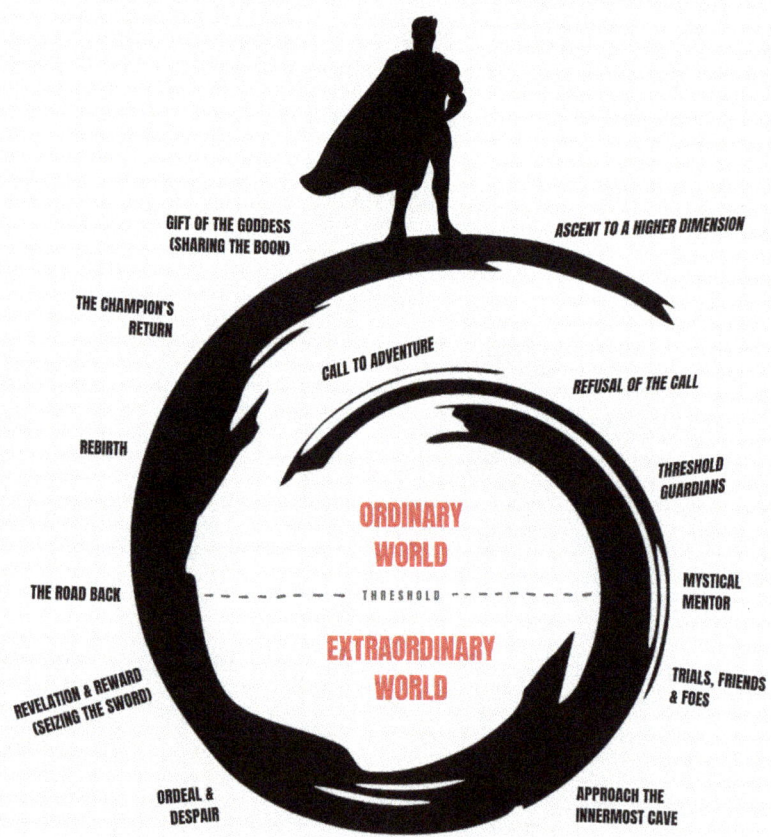

THE *HERO'S* JOURNEY

GIFT OF THE GODDESS
(SHARING THE BOON)

ASCENT TO A HIGHER DIMENSION

THE CHAMPION'S
RETURN

CALL TO ADVENTURE

REFUSAL OF THE CALL

REBIRTH

THRESHOLD
GUARDIANS

ORDINARY
WORLD

THRESHOLD

THE ROAD BACK

MYSTICAL
MENTOR

EXTRAORDINARY
WORLD

REVELATION & REWARD
(SEIZING THE SWORD)

TRIALS, FRIENDS
& FOES

ORDEAL &
DESPAIR

APPROACH THE
INNERMOST CAVE

Figure 1.1: The Hero's Journey Cycle. The map you didn't know you needed. This circular path shows how heroes (yes, including you) move through transformation— leaving the familiar, facing trials in the unknown, and returning changed. Spoiler: the journey never really ends; it just spirals deeper.

THE HERO'S JOURNEY: 3 STAGES, 13 STEPS FOR THE MODERN HERO

Stories across time and cultures share a common pattern—what Campbell called the Hero's Journey. From ancient myths to modern blockbusters, this pattern shows up again and again because it mirrors something real about how we grow and change.

While Campbell studied these patterns in traditional myths featuring supernatural heroes, this same framework applies perfectly to us as modern heroes—those everyday individuals navigating internal struggles, confronting personal flaws, and striving for self-understanding. Our battles may be in boardrooms rather than battlefields, our demons may be self-doubt rather than fire-breathing dragons, but the core structure of transformation remains remarkably consistent.

Campbell mapped this journey into three main stages—the departure stage, the initiation stage, and the return stage—with each containing smaller steps that mark the hero's path. But don't let the neat structure fool you. These aren't rigid boxes to check off; they're more like landmarks on a winding trail, sometimes visited out of order, sometimes circled back to, sometimes barely recognizable until you've passed them.

What makes this framework so valuable for us modern heroes isn't its neat structure but its practical truth. These stages reveal pathways through our inner worlds, showing us how transformation actually works as we search for genuine meaning and our authentic Self in a complex, often disconnected modern world.

STAGE 1: DEPARTURE—LEAVING WHAT YOU KNOW

Have you ever felt that restless itch that something needs to change? That's where the Hero's Journey begins—with departure.

For us modern heroes, the departure stage marks the beginning of our journey toward authentic living. It's that first bold (or terrifying) step away from the familiar and into the unknown—leaving the comfort of certainty for the discomfort of possibility.

While fictional heroes like Luke Skywalker gaze at alien suns or Neo takes the red pill, our departures rarely come with special effects. Maybe yours looks like questioning a career path that society approves of but leaves us empty, or perhaps examining a relationship pattern that repeats but never fulfills, or challenging belief systems we've inherited but never truly examined. The modern hero's departure usually happens inside us before it shows up in our actions.

The thing I've noticed about departure—both in my own life and watching others—is that we fight this stage like hell. Our brains are hard-wired to cling to the known, even when the known is slowly draining our souls. I've found that, for the modern hero, it often takes a significant disruption—a health scare, a relationship breakdown, a career setback, or simply that quiet but persistent voice whispering "there must be more than this"—to shake us loose from our comfortable patterns and get us moving.

Step 1: The Ordinary World—Where We Begin

Every hero starts somewhere ordinary. Before any hero embarks on their extraordinary journey, they first must exist in what Campbell calls "the ordinary world"—the realm of the familiar, the routine, the expected. This is the starting point, the status quo that will eventually be disrupted.

For Luke Skywalker, it was a dusty farm on a forgotten planet. For Bilbo Baggins, the cozy comforts of his hobbit hole. For me, it was a soul-sucking job at a TV shopping network in a small English town, where I spent my days helping to sell questionable gadgets to insomniacs and spent my evenings wondering if this was really all life had to offer.

I can still feel the weight of that tie each morning—shuffling through corporate pleasantries, sitting in fluorescent-lit meetings where minutes dragged endlessly, tracking sales figures of abs-of-steel gadgets that probably belonged in a museum of dubious inventions. Meanwhile, my friends were off having gap-year adventures.

Desperate to inject some excitement into my life, I made the question-able choice to appear on reality TV—a decision that resulted in mortifying footage of me giving a lap dance on national television while sporting a regrettable haircut that made me look like a confused sheepdog. Not my finest moment. But even this embarrassing bid for escape only highlighted how desperately I needed a real change.

The ordinary world isn't inherently bad. For some, it's a place of comfort and security. But for the hero-in-waiting, it eventually becomes too small, too limiting. There's a growing awareness that something essential is missing, a restlessness that can't be soothed by the usual distractions.

I felt this strongly during my snowy evening commutes, the haunting lyrics of a song "Everybody's Changing" striking a chord so intense I couldn't ignore it anymore. My friends' tales of adventures made me feel like a caged animal, pacing the ever-shrinking confines of a life I was outgrowing by the day.

What about your ordinary world? Maybe it's a relationship that once worked on paper but lacks real connection. Perhaps it's a belief system that once provided certainty but now feels hollow, or a community that once embraced you but now expects conformity. Whatever form it takes, the ordinary world is the starting point we must eventually leave behind to discover who we truly are.

Step 2: The Call to Adventure

The call to adventure is that key moment when the universe taps you on the shoulder (or sometimes smacks you square in the face) and says: "It's time for something different." This call disrupts the ordinary world, presenting an opportunity or challenge that requires you to venture beyond your comfort zone.

Sometimes the call comes as a whisper—a book that changes your perspective, a chance encounter that plants a seed of possibility, a recurring dream that sticks with you. Other times it arrives as a shout—a job loss, a health crisis, the end of a relationship. Whether gentle invitation or forceful ejection, the call to adventure marks the point where the familiar path forks, and a new possibility emerges.

My call came in the form of my childhood friend Danny bursting through the door of our shared Australian apartment, eyes gleaming with that particular mix of mischief and opportunity I'd come to both love and fear. "Pack your bags, Lee. I've found us a ride East," he announced, "but there's a twist—you're going to fight along the way."

I'd like to say I responded with immediate heroic enthusiasm; but the truth is closer to stunned disbelief. Me? Fight? My combat experience consisted of a few schoolyard scraps and wrestling matches with my brothers. The idea of stepping into a boxing ring with actual fighters seemed like madness. And yet, beneath the fear was a spark of curiosity, a whisper of "what if?" that I couldn't quite silence.

This is the nature of the call to adventure—it simultaneously terrifies and intrigues us. It speaks to something beyond our usual rational thoughts, something that recognizes the call as an invitation to become more fully ourselves, even as our logical minds catalog all the reasons to decline.

Think of Neo in *The Matrix*, presented with the choice between the blue pill (return to comfortable illusion) and the red pill (embrace a disturbing reality). Or Frodo Baggins, offered the burden of the One Ring. The call asks something significant of us—courage, sacrifice, trust in the unknown—and in doing so, it reveals the potential hero within the ordinary person.

Your call to adventure might be subtle—a persistent dissatisfaction with the status quo, a creative urge that won't be silenced, a relationship that challenges your assumptions. Or it might be dramatic—a diagnosis that changes everything, an unexpected opportunity in a distant place, a loss that reshapes your world. Whatever form it takes, the call invites you to a larger life, one that can't be lived from the safety of what you already know.

Step 3: Refusal of the Call

Let's be honest—I've never met anyone who immediately jumped at the call to adventure with open arms and a confident smile. Have you? Our first response is often resistance, hesitation, or flat-out refusal. And thank goodness—because this isn't weakness; it's a natural human reaction to the prospect of leaving our zone of comfort and competence for the terrain of uncertainty.

The refusal of the call represents that part of us that clings to the familiar, even when the familiar has become stifling. It's the voice of caution that catalogs all the risks, the inner critic that questions our capabilities, the social programming that prioritizes security over growth.

When Danny proposed the boxing tent adventure, my inner refusal was immediate and forceful. The parade of self-doubts marched through my mind with military precision: "You'll get hurt. You'll embarrass your-self. You're not a fighter. You're not strong enough, tough enough, brave enough." These weren't just idle concerns—they were my brain's way of protecting me from potential harm and humiliation.

What's fascinating about this stage of the journey is that the refusal often reveals exactly what we need to overcome to grow. My hesitation wasn't just about physical danger—it was about confronting my fear of not being good enough, my reluctance to be vulnerable, my avoidance of situa-tions where I couldn't control the outcome.

We see this refusal clearly in countless stories. Think of how Bilbo initially closes his door on Gandalf's invitation to adventure, preferring the predictable comforts of his hobbit hole. Remember that moment when Peter Parker shocked everyone by turning down Tony Stark's offer to become a full-fledged Avenger at the end of *Homecoming*? He chose to remain in his more manageable role as a "friendly neighborhood Spider-Man." That's the refusal playing out perfectly.

The refusal isn't a failure—it's a natural part of the process, a moment of reckoning where we weigh what we might gain against what we must risk. Sometimes the refusal persists, and the adventure is delayed until a later calling. But for those who eventually move forward, the refusal serves as important preparation, forcing us to name our fears before we face them.

My own refusal didn't last long—partly because the alternative (staying in our small outback town with dwindling funds) seemed increasingly untenable, and partly because beneath my fear was a growing hunger for experience, for challenge, for discovery. Sometimes we overcome the refusal not because our fears disappear, but because our desire for growth finally outweighs them.

Step 4: Crossing the First Threshold

Crossing the first threshold is the moment of commitment, where contem-plation ends and action begins. It's the point of no return, where you leave the boundaries of your ordinary world and step fully into the adventure. This crossing often feels momentous—a palpable shift from the known to the unknown, from the familiar landscape of your previous life to terrain unmapped and unexplored.

For me, that threshold was both literal and symbolic—climbing aboard that bizarre Mad Max vehicle with its welded-together cab, makeshift bunks, and shipping container strapped to the back. As I stuffed my life into a backpack and settled into that ramshackle truck beside fighters with scabbed knuckles and wary eyes, I knew I was leaving behind not just a place, but a version of myself—the cautious English lad who prioritized safety over experience.

The threshold crossing rarely feels clean or confident. It's usually messy, marked by equal parts excitement and terror. As our makeshift caravan rumbled down dusty outback roads, the truck's door secured by nothing more than a frayed rope and a screwdriver, I felt utterly out of my depth. I was venturing into a world with unwritten rules and unfamiliar dangers, where my previous experience offered little guidance.

This is the essence of the threshold—it demands that we leave behind our old tools and certainties. The skills and strategies that served us in the ordinary world often prove inadequate for the challenges ahead. Crossing the threshold requires a willingness to be a beginner again, to embrace vulnerability and not-knowing.

In *Star Wars*, Luke's threshold crossing comes when he leaves Tatooine with Obi-Wan, venturing into the wider galaxy. For Bilbo Baggins, it's the moment he runs out his door without a handkerchief, contract in hand, calling out that he's going on an adventure. These moments are simultaneously terrifying and liberating—the hero has committed to the journey, even without knowing where it will lead.

Your own threshold crossing might not involve a physical journey, but it will likely share that quality of decisive action in the face of uncertainty. It might be leaving a secure but soul-deadening job, ending a comfortable but stagnant relationship, speaking a truth you've long kept silent, or pursuing a passion you've always deferred. Whatever form it takes, crossing the threshold marks your true entry into the Hero's Journey—the point where you stop contemplating change and start living it.

Step 5: Trials, Friends, and Foes

Once you've crossed the threshold, the journey intensifies. The trials, friends, and foes stage is where the hero encounters a series of challenges and tests, meets allies who provide assistance and enemies who create obstacles, and begins the process of transformation through these experiences.

This stage isn't about a single challenge but a series of increasingly difficult tests that force growth and adaptation. Each trial strips away another layer of the old identity, making space for something new to emerge. Each ally provides a gift—whether knowledge, support, or a new perspective—that proves essential for the journey. And each enemy, interestingly, serves as a catalyst for development, revealing weaknesses that must be addressed and strengths that have yet to be claimed.

My boxing tent adventures were like living through this stage with almost ridiculous precision. The whole carnival setup was basically one long gauntlet of trials—getting my head knocked about nightly was just the obvious bit. The real psychological minefield was being the "Pommy" (Aussie slang for a Brit, and not always said with affection) in a world where I was clearly cast as the evening's entertainment and the sacrificial lamb thrown to the wolves to whet the crowd's appetite for violence.

The Indigenous fighters I faced became both foes and unexpected teachers. Their fists delivered painful lessons about resilience and adaptability, while their eyes reflected a history of oppression and resistance that gave our encounters a depth beyond mere sport. Each match was a confrontation not just with their physical prowess but with my own limitations and untapped potential.

And then there was Danny, my best friend and fellow traveler, who became both ally and opponent when we faced each other in the ring. That fight tested not just our bodies but the very foundation of our friendship. Trading blows with someone who knew all my weaknesses and vulnerabilities raised thought-provoking questions about trust, loyalty, and the nature of true connection. Like Simba facing Scar (though with more sweaty headlocks and fewer singing hyenas), I had to confront both an external challenge and an internal struggle.

The trial stage often feels chaotic and overwhelming. There's no clear roadmap, no certainty about which challenges matter most or how to navigate them successfully. This disorientation is intentional—it forces the hero to develop new capabilities, to see with fresh eyes, to discover resources they didn't know they possessed.

In "Top Gun: Maverick," Pete Mitchell (Tom Cruise) faces a number of challenges both in the air and on the ground while navigating complex relationships with his new trainees, particularly Rooster, the son of his deceased friend, Goose. Each trial reveals something new about Maverick's character, pushing him to confront his past failures, mortality, and responsibility. These aren't random obstacles but formative experiences that gradually transform him from a rule-breaking aviator clinging to his past into a mentor willing to sacrifice for the next generation. From someone haunted by guilt to someone who's finally found peace.

Your own trials, friends, and foes might look very different from mine or Maverick's, but they'll serve the same function in your journey. The difficult boss, the health challenge, the creative block, the financial setback—these aren't just annoyances to be overcome but invitations to develop new strengths. The unexpected mentor, the supportive friend, the community that welcomes you—these aren't just pleasant additions to your life but essential guides who offer what you cannot provide for yourself. Even your antagonists—the critic, the competitor, the person who triggers your deepest insecurities—serve as mirrors reflecting what you most need to address or integrate.

This stage of the journey isn't about eliminating challenges but learning to engage with them differently. It's about recognizing that the path of transformation isn't smooth or straight but winding and rocky—and those very difficulties are what shape you into the person you're meant to become.

Step 6: Magical Mentor (or the Mentor with Supernatural Aid)

In the Hero's Journey, the mentor figure provides guidance, wisdom, and often tangible aid that proves essential for the hero's success. This mentor typically possesses knowledge, experience, or abilities that the hero lacks —qualities that may seem almost magical or supernatural from the hero's perspective.

The mentor isn't always a kindly wizard or wise elder (though they certainly can be). Sometimes they appear in unexpected forms—a gruff trainer, a demanding teacher, an antagonist whose challenges force growth or even a spirit animal. What defines the mentor isn't their appearance or manner but their function: they see potential in the hero that others (including the hero themselves) might miss, and they provide exactly what's needed to help that potential unfold.

In my boxing tent saga, my unlikely mentor emerged in the towering form of Michael, our carny ringleader. With his weathered face and hands like shovels, he was no Obi-Wan Kenobi offering gentle wisdom. His mentorship came in the form of tough love—throwing me into the ring with opponents who outmatched me and expecting me to survive through sheer determination.

At first glance, Michael's approach seemed more sadistic than supportive. Was this mentorship or exploitation? But looking back, I recognize that his harsh methods contained a hidden gift. By placing me in situations where failure seemed inevitable, he forced me to tap into resources I didn't know I possessed. Each fight that I survived built not just physical resilience but something deeper—a stronger confidence. Not the superficial confidence of never being challenged, but the earned confidence of facing difficulty and finding a way through.

Unlike the idealized mentors of fiction, real-life magical mentors rarely announce themselves as such. They don't arrive with a staff and flowing robes, announcing their intention to guide you to greatness. More often, they appear as the boss who pushes you beyond your comfortable capabilities, the friend who tells you the truth when others offer empty comfort, the teacher who sees past your excuses to your potential.

The mentor's magic lies not in supernatural powers but in their ability to see you more clearly than you see yourself—to recognize abilities within you that remain dormant until the right challenge awakens them. Their guidance isn't always comfortable or welcome in the moment. Look at how Yoda pushed Luke to his absolute limits on Dagobah—nothing easy or pleasant about hanging upside down while lifting rocks with your mind! But the cranky green guru provided exactly what Luke needed to develop his abilities and prepare for greater challenges.

Your own magical mentor might be formally designated—a therapist, a coach, a teacher—or they might appear in unexpected guises throughout your journey. They might offer explicit instruction or simply create conditions that demand your growth. They might walk alongside you for years or appear briefly at a decisive moment. However they manifest, their presence marks a significant shift in your journey—from floundering in unfamiliar territory to gaining the tools and perspective needed to navigate it successfully.

STAGE 2: INITIATION—FACING YOUR TRIALS

If the departure stage is about leaving the familiar, the initiation stage is about diving head first into the unfamiliar—plunging into the depths of challenge and transformation. This is where the real work happens, where the hero faces their greatest tests and undergoes the most meaningful changes.

The initiation often involves a symbolic death and rebirth. The old identity, with its limitations and illusions, must die to make way for something new to emerge. This death can be terrifying—it feels like losing yourself, like everything you've relied on is crumbling away. But this breaking down is necessary; you cannot become who you're meant to be while clinging to who you've been.

This stage often feels like a descent into darkness, an encounter with the shadow parts of yourself and your world. Like Jonah in the belly of the whale or Odysseus in the underworld, the hero must journey into the depths before they can rise transformed. It's in this darkness that the most valuable treasures are found—insights, capabilities, and strengths that were hidden from the surface level of ordinary awareness.

Step 7: Approach the Innermost Cave

As the Hero's Journey progresses, there comes a point where the preliminary challenges give way to something more essential. Campbell calls this "approaching the innermost cave"—the movement toward the heart of the adventure, the core challenge that contains both the greatest danger and the greatest potential reward.

The innermost cave isn't necessarily a physical location (though it can be). More essentially, it represents the confrontation with whatever lies at the center of your quest—the truth you've been avoiding, the fear that's been holding you back, the pattern you need to break, the question you need to answer. It's the heart of darkness that contains the most important light.

In my boxing tent saga, the innermost cave was the ring itself—that sawdust-strewn square where I faced not just physical opponents but my deepest insecurities and self-doubts. Each time I stepped between those ropes, I entered a space where pretense fell away and only the raw truth remained. There was nowhere to hide, no way to fake it. The ring stripped me bare, exposing everything I was and wasn't.

The Indigenous fighters I faced became reflections of my own fears—their strength highlighting my weakness, their skill revealing my limitations, their fury forcing me to confront parts of myself I'd kept hidden. Each bout was a descent into my personal underworld, a face-off with the shadow Self I'd long avoided.

What made these encounters so transformative wasn't just their difficulty but their honesty. There's something brutally sobering about getting punched in the face repeatedly. It cuts through intellectual defenses and social masks, revealing what's actually there beneath the layers of persona. Some nights I discovered courage I didn't know I possessed; other nights I found limitations I'd been denying. Both discoveries were valuable.

That scene in *Black Panther* where T'Challa enters the ancestral plane and confronts his father? Pure innermost cave territory. That spiritual and psychological space forces him to question inherited wisdom and establish his own path as a leader. It's not a physical battle but an internal struggle with legacy, identity, and purpose. We all have our own version of that ancestral plane, don't we?

The approach to your innermost cave might come as a period of intensifying challenge or a quiet moment of truth that can no longer be avoided. It might involve confronting a relationship pattern that repeatedly creates suffering, facing an addiction that you've been downplaying, acknowledging a dream you've been too afraid to pursue, or questioning beliefs that no longer serve you but provide comfortable certainty.

What makes this stage both crucial and difficult is that approaching the innermost cave requires vulnerability. The defenses and strategies that have protected you must be lowered for genuine transformation to occur. This is why the approach often brings up intense resistance—the closer you get to the core issue, the more strongly the psyche's defense mechanisms activate to maintain the status quo.

But it's precisely this vulnerability that makes the approach so powerful. By willingly entering the space of your deepest challenges and fears, you create the possibility for healing and connection that cannot occur while you're running or hiding. The cave may seem dark and scary, but it contains exactly what you need for the next phase of your becoming.

Step 8: Moments of Ordeal & Despair

At the heart of the modern Hero's Journey lies the ordeal—the biggest crisis where everything hangs in the balance. You know that moment when your stomach drops and you think, 'I can't do this'? This is the darkest point, when failure seems not just possible but imminent, when resources are depleted, allies are distant, and we must face our greatest challenge alone. Or at least it feels that way.

For us modern heroes, the ordeal isn't typically a battle with a dragon or a duel with a villain—it's an existential reckoning. It tests not just what we can do but who we are at our core. When all external supports are stripped away, what remains? What will we stand for? What will we sacrifice? What depths of courage, resilience, or wisdom can we access when everything is on the line?

The modern hero's ordeal might be facing a devastating diagnosis, enduring the breakdown of a marriage, confronting an addiction, or acknowledging a significant failure. These moments feel like endings, but they actually contain the seeds of our most meaningful transformations.

Of course, my ordeal came in those brutal fights, night after night of relentless pummeling at the hands of unpredictable prizefighters. To them, I represented more than just an opponent; I was a "Pommy," a symbol of colonial oppression they sought to fight back against with every punch. Each fight tested the limits of my resolve, my stamina, and my ability to take a punch without crying for my mum (a feat I managed... most nights).

But the true ordeal, the moment of deepest darkness, emerged in the fight against Danny, my best mate and closest ally. Facing off against him challenged not just our friendship but my very sense of Self. As we traded blows, I questioned everything—our bond, my purpose, and my place in the world. It was an excruciating descent into the abyss of doubt.

The bruises and blood were real enough, but the deepest pain came from within—the inner voice of doubts and questioning. What am I doing here? Am I going to be safe? Does Danny even really like me? Had I got this all wrong? Was this journey a terrible mistake? In those moments, the ground seemed to fall away beneath me, leaving nothing solid to stand on.

This is what the ordeal does—it creates a vacuum where old certainties dissolve, forcing an encounter with more authentic truths. It's a psychological and spiritual death that precedes rebirth. Something essential must be surrendered—an outdated identity, a limiting belief, an attachment to control—before something new can emerge.

"Stereotypical" *Barbie's* ordeal in the 2023 film was a really fun example of this stage—that moment when she chooses to leave the fantasy of Barbie Land and become human. Think about what's at stake there: she surrenders perfection and immortality to confront the messy reality of human existence with all its limitations. It's not her constant cheerfulness or impossible proportions that finally satisfy her, but her courage to embrace reality in all its complexity and imperfection. That's the essence of our ordeals too—choosing authenticity over comfortable illusion.

Your own ordeal might not involve physical danger, but it will likely share that quality of existential challenge. It might come as a betrayal that shatters your trust, a failure that destroys your self-image, or a loss that seems unbearable. Whatever form it takes, the ordeal feels like the end—of your quest, your hope, perhaps even your Self as you've known it.

And yet, this apparent ending contains the seeds of a new beginning. The ordeal's purpose isn't to destroy but to transform. By bringing you to your knees, it creates the possibility for surrender—not as defeat, but as opening to something greater than the limited Self that entered the journey. The hero who emerges from the ordeal is fundamentally changed, possessing a depth, humility, and authenticity that wasn't possible before this confrontation with their limits. They become more fully human, and more heroic.

Step 9: Reward (Seizing the Sword)

After enduring the ordeal, the hero claims their reward, or "The Ultimate Boon"—the prize that makes their struggles meaningful. In classic myths, this might be a literal treasure—a golden fleece, a magical elixir, a powerful weapon. But for the modern hero, the more valuable reward is internal—a new understanding, ability, or quality of being that transforms them from within.

Campbell calls this "seizing the sword," referencing the mythic imagery of the hero claiming a weapon of power. But the sword isn't just a tool for battle; it's a symbol of clarity, wisdom, and the ability to cut through illusion to truth. The modern hero returns from the ordeal with sharper vision, able to see what was previously hidden and to act from a place of greater wisdom.

For me, the ultimate reward from my ordeal wasn't just keeping all my teeth intact (though that was a nice bonus). It was a newfound sense of Self, forged in the fiery furnace of the boxing tent. I had gone in a naive, restless kid searching for thrills and validation; I emerged a young man with a greater understanding of my own strength and resilience. The physical bruises faded, but the inner transformation remained—an unshakable sense of my own worth and potential that no external validation could provide or take away.

But the true reward went beyond just personal growth. Through the bonds formed in the boxing tent—with Danny, the Indigenous fighters, and even Michael, our carny ringleader—I discovered the power of authentic connection and brotherhood. We were all heroes on our own journeys, facing our own challenges and demons, but we weren't alone. The greatest reward was the realization that our struggles, our triumphs, and our transformations were all connected, part of a larger web of human experience.

In the end, the ultimate reward was a shift in perspective, a new way of seeing myself and my place in the world. I had stripped away the masks and illusions, confronted my deepest fears and doubts, and emerged with a truer, more authentic sense of Self. Much like Neo mastering *The Matrix* or Frodo destroying the One Ring, this, my friends, is a reward you can't put a price on—a treasure beyond comparison that I hold close to this day.

It serves as a reminder of the inherent hero within each of us, poised to be unleashed.

I still get goosebumps thinking about when Neo finally understands the true nature of *The Matrix*. His reward isn't just the flashy ability to dodge bullets and manipulate the simulated world—it's the clarity to see reality as it truly is. He can perceive both the constructed nature of *The Matrix* and his own unlimited potential within it. That's what makes his story so compelling—his greatest power isn't bending spoons but seeing through illusion. I think that's why that story resonates with so many of us —we all hunger for that moment of seeing beyond our limiting beliefs.

When you reach this stage, you might be surprised by how your reward shows up—maybe it's a newfound clarity about your life's direction, the courage to make a necessary change, a richer capacity for intimacy, or simply the quiet confidence that comes from having faced your fears and survived. Whatever form it takes, this reward represents more than just the spoils of your journey—it's the manifestation of your transformation, the evidence that you are no longer the same person who first heard the call to adventure.

STAGE 3: RETURN—BRINGING IT ALL BACK HOME

The final stage of the modern Hero's Journey is the return, where we bring back what we've gained from our quest and blend it into our everyday lives. This isn't about returning to the status quo—the hero who returns is not the same person who left, and the ordinary world can never look the same to them again.

The return often involves struggles of its own. How do you bring back wisdom from the mountaintop to a world that hasn't shared your experience? How do you translate insights gained in extraordinary circumstances to the rhythms of ordinary life? How do you remain true to your transformation when old patterns and expectations press in from all sides?

These challenges make the return not just an end to the journey but a crucial part of its meaning. The modern hero's task isn't just personal transformation but bringing gifts back to their community—whether that's literal knowledge and skills or simply a new way of being that inspires others.

Step 10: The Road Back

After claiming the reward, the hero must begin the journey home. This road back isn't usually a simple return trip—it often involves challenges, pursuits, and final tests that bridge the special world of adventure and the ordinary world left behind.

For the modern hero, the road back represents the challenge of bringing together what we've learned during our transformative experiences with our everyday lives. It's one thing to have an insight on a meditation retreat, during a period of crisis, or in the heat of a life-changing adventure; it's quite another to live that insight amid the demands and distractions of normal life.

Remember when I shared how Danny and I parted ways after reaching that paradise on Australia's Sunshine Coast? That moment perfectly shows the "Road Back" stage of the Hero's Journey. While I clung to our friendship like a life raft, Danny, like an older brother, recognized something I couldn't yet see—that our paths needed to split for true growth to continue. The painful separation I experienced wasn't just about losing a travel companion; it represented an important test in my journey.

Looking at it through Campbell's framework, this parting marked the beginning of my road back—the challenge of bringing together what I'd learned in the boxing tent with my new independent life. Like Neo returning to *The Matrix* with new abilities or Dorothy waking up in Kansas with a transformed perspective, I had to navigate the challenges of re-entry, finding ways to bring extraordinary insights into ordinary reality without the structure and support that had carried me this far.

I've seen people navigate this stage in countless ways—returning to work after a transformative sabbatical, redefining relationships after a personal breakthrough, or applying insights from therapy to daily challenges. For you, the road back might look completely different, but the essence is the same: building bridges between your deepest truths and your everyday reality, finding ways to live authentically even when the environment hasn't changed as much as you have.

This road isn't always smooth. You may face resistance—from others who prefer the version of you they knew before, from systems designed to maintain the status quo, or from your own habits and comfort zones pulling you back to familiar patterns. The road back tests whether your transformation was just temporary or has really become part of who you are.

Step 11: Rebirth & The Champion's Return

The champion's return marks the final threshold the hero must cross before completing their journey. This ultimate test often requires facing death one last time—whether literal or symbolic—drawing upon everything learned to emerge victorious. It represents a final rebirth, the hero fully shedding their old identity and embracing their new Self and role.

For the modern hero, this rebirth often comes when we're tested to see if we'll revert to old patterns under pressure or truly embody our transformation. It's the moment when what we've learned becomes not just knowledge but wisdom, not just an experience we've had but an integral part of who we are.

In my own journey, this rebirth didn't come in a single, dramatic moment, but in the quiet unfolding of countless days spent exploring the sun-drenched coast of Australia. Freed from both the confines of the boxing tent and the suffocating constraints of my former office life back in England, I threw myself into the laid-back rhythms of beach life, creating deep friendships and savoring the simple joys of life. The fluorescent lights, sales reports, and soul-crushing meetings that had once defined my days seemed like artifacts from someone else's life—a person I barely recognized anymore.

With each passing day, I could feel myself shedding the skin of my old life, growing more connected to the person I was meant to be. Gone was the wide-eyed, bumbling British lad who couldn't throw a punch without apologizing. In his place stood a young man who had stared down his demons, conquered his fears, and learned that sometimes, the greatest victories come from within.

But true transformation is never easy, and there were moments when the old fears and doubts would resurface, threatening to drag me back into the shadows. The struggles I faced—finding work, making new connections, creating a life on my own terms—were constant reminders of the challenges ahead. It was in those moments that I drew upon the lessons of the boxing tent—the grit, the resilience, the unshakable belief that no matter how tough things get, I could find a way through.

I had learned to roll with the punches—both literally and figuratively. And with each new obstacle I overcame, I felt myself growing stronger, more resilient, and more capable of handling whatever life threw my way.

Think about that crazy moment in *Severance's* season finale when Mark starts to recognize the truth about his situation. For those who missed this brilliant series, it's about employees who undergo a procedure that completely separates their work and personal memories—at work, they have no idea who they are outside the office, and at home, they can't remember anything about their job. There's something moving about watching those artificial walls between Mark's work Self and home Self begin to crumble. After living a literally divided existence—no memory of work at home, no memory of home at work—the fragments of his identity finally start reaching toward each other. What makes this such a perfect rebirth moment is how it shows transformation isn't about escaping our problems or becoming someone else entirely, but bringing together the disconnected parts of ourselves into something more complete and real.

When was the last time you handled something that would have crushed you a year ago? For me, I love watching or hearing about these rebirth moments in people's lives—like when they face a situation that would have once defeated them but now reveals how much they've grown. Maybe you've already experienced this: standing your ground in a difficult conversation that once would have left you silent, pursuing a dream you'd previously abandoned out of fear, or finding peace in circumstances that once would have felt unbearable. These moments mark not just changes in what you do, but transformations in who you are.

Step 12: Gift of the Goddess

The Hero's Journey comes full circle when the personal reward from Step 9 (Seizing the Sword) transforms into something greater—a gift they can now share with their community. While the Reward was something we earned for ourselves during our ordeal in the special world, the Gift represents what we contribute back to the ordinary world upon our return.

Think of it as the difference between conquering a mountain to plant your flag and conquering it to build a lighthouse that guides others. Both achievements require courage, but only one lights the way for those who follow.

For the modern hero, this gift isn't usually a material object but a quality of being—a greater capacity for love, a clearer sense of purpose, a hard-won wisdom that can benefit others. It represents the moment when personal transformation expands beyond the Self, creating ripples that touch the lives around us.

The treasure I pocketed from my stint as the boxing tent's warm-up whipping boy? As a young lad not even in my twenties yet, I couldn't have named it clearly. I felt different—more authentic, more resilient—but I didn't yet understand how these changes might benefit anyone beyond myself. That's the thing about the gift stage of the journey—sometimes it takes years, even decades, to fully unwrap and understand.

In retrospect though, I see that those early adventures planted seeds that would grow through many more cycles of departure, initiation, and return. With each new journey, the gift has clarified and strengthened. What began as personal resilience gradually transformed into something I could share—first unconsciously through how I showed up in relationships, later more deliberately through mentoring others facing their own challenges.

The writing of this book itself represents another cycle in that spiral—taking what I've learned across many journeys and offering it as a map for fellow travelers. The gift isn't about positioning myself as having all the answers, but about creating a space where others might recognize their own heroic potential. Consider this my lighthouse atop the mountain.

This Gift of the Goddess stage appears everywhere from ancient myths to today's streaming hits—it's the moment when heroes share their hard-won wisdom with their community. In Greek mythology, Prometheus stole fire from the gods specifically to share it with humanity. The Buddha, after achieving enlightenment under the Bodhi tree, spent decades teaching others the path he'd discovered. King Arthur established the Round Table to share his vision of justice with his kingdom.

We see the same pattern in our most beloved modern stories. Think about Tony Stark's ultimate sacrifice in *"Avengers: Endgame,"* when he uses the knowledge and technology he's developed to save not just his friends but the entire universe. Or consider how *Moana* returns the heart of Te Fiti, restoring harmony to her people and the ocean. Even in *The Lord of the Rings*, it's brilliant how the hobbits return to save the Shire using the courage and wisdom they've gained on their journey.

Many of us discover our gifts gradually, often in surprising forms. Think about what comes so naturally to you that you might not even see it as special—maybe it's the way you inspire people around you without even trying. Perhaps you're the friend everyone calls when they need someone to listen without judgment, or you have this knack for seeing solutions that escape everyone else. Maybe you're the person who can explain complicated things in a way that suddenly makes them crystal clear. Or maybe your gift hasn't fully revealed itself yet. For some, it emerges through creative expression that shifts how people see the world, or through practical solutions to problems nobody else could solve. Each hero's gift is as unique as their journey, but they all share one quality— they transform our personal adventures into something that benefits others.

Step 13: Ascent to a Higher Dimension

The ascent to a higher dimension represents the ultimate destination of the Hero's Journey—the point where we transcend the limitations of our old life and step into a new reality. I don't mean this in some mystical, floating-above-the-clouds way. It's a moment of awakening to the inter-connectedness of all things and the power we each hold to shape our world. It's seeing the same reality but with new eyes.

For the modern hero, this ascent rarely means leaving the material world behind or achieving some perfect enlightened state. Instead, it represents a basic shift in awareness—perceiving familiar territory through an entirely new lens, engaging with the same old challenges but from a place of greater freedom, wisdom, and compassion.

For me, this ascent wasn't a single, blinding moment of revelation, but a gradual unfolding of understanding. Each new adventure, each connection formed and lesson learned, brought me closer to a sense of unity with the world around me. I began to see the Hero's Journey not as a solitary quest, but as a collective unfolding—a dance in which we are all partners.

As I continued to grow and evolve, I found myself drawn to the frontiers of human potential—to the cutting edge of science and spirituality, and to the wisdom of elders and visionaries who had glimpsed the furthest reaches of our capabilities. I became a student of the human condition, seeking out patterns and principles that could help us navigate our individual and shared journeys with greater awareness and purpose.

This, then, is the final lesson of the Hero's Journey—that the power to transform ourselves and our world lies within us all. That by stepping into the arena of our own lives, by embracing the challenges and opportunities that come our way, we can tap into a wellspring of potential beyond our wildest dreams.

This ascent isn't some distant mountain peak—it's happening in small moments all around us. When you suddenly realize your personal struggles and triumphs are connected to larger patterns, that's it happening. When you find yourself seeing beyond superficial differences to our shared humanity, that's it too. And when you see how your particular gifts and challenges have prepared you for a specific role only you can fill—you're experiencing the ascent right there.

The ascent to a higher dimension isn't about escaping the messiness of human existence or achieving some perfect state of being. It's about embracing life more fully, with greater awareness, compassion, and purpose. It's about recognizing that we are all on this journey together, each playing our part in the unfolding story of what it means to be human.

COMING FULL CIRCLE: THE MODERN HERO IN ALL OF US

So here we are, having traveled through the stages and steps of the Hero's Journey together. What started as an ancient mythic pattern turns out to be the blueprint for our very modern lives. This isn't some template for stories about supernatural beings with magical powers—it's a map for understanding our own path toward living with authenticity, purpose, and meaning in a world that keeps pulling us toward conformity and comfort.

The battles we face as modern heroes rarely make headlines. We battle not dragons but depression, not evil empires but stubborn habits, not external villains but internal voices of doubt and fear. Our journeys involve navigating loneliness, creating space for reflection, and recognizing that true heroism often means admitting when we need connection and support.

Through my own journey—from the stifling walls of a corporate cubicle to the sweat-soaked canvas of a carnival boxing tent, from the naive youth seeking thrills to the man seeking truth—I've experienced firsthand how this ancient pattern of transformation applies to our modern lives. The lessons I learned, the allies I found, and the tests I endured didn't make me superhuman—they made me more fully human.

But my journey as a modern hero is far from over, and yours isn't either. The Hero's Journey isn't a one-time adventure but a spiral of continuous becoming. It invites us not to achieve perfection but to engage with life's deepest questions and challenges with courage and an open heart.

The modern hero understands that the power to transform doesn't come from supernatural abilities or divine bloodlines, but from our willingness to look honestly at ourselves, to venture beyond our comfort zones, and to bring our authentic gifts to a world in need of them.

So let us embrace the modern hero within each of us—not the flawless champion of myth but the beautifully imperfect human being with the courage to grow. Let us remember that heroism today isn't about conquering others but about facing ourselves, building meaningful connections, and contributing to something larger than our individual concerns.

The path of the modern hero is challenging, with obstacles both external and internal, but its rewards are powerful—a life of authenticity, purpose, and genuine connection. With the wisdom of ancient patterns guiding our own everyday journeys, we can navigate the complexity of modern existence while staying true to the timeless human quest for meaning and wholeness.

WHERE ARE YOU ON YOUR HERO'S JOURNEY?

So where might you be on this ancient path that continues to shape our modern lives?

Take a moment right now. Close your eyes if you can and ask yourself:

What's my current relationship with comfort and challenge? With the familiar and the unknown?

Perhaps you're still in the Campbellian Cave of the Ordinary World—that comfortable yet somehow limiting space where routine provides security but your soul hungers for something more. You sense a stirring, a restlessness that can't be soothed by another scroll through social media or another purchase that promises fulfillment. You know this feeling, right? That sense that something's missing even though everything looks fine on paper? The walls of this cave aren't physical—they're made of expectations (yours and others'), of fears carefully disguised as practicality, of patterns that once served but now limit you.

Or maybe you recognize this: You've heard the Call to Adventure and find yourself frozen at the threshold, one foot raised to step into the unknown, the other firmly planted in familiar ground. This hesitation isn't weakness—it's a natural response to the enormity of what lies ahead. The primitive parts of our brain, wired for survival, sound alarm bells when we approach the boundaries of our comfort zone. Those bells don't mean danger—they signal growth. So ask yourself: What opportunity or challenge has been knocking at my door that I've been hesitant to answer? What's holding me in place?

Perhaps you're already deep in the Special World of trials and challenges, facing opponents both external and internal. These battles rarely look like literal boxing matches. More often, they appear as difficult conversations you've been avoiding, creative risks that expose you to criticism, relationships that require vulnerability when you'd rather remain armored, or inner demons that finally demand facing after years of successful avoidance.

Wherever you find yourself, know this: there is wisdom in that precise location. You're exactly where you need to be in this moment of your unfolding story.

THE PRIMARY INGREDIENT: ADVERSITY AND CHALLENGE

Problems and adversity aren't unfortunate detours on the Hero's Journey —they're the main driver for growth and development. In both literature and life, the journey isn't complete until we've faced and overcome significant challenges. The hero must confront their fears and take control of the situation to resolve the conflict and complete their journey. This truth contradicts our natural inclination to seek comfort and avoid difficulty, yet it's the resistance of the cocoon that gives the butterfly the strength to fly.

The journey isn't just about external obstacles either. It's equally about reconciling our inner Self with our outward journey—coming to terms with personal difficulties and breaking free from old patterns in order to mature and reach our full potential. This process of psychological development, though challenging, ultimately leads to the rewards of personal growth and reaching our true human potential.

Few people consciously choose to embark on the Hero's Journey. We're hardwired to move away from pain and toward pleasure—a survival mechanism that serves us well in many contexts but becomes an obstacle on the path of transformation. It's far more common to put off our quest until we "feel ready"—which, if we're honest, might mean never. We procrastinate by putting important matters aside, using clever delay tactics, filling our downtime with distractions, making reasonable-sounding excuses, or simply choosing to do nothing.

Yet even as we resist, there's often an internal tension brewing within us, a conflict that intensifies with each passing moment. We can sense this inner battle, feeling opposing forces at play whenever we confront the misalignments between who we are and who we're becoming. To resolve this tension, we eventually must act and seek resolution, either consciously or unconsciously.

The good news? We all find ourselves on a Hero's Journey, whether current or past. What matters most isn't where we've been but what we do today, in this present moment. It's never too late to embrace the challenges and opportunities of the journey and take steps toward reaching our true potential.

RECOGNIZING YOUR STAGE & HEARING THE CALL

How do you identify where you stand on this circular path? Listen to the questions that occupy your mind. They reveal your current terrain more accurately than any external measurement.

If you're in the Ordinary World, your questions might sound like:

- *"Is this all there is?"*
- *"Why do I feel restless despite having everything I'm 'supposed' to want?"*
- *"What's this nagging feeling that something important is missing?"*

If you're hearing the Call to Adventure, you might be asking:

- *"What would happen if I actually pursued that dream/had that conversation/made that change?"*
- *"Am I crazy to want something different when what I have is perfectly fine?"*
- *"How can I tell if this urge is a distraction or a genuine calling?"*

In the midst of Trials and Challenges, your questions often shift to:

- *"Why is this so much harder than I expected?"*
- *"Have I made a terrible mistake?"*
- *"How do I keep going when I can't see the way forward?"*

And if you're approaching the Return with your hard-won insights, you might wonder:

- *"How do I bring together what I've learned with my everyday life?"*
- *"Will others understand how I've changed?"*
- *"How do I honor this transformation without either downplaying it or becoming self-important about it?"*

LISTENING FOR THE CALL

The modern hero isn't the one who skips stages or navigates them perfectly—they're just the one who keeps showing up, step after uncertain step. Here's how Abraham Maslow put it—and boy, did he nail it:

"We grow forward when the delights of growth and anxieties of safety are greater than the anxieties of growth and the delights of safety."

— ABRAHAM MASLOW

I know, a bit of a tongue twister, but stick with me. This happens outside your comfort zone, where you discover strengths and abilities you never knew you possessed.

But how do you actually recognize when life is calling you toward something greater? The call to adventure rarely arrives with trumpets and clear instructions. More often, it whispers through these sneaky little channels that we've got to learn to hear:

Restlessness and Strange Sounds

Sometimes that restless feeling might just show up in unexpected physical ways—persistent ringing in your ears, unusual sounds, unexplained sensations. Of course, these could be medical or neurological, and it's always worth checking with a doctor if you're concerned. But who's to say your neurology isn't how the hero within you tries to break the surface? Even ancient traditions recognized that emotional or spiritual unrest often manifests physically. The Greeks called it "soma," the Chinese medicine masters mapped how different emotions affected different organs, and Indigenous healers worldwide have always treated physical symptoms as potential messages from our inner world. Sometimes what shows up in our bodies is actually our psyche trying to get our attention.

Which makes me wonder: what if sometimes—not always, but sometimes—these outer sensations are also connected to that inner restlessness we've been talking about? Like how Neo kept seeing that same black cat twice, that glitch in *The Matrix* that told him something was off before he understood what it meant? What if it's that deeper part of you saying you've outgrown where you are? And what if your body sometimes joins the conversation? Could some of these experiences be another way the call to adventure tries to reach us? Like something inside going *"Oi! Pay attention! There's more to explore!"* through whatever channel it can find.

Unusual Encounters

You know those moments that make you stop and go "okay, what was that about?" A butterfly landing on your shoulder right when you're thinking about making a big change. A path in the woods that seems to practically call your name.

The ancient world was full of people reading signs in nature—Greeks at Dodona listening to oak leaves, Celts watching bird flight patterns. Were they all delusional? Or did they know something we've forgotten in our rush to explain everything away?

Here's what I've noticed: these weird encounters tend to cluster around times of transition. Like the universe starts getting less **subtle** when you're approaching a threshold. That butterfly might just be a butterfly. Or it might be life saying, "psst, pay attention here." Both can be true, can't they?

Life Curveballs and Plot Twists

Life has this habit of throwing curveballs right when you think you've got things figured out. The job loss, the surprise opportunity, the relationship that implodes or appears from nowhere. Buddhism calls obstacles "the path itself." The Stoics treated setbacks as training. Even Campbell noticed that heroes only become heroes after their normal life gets proper disrupted.

Makes me think of Luke Skywalker—would he have ever left Tatooine if his aunt and uncle hadn't been killed? Horrible way to start an adventure, but there it is. Sometimes the worst thing that happens to you becomes the thing that finally sets you free. Not always. Not even usually. But sometimes.

Dreams and Recurring Symbols

That dream you keep having? The one with the same theme playing out in different costumes? Every culture from the Aboriginal Dreamtime to Egyptian dream temples took these seriously. Some psychologists spend their whole lives studying them.

Your unconscious mind doesn't really do reruns for no reason. Those recurring dreams aren't just your subconscious running out of creative material—they're more like urgent messages trying to break through. It's as if there's a wiser part of you writing these dream stories, connecting dots that your waking mind hasn't quite figured out how to see yet.

Think of it like when someone keeps bringing up that thing you did three years ago—there's unfinished business there. Those recurring symbols might be something inside you going, "Hey, we need to talk about this." Sometimes in really weird ways involving teeth falling out or being late for exams you took twenty years ago.

When Your Gut Keeps Trying to Tell You Something

The quiet intuition that speaks in moments of stillness and the recurring patterns that seem to follow you through life often point to areas of growth wanting your attention. That inner knowing—so easily dismissed as "just a feeling"—is often the voice of your own wisdom trying to get through.

Then there are those patterns that keep repeating. Same relationship dynamics, different person. Same work situation, different company. It's like Groundhog Day but spread across years instead of days. These patterns are calls to adventure because they're showing you exactly where your Hero's Journey needs to happen. Each time that familiar situation shows up, it's life saying, "Here's your quest again—are you ready to face it differently this time?" The pattern keeps calling until you finally answer by doing the inner work to break it.

Think about it—the Hero's Journey often starts when someone realizes they can't keep living the same way. These recurring patterns are life's way of making that unbearably clear. They're not random; they're more like highlighted passages in the book of your life, emphasizing exactly where your transformation needs to begin.

Synchronicities (When the Universe Winks at You)

Those meaningful coincidences that seem way too specific to be random? You're thinking about someone, they call. You're pondering a big decision, suddenly every conversation seems related to it. These moments when events connect through meaning rather than obvious cause-and-effect have fascinated thinkers throughout time.

Our brains love patterns, sure. Confirmation bias is real. But Indigenous cultures have always known everything connects in ways our linear thinking struggles with. What if synchronicities are moments when we accidentally tune into that bigger frequency? When the boundaries between our individual awareness and something larger get a bit thin?

Not every coincidence is cosmic. But when they start piling up, when the winks from the universe get less subtle... well, even the skeptic in me starts wondering what's really going on.

Remember, the call to adventure often disguises itself in ordinary moments. Like the heroes of ancient tales who found magic rings in fish bellies or received quests from seemingly ordinary strangers at crossroads, your call may arrive wrapped in the mundane, recognizable only to the eyes and ears alert enough to see its significance.

As you set out on your journey, don't forget that most important companion: a sense of humor. The path of transformation is rarely a straight line. You'll face unexpected twists, humbling setbacks, and moments of surprising joy. You might find yourself temporarily lost in the equivalent of a dark forest, or facing your own version of a clever trickster who speaks in riddles. In those moments, when the journey seems most challenging, laughter can be as powerful a tool as any sword or shield.

THE ESSENTIAL SPACE BETWEEN

Remember the sailor's wisdom that opened this book? They called it "leeway": that protected space where winds calm and waters settle, creating crucial room to readjust course amid unpredictable forces. It's the margin sailors build into their journey—not as luxury but as necessity—knowing that storms will blow them sideways and they'll need room to recover.

When we apply this wisdom to our Hero's Journey, it reveals something Campbell's neat framework misses—the key importance of intentionally creating protected spaces between stages. This isn't about taking breaks or pausing randomly. It's about building in the shelter, space, and support needed for real growth to happen.

In Campbell's framework, the stages flow one into another in neat succession. But my experience tells me there's something important that happens between these stages—in the protected spaces where we can process what we've been through. This is where meaning forms from experience, where the lessons sink from our heads into our bones, where the seeds of the next adventure grow in darkness.

Modern life, with its relentless pace and constant connectivity, wages war against this essential practice. We're endlessly bombarded with new calls to adventure before we've properly understood the last one. No shelter from the storm of constant stimulation. No space to process. No time to find the support we need. The result? A scattered, shallow engagement with our own becoming.

I discovered the power of leeway quite by accident during those months after Danny and I parted ways. Without his constant companionship, I initially felt adrift. The emptiness was uncomfortable—I filled it with booze-fueled partying in beachside bars, nightclubs, casual friendships, and all the other shenanigans that marks a young man's search for meaning in a fun coastal beach town.

But gradually, something shifted. In that unstructured time—sunset walks along empty beaches, quiet mornings with nothing planned—my experiences began to merge into understanding. The boxing tent's lessons of resilience, the challenges of severed friendship, the disorientation of being a stranger in a strange land—all these began to speak to me in a language deeper than words.

This growth wasn't something I could force or schedule. It happened because I'd accidentally created the conditions for it: the shelter of that beach town, the space of unstructured time, and eventually, the support of new friendships.

This is what LeeWay offers the modern hero—not just rest, but the conditions for transformation. Not escape from the journey, but the important margin that makes the journey sustainable.

Can you create this in your own life? Can you resist the cultural pressure to be constantly in motion, perpetually productive, always onto the next thing? Can you build in the shelter, space, and support you need not just to survive your adventures but to understand them?

Your journey needs both movement and pause, both challenge and understanding. Without leeway—without consciously creating these protected spaces for processing and growth—even the most heroic efforts lead only to exhaustion, not growth.

THE INCOMPLETE HERO: MODERN MEDIA'S MISSING RETURN

Our culture's storytelling reveals much about our shared values and blind spots. Have you ever noticed how many popular film franchises—particularly in the superhero genre—present an incomplete version of the Hero's Journey? Characters in Marvel and DC films tend to remain frozen in a constant adolescence, cycling through new challenges without evolving into fully integrated adults. Batman saves Gotham for the fiftieth time, but still can't process his childhood trauma. *Iron Man* builds a new suit but stays stuck in the same emotional patterns.

This incomplete storytelling pattern is more than just a convenient formula for endless sequels—it reflects and reinforces our cultural mixed feelings about the complete arc of adult development. We celebrate the departure, the struggle, and the victory, but grow strangely quiet about what comes after.

What happens to the hero who completes their mission? What does integration and maturity look like? How does individual achievement transform into helpful contribution? These questions remain largely unaddressed in our most popular myths.

Batman may save Gotham repeatedly, but he rarely grows beyond his basic wound. *Iron Man* might develop new suits, but his core character remains stuck in the same psychological patterns. The commercial need for these characters to remain recognizable and marketable keeps them locked in an endless middle-stage of the journey.

This creates a troubling gap in our cultural imagination. Without complete examples of the return and integration stages, we're left without maps for our later life transitions. No wonder so many adults feel stuck, unable to imagine evolution beyond the initial adventures of early adulthood. No wonder we struggle with the shift from achievement to contribution, from individual heroics to community leadership.

When our heroes never entirely mature—never evolve beyond the endless cycle of crisis and response—we lose sight of what might lie beyond our own current challenges.

The few exceptions in popular media stand out precisely because they complete the full circle. In *Logan*, we finally see Wolverine confront his mortality and legacy, finding purpose not in another battle but in ensuring the future for the next generation. *The Lord of the Rings* trilogy, unlike most franchises, courageously shows us the return—Frodo forever changed, unable to easily resume his former life, ultimately departing to find healing beyond the bounds of his familiar world.

These complete journeys stay with us differently. They resonate with a larger truth about the nature of transformation—that it doesn't just make us better at what we already do, but fundamentally changes who we are and how we relate to the world.

The true Hero's Journey doesn't actually end with the climactic battle or claiming the magical elixir. It continues through return, integration, and ultimately, giving back—the stage where personal achievement transforms into contribution. Without these final chapters, we're left with an incomplete template for our own becoming.

Next time you watch a superhero film or binge a popular series, notice how often the story cycles through departure and initiation while avoiding the return. Notice how rarely we see our cultural heroes engaged in the vulnerable, complex work of integration—of bringing their gifts back to community, of mentoring the next generation, of finding meaning beyond the adrenaline of adventure.

And then ask yourself: what might lie beyond the battle in your own Hero's Journey? What would true integration and growth look like for the gifts and wisdom you've earned through your trials?

THE SPIRAL NATURE OF GROWTH

One of the most liberating realizations about the Hero's Journey is that it's not linear but spiral. We don't complete it once and arrive at some perfect, finished state. We circle back through similar terrain at different levels, encountering familiar challenges with new resources, revisiting old wounds with greater perspective.

This spiral nature explains why we can feel both advanced and beginner, why we can teach others what we're still learning ourselves, why we can be wise in one domain while fumbling in another. We're not moving in a straight line toward perfection but in a spiral toward integration and wholeness.

I've returned to the Ordinary World and heard new Calls to Adventure countless times since my younger years. Each cycle has strengthened my understanding of myself and my place in the world. Each return has brought gifts I couldn't have imagined when I first set out. Each new departure has required its own courage.

And here's the beautiful oddity: as the journey becomes more familiar, it also becomes more mysterious. The outer limits may narrow, but the inner ones expand. The questions become less about what to do and more about how to be. The adventures shift from conquering external obstacles to embracing internal conflicts.

YOUR JOURNEY, YOUR WAY

As a fellow traveler rather than an expert guide, I offer these reflections not as definitive maps but as potential lanterns for your unique path. I'm still finding my way too. The Hero's Journey provides a framework, but you'll discover territories Campbell never named, encounter challenges no myth has recorded, and bring back gifts uniquely yours to offer. Your Hero's Journey won't look like mine, and thank goodness for that. It likely won't look like anyone else's too. It will be shaped by your particular wounds and gifts, by the specific calls that speed up your pulse, by the challenges that both terrify and attract you. There's no standardized route to becoming yourself.

What matters isn't that you follow some prescribed path but that you engage authentically with wherever you find yourself. The hero's way teaches that showing up fully—even with bruises and uncertainty— matters more than perfect technique or guaranteed victory. It's about reclaiming the parts you've hidden or denied, integrating the shadows and the light, and bringing your whole Self to this brief, beautiful experience of being human.

So wherever you stand today in your own unfolding story—know that you're not alone. Across time and culture, countless others have walked similar paths, faced similar doubts, and discovered similar truths.

The modern hero isn't some exceptional being with supernatural powers. The modern hero is you—showing up for your life with courage, vulnerability, and an open heart, willing to be changed by what you encounter, ready to offer your unique gifts to a world that needs exactly what only you can bring.

In Chapter 2, we're going to dig into why we're wired for this journey in the first place. Not with fancy academic jargon that puts you to sleep, but through real stories and practical insights about how growth is literally coded into our DNA. I promise to give your eyes a break from boxing metaphors—I think I've stretched that canvas as far as it can go without snapping. By examining the principles of growth and evolution through the lenses of psychology, biology, and social science, we will uncover the mechanisms driving our relentless pursuit of personal development. This exploration will deepen our understanding of the interconnectedness between our individual journeys and the grand unfolding of the universe itself. Get ready to dive deep into what makes us tick!

———

CHAPTER 1 SUMMARY

So, we've made it through Chapter 1, where I dragged you along on my dubious adventure of getting repeatedly punched in the face in an Australian boxing tent—and yes, I used it as an example way too many times! But beyond my embarrassing tales of flying sweat and questionable life choices, we uncovered something pretty significant: that ancient pattern every hero walks, whether they know it or not.

KEY LEARNINGS:

- The Hero's Journey isn't just for caped crusaders—it's for everyday people brave enough to grow
- Your biggest challenges aren't random cosmic jokes but essential stations on your path
- That uncomfortable "something's missing" feeling? That's your call to adventure

- We all need "leeway"—sacred space between action where meaning actually forms

KEY TAKEAWAYS:

- Real heroism is facing your demons with shaky knees and doing it anyway
- The journey spirals—you'll revisit similar territory at deeper levels
- Your story won't look like mine or anyone else's, and thank God for that
- Sometimes your best mate has to punch you in the face for deeper truth to emerge

Reflective Question: What's your boxing tent—that thing challenging you to step beyond comfortable into the territory where real growth happens? And what might be waiting for you on the other side of that fear?

WHAT'S REALLY BEHIND THAT "SOMETHING MORE" FEELING

Remember that scene in *The Matrix* where Neo sits in his cubicle, staring through his monitor like it's a window to nowhere, his soul slowly dissolving into corporate gray? If you've ever felt that bone-deep certainty that you're meant for something more—that maddening itch you can't quite scratch—then it's important to understand that this feeling isn't a flaw in your programming; it's the whole point.

You see, deep within the heart of every human being lies a powerful yearning—an innate drive for growth that, once awakened, can propel us forward on a transformative journey across all aspects of life. This desire for growth shapes our choices and aspirations. And honestly? I've spent way too many nights wondering where this yearning comes from—this restless feeling that there must be more to life than just surviving day to day. In this chapter, we'll explore where this drive actually comes from, viewed through the lenses of psychology, biology, and social science. By looking under the hood of the complex mechanisms and motivations behind this desire, maybe we'll better understand why we relentlessly pursue the path of personal evolution.

So let's get straight to it: where does this drive actually come from?

I discovered that this restless feeling isn't just personal—it's actually cosmic. The same force that drove the first atoms to bond together, that pushes plants toward sunlight, and that builds galaxies is the exact same energy driving your 2 a.m. existential crisis. Once you see this connection, you can't unsee it. And more importantly, you can work with it instead of against it.

From the explosive inception of the cosmos during the Big Bang, the universe has been ever-expanding, continuously adapting to shifting circumstances. As the physical world evolved from pure energy to atoms, molecules, cells, organisms, and ultimately conscious beings like us, our inner worlds have undergone a corresponding transformation.

As Moby sang, "We are all made of stars!" The very energy and matter that make up the cosmos have given rise to the complex, self-aware beings we are today. I find it humbling to consider that the same forces that formed stars are at work in our own desire to grow. We're not separate from this cosmic unfolding—we're an expression of it. Think about that for a moment: our personal growth journey is literally the universe becoming more conscious of itself through us.

Across all scales of this unfolding universe, a fundamental principle emerges: the constant drive to maintain internal stability and external equilibrium while adapting to external circumstances. This principle shows up everywhere—from atoms to human psychology to the Hero's Journey we explored in Chapter 1. It's the same pattern that psychologists have mapped in how we develop as individuals, in how our basic human needs are structured, and that you'll recognize in your own growth spurts and setbacks.

This principle, essential for survival and growth, is beautifully demonstrated in nature. Take the humble tree, for example. With roots reaching deep into the earth, the tree draws nutrients and water from the soil, transforming them into life-sustaining energy through photosynthesis—a powerful act of internal stability. Try it sometime: stand beneath an old oak and place your hand on its trunk. Feel the rough bark, cool and solid. Listen to the whisper of its leaves. That tree embodies a deep understanding of balance that humans are still striving to learn. At the same time, it engages with its environment, releasing oxygen into the atmosphere and providing shelter and sustenance for countless organisms, achieving a delicate external equilibrium that allows it to thrive in harmony.

Our immune systems are another brilliant example. Right now, as you're reading this, they're fighting off nasties we don't even know exist while keeping all the good bacteria happy—basically, a constant dance of internal stability and external equilibrium. Our bodies are doing all this without us even thinking about it. Makes you wonder what else is going on in there, right?

THE THREE STAGES: HOW EVERYTHING LEARNS TO GROW

Believe it or not, there's actually a pattern running through all of this growth and development, from the very first atoms right up to whatever personal growth challenge we're wrestling with right now.

I spent way too much time trying to figure this out, honestly. Like, why do I keep feeling this restless itch for something more, even when things are going well? Why does growth feel so necessary but also so damn difficult? And then I stumbled across this three-stage pattern that shows up everywhere—and I mean everywhere—in nature, and suddenly a lot of things started making sense.

Whether we're talking about atoms figuring out how to stick together or us trying to navigate a career change, the same basic process keeps showing up. It's like the universe has this one operating system that it uses for everything, and once you see it, you can't unsee it. Kind of like when someone points out that arrow in the FedEx logo—suddenly it's all you can see. Except this pattern is in literally everything.

Stage 1: Establishing Viability (Internal Stability)

Okay, so the first stage is basically about individual entities learning to become viable within their own conditions—which sounds fancy, but really just means learning to exist without falling apart. I know that might sound obvious, but think about it: every single thing in the universe has had to solve this problem before it could do anything else.

At the atomic level, those first atoms after the Big Bang? They had to figure out how to maintain their structure despite incredible heat and chaos. It's like the universe's first lesson in "getting your shit together"—excuse the language, but that's essentially what had to happen. If they couldn't hold themselves together, there'd be no molecules, no cells, and no you reading this right now. At the molecular level, water molecules had to learn to keep their bonds stable under different conditions. At the cellular level, early cells had to develop all their internal systems—metabolism, reproduction, waste management—just to stay alive.

At the organism level, early humans had to master fire and hunting skills, while other organisms developed their own survival strategies—birds learning to fly, plants developing root systems, animals mastering their environmental niches. Each species had to achieve basic competence within their framework.

And for us personally? This is the foundational work we all have to do —building self-awareness, dealing with our trauma, developing emotional regulation, learning practical life skills. It's establishing what that principle we talked about calls "internal stability"—getting our inner world organized enough that we're not constantly in crisis mode. You know, actually having our shit together for five minutes before the universe throws another curveball.

Stage 2: Finding Your People (Compatible Bonding)

Once we've got some basic stability sorted—and this is key, we can't really skip Stage 1 no matter how much we want to—then something interesting happens. As conditions become more complex or threatening, we start reaching out, looking for connections with others who get us, who share our values, who can support our growth rather than drain our energy. This isn't just nice to have—it's how we increase our resilience when the framework conditions of life get more challenging.

At the atomic level, this is when hydrogen bonds with oxygen to create water—something completely new and more capable than either could be alone.

At the molecular level, simple organic compounds started combining into complex proteins and the sophisticated molecular machinery we find inside living cells.

At the cellular level, individual cells began specializing and working together to become multicellular organisms—some becoming heart tissue, others becoming brain tissue, each contributing unique capabilities to the whole.

At the organism level, animals formed packs, hives, and communities. Wolves hunt together, bees create colonies, even plants form symbiotic relationships with fungi in their root systems.

For humans specifically, we developed language, shared beliefs, and cultural traditions. We figured out that we could survive and thrive better together, but—and this is crucial—only when we bonded with compatible others. This is where we recognize that we can't go it alone. We need others—not just for emotional support, but for survival itself.

Stage 3: Cooperating

The final stage is where different bonded groups learn to work together on challenges that are bigger than any single group can handle. As the framework conditions become even more complex and threatening, groups themselves have to adapt by cooperating with similar but compatible groups. This is where we create communities, organizations, movements —the collective structures that allow us to tackle challenges too big for any small group to handle on their own.

At the molecular level, different molecular systems cooperate in complex chemical reactions—like photosynthesis or cellular respiration— that make life possible.

At the cellular level, different types of specialized cells work together as organs and organ systems, creating the incredible coordination we see in complex organisms.

At the organism level, different species cooperate in ecosystems that maintain balance across entire environments—predator-prey relationships that prevent overpopulation, pollination partnerships between plants and insects, decomposer organisms that recycle nutrients for the whole system.

At the social level, human tribes and nations are now learning to cooperate on global challenges—climate change, pandemics, economic systems —stuff that crosses all boundaries and requires coordination our species has never attempted before.

On a personal level, this is about contributing to something larger than our immediate concerns—whether through our work, creative expression, how we raise our kids, or service to causes that transcend personal benefit. It's that shift from asking "What can I get?" to "What can I give?"

This is the stage where the hero returns with the elixir, where what we've learned becomes a gift we can offer to others. It's where our individual journey starts serving the collective journey of human evolution.

THE COSMIC PATTERN IN HUMAN HISTORY

Now here's where it gets pretty fascinating. This exact same three-stage pattern hasn't just shaped individual growth—it's shaped the entire story of human civilization. And understanding this progression is crucial for grasping our own personal growth journey, because we're literally living through the same process that has unfolded over hundreds of thousands of years.

Stage 1: Individual Mastery and Early Human Viability (300,000 - 10,000 BCE)

For most of human history, our ancestors' primary challenge was establishing individual and small-group viability. Think about what "getting your house in order" meant for early humans: mastering fire, developing hunting and gathering skills, creating basic tools, learning to read weather patterns and animal behavior.

This wasn't just about physical survival—it was about developing the cognitive and emotional frameworks that would later enable larger social cooperation. Early humans had to learn emotional regulation (panic gets you killed), delayed gratification (storing food for winter), and basic trust (sharing resources with their immediate group).

Archaeological evidence shows that early human groups were small—typically 20-50 individuals—because larger groups required social technologies that hadn't yet developed. Each person needed to be essentially self-sufficient within their small band.

Stage 2: Tribal Bonding and the Agricultural Revolution (10,000 BCE - 1500 CE)

Around 10,000 years ago, something remarkable happened: humans had become so individually viable that they could support larger, more permanent social bonds. The Agricultural Revolution wasn't just about farming —it was about humanity's transition from individual viability to systematic bonding and cooperation.

Suddenly, humans could form settlements of hundreds, then thousands of people. But this required entirely new social technologies: complex language systems, shared religious and cultural beliefs, social hierarchies, laws, and governance structures. These weren't luxuries— they were survival necessities for managing the increased complexity of larger groups.

Think about the development of written language, legal codes like Hammurabi's Code, religious traditions, and early forms of democracy in places like ancient Athens. These were all social bonding technologies that allowed humans to cooperate in groups far larger than our brains can naturally manage through personal relationships alone.

Stage 3: Global Cooperation and Planetary Challenges (1500 CE - Present)

The last 500 years represent humanity's awkward adolescent transition into Stage 3: learning to cooperate across tribal, national, and cultural boundaries to address challenges that transcend any single group's capacity to solve alone.

The forces driving this transition were largely technological and environmental, such as global trade networks, industrialization, population growth, and environmental challenges that crossed all boundaries. Suddenly, the challenges facing human civilization—climate change, nuclear weapons, pandemics, economic interdependence—required cooperation between groups that had been competitors for millennia.

We've developed impressive tools for planetary cooperation: international law, global communication networks, scientific collaboration across borders, and international organizations. Yet we're still learning how to use these tools effectively. Climate change, trade wars, and uneven pandemic responses all show our continued struggle to fully master plane-tary-scale cooperation.

But the thing is—this is exactly where we are in human development right now. We're learning to cooperate at the species level. Think about it: the baton of evolution has been passed to us, and we've become the most advanced cooperators in the known universe. We're now responsible for continuing that same pattern we've been exploring—from cosmic evolu-tion to conscious evolution. No pressure or anything.

WHY OUR PERSONAL JOURNEYS MATTER NOW MORE THAN EVER

Here's where this big-picture view connects directly to our personal growth: we're all simultaneously navigating these three evolutionary stages in our own development while living within a civilization that's struggling with the same transitions.

Remember our discussion of the modern hero from Chapter 1? Unlike the classic hero with supernatural powers, the modern Hero's Journey centers on overcoming internal struggles, confronting personal flaws, and striving for self-understanding. This is exactly what these three stages represent—our evolution from surviving to thriving to serving.

At the individual level, we're working to establish our own viability—developing the psychological, emotional, and practical skills needed to thrive in a complex modern world. This is our personal Stage 1 work: building self-awareness, healing trauma, developing competence, and creating internal stability.

At the same time, we're learning to form authentic bonds with others —finding our tribes, building meaningful relationships, and contributing to communities that share our values. This is our personal Stage 2 work: moving beyond pure self-interest toward mutual support and collab-oration.

And finally, we're being called to contribute to challenges larger than ourselves or our immediate communities—whether through our work, creative expression, parenting, or service to causes that transcend personal benefit. This is our personal Stage 3 work: aligning with something greater than our individual ego's agenda.

What makes this particularly challenging is that we're living through a time when our civilizational structures haven't yet caught up to our planetary challenges. The very institutions that helped us succeed at Stage 2 are now obstacles to Stage 3 cooperation. This creates both external stress (living in systems that aren't designed for current challenges) and internal stress (feeling called to contribute to solutions that seem impossibly complex).

Our individual Hero's Journeys? They're actually part of humanity's collective Hero's Journey toward a more evolved form of civilization. Which helps explain why our personal growth sometimes feels so bloody urgent and necessary. We're not just working on ourselves for selfish reasons—we're developing the consciousness and capabilities that our species needs to navigate this transition.

There's a principle that captures this perfectly: "Establishing internal stability and external equilibrium are the universal conditions necessary for evolutionary progress." Whether we're talking about atoms, cells, organisms, or human consciousness, one factor has been critical for evolution: if an entity at a particular plane of being is unable to establish itself in its framework of existence—to manage its internal stability and external equilibrium—then any attempts it makes to grow and develop by building a group structure will fail.

This is why the foundational work matters so much and why every Hero's Journey begins with getting our house in order before venturing into the unknown.

The same pattern that created stars, cells, and civilizations is now calling us forward on our own transformative journeys. The difference is, now we know we're part of something much bigger than our individual stories—we're part of the universe itself becoming more conscious, more connected, and more capable of creating the future we all need.

THE POWER OF ROOTS: GROWING TALL BY DIGGING DEEP

Remember those difficult trials our hero faced in Chapter 1? There's a reason why the journey always involves a descent before the triumphant climb. Every hero must go down before they can truly rise up.

I love to use the analogy of a tree to illustrate this important point. For a tree to grow tall and reach for the light, it must first sink its roots deep into the dark, rich soil of the earth. Or as Nietzsche so eloquently put it:

> "It is the same with the human being as with the tree. The higher they climb into the height and light, the more strongly their roots strive earthward, downward into the dark, the depths—into evil."

> — NIETZCHE

This truth is embedded in the ancient Tree of Life symbol found across spiritual traditions worldwide—from Norse mythology's Yggdrasil to the Kabbalistic Sephirot to the Mayan Wacah Chan. These diverse cultures independently recognized the same wisdom: growth requires both darkness and light, both descent and ascent, both roots and branches working in perfect balance.

Figure 2.1: The Tree of Life (Yggdrasil). Yggdrasil—the Norse World Tree that's been trying to tell us the whole time: your roots need to go as deep as your branches reach high. Those ancient myths weren't being poetic; they were being literal about how growth actually works.

You'd think with this universal truth staring at us from every tradition, we'd have figured out how to grow properly by now. But walk into any bookstore's self-help section and what do we see? Often it's shiny promises of "10 Steps to Success" or "Manifest Your Best Life Now!" Much of the industry has become a machine designed to sell us the next hit of inspirational dopamine. We've all been there—buying these books by the dozen, highlighting profound-sounding quotes, feeling that rush of "this is it!" motivation...only to then watch it evaporate a week later.

Many of these books seem brilliantly designed to feed our ego's hunger for quick fixes while carefully stepping around the messy work of genuine transformation. It makes sense from a business perspective—temporary inspiration often proves more profitable than lasting transformation. After all, a book that genuinely solved all our problems might eliminate the need to buy the author's next five titles.

I should know about this self-help dopamine loop—I was literally paid to participate in it.

At my first job as a young impressionable 18-year-old, there was this bonus scheme where I could literally earn money for reading self-help books and writing reports. Read a book, write a report, collect cash. But it went further—they'd also pay us to attend yoga classes, meditate, even eat healthily. Teenage me thought I'd discovered the world's best hack—getting paid hundreds of dollars to 'improve myself'? Brilliant.

Naturally I dove in head first, devouring Tony Robbins and Napoleon Hill, Deepak Chopra, all the usual Law of Attraction stuff, writing earnest reports about positive thinking, collecting my bonuses while doing downward dogs and sipping green juice. Looking back now, the whole setup was oddly ahead of its time—this was before corporate wellness programs, before yoga studios on every corner. But it still felt a little off.

The person behind this program was actually quite well-known in the 'law of attraction' world. One of those guys whose name you might recognize if you were into that scene in the early 2000s. Charismatic, charming, wealthy, the full 'I've manifested abundance' package. But even as a teenager, watching him preach positive thinking while wielding power and wealth in ways that felt... transactional... planted a seed of skepticism I couldn't yet articulate.

It took me years—and definitely no manifestation of abundant wealth

—to realize I was caught in a pattern. After cycling through dozens of these books, watching that familiar post-inspiration slump return again and again, I began searching for more meaningful approaches. What I discovered is that lasting transformation often requires more than uplifting quotes and morning affirmations. It requires work. Deep, difficult work. Lasting transformation asks us to face the shadows, examine wounds, challenge core beliefs—the psychological equivalent of sending roots down into dark soil.

That's not to say those law of attraction gurus, or manifestation warriors were a sham. Quite the opposite in fact. Sure, I may occasionally roll my eyes at those same gurus I once admired or find those TikTok manifestation influencers cringe now but they had their place and served their purpose for me. They met me—a sheltered Yorkshire lad who'd been taught to know his place—where I was at that particular moment in time and cracked open my working-class worldview in ways that nothing else had. They were doorways, the first steps on a longer path to where I am now, writing my own doorway. But there's a difference between a doorway and a home. Many of us get stuck in the hallway, continuously opening new doors but never fully entering the rooms of deeper work, never making ourselves at home in any practice.

WHY WE OFTEN AVOID THE DARKER TERRITORY

So why do many self-help approaches tend to sidestep the darker territory? Sure, it's partly about sales—inspirational quick fixes often sell better than books about the hard work of confronting our shadows. But I think it goes deeper than commerce. It reflects our collective discomfort with authentic human struggle. And our culture has created a powerful taboo around discussing these darker aspects of growth.

We see this discomfort everywhere, from casual conversations to corporate boardrooms. I've seen this play out countless times: the moment someone begins speaking honestly about depression, childhood trauma, or their darker emotions, the room grows tense. People begin fidgeting nervously in their seats. Try mentioning in a job interview that you've struggled with anxiety—suddenly you might be seen as a "liability." Share with your sports team that you're working through grief, and watch how quickly they might question your commitment or mental toughness.

This judgment isn't just obvious stuff, either. It's often woven right into the structure of our institutions. I once mentioned scheduling around a therapy appointment in a corporate environment where leadership praised 'authenticity' and 'bringing your whole self to work' in mission statements. The subtle shift in how I was perceived was unmistakable.

What makes this particularly challenging is how it can drive us further into isolation. When someone finally musters the courage to share their authentic experience and is met with judgment or dismissal, they don't just stop sharing—they retreat further into shame. "See?" the inner critic whispers. "This is why you shouldn't have said anything. You're too much. You're broken."

Our culture's positivity preference has made many of us uncomfortable with difficulty. We're often told to "focus on the good," "just be positive," and "fake it till you make it." The result? We're living in a time where many feel fundamentally flawed because our natural human struggles don't match the polished success stories surrounding us. When we can't show our struggle, it becomes harder to heal it.

This might be why much of the self-help industry gravitates toward quick fix, surface-level solutions—addressing the real issues would mean confronting the darkness we've been taught to fear. It would mean admitting that growth often hurts, that transformation requires loss, that becoming who we're meant to be sometimes means letting parts of ourselves die.

THE THREE FACES OF AVOIDANCE

So what exactly does this surface-level approach look like? Let me name it clearly, because once you can see it, you can catch yourself doing it.

Spiritual bypass is a term coined by psychologist John Welwood. It's using spiritual concepts to avoid psychological work. Instead of feeling the grief, you "accept what is." Instead of processing anger, you "send love and light." The concept isn't wrong—acceptance and love are genuine practices. But they're being used to skip the messy human work of actually feeling what you feel.

Toxic positivity is the refusal to acknowledge that anything is wrong. "Good vibes only." "Everything happens for a reason." It's emotional suppression wearing a smiley face.

Toxic manifestation is lying to yourself and calling it faith. "Speak it into existence." "The universe doesn't know the difference between reality and visualization." It takes a genuine insight—that our beliefs shape our experience—and turns it into magical thinking that bypasses honest self-assessment.

All three are branches without roots. They're the hallway, not the home.

EARLY EMBERS OF CHANGE

I have a lot of hope, though. I'm seeing early embers of something different, particularly with Gen Z. These digital natives have grown up swimming in a sea of toxic positivity—Instagram perfection, LinkedIn success theater, and "good vibes only" culture. But here's what's interesting: they're not all buying it anymore.

They've watched millennials burn out chasing happiness hacks and morning routines. They've seen their parents' generation struggle in silence while posting motivational quotes. And they're increasingly calling bullshit on the whole performance.

Their exhaustion with toxic positivity is creating a genuine hunger for authenticity that traditional self-help simply doesn't provide. They want to talk about trauma, not transcend it with affirmations. They want to examine systemic issues, not just manifest individual success. They want to do the shadow work that previous generations swept under the rug of "positive thinking."

This desire for authenticity—for permission to be human—is spreading beyond Gen Z. I'm witnessing it in unexpected places, like workshops where successful entrepreneurs confess they've read every self-help and leadership book on the market, yet still feel empty inside. One founder recently told me, "I've applied all the techniques, reached all my goals, built the company, but I still feel like I'm playing a role rather than living my life." His bookshelves were full, but his inner life was hollow because few books had guided him to examine the childhood wounds driving his relentless need to prove himself.

These entrepreneurs are discovering what the younger generation already senses: we can't optimize our way out of pain we haven't let ourselves feel. We can't scale our way past trauma we haven't processed. We can't hustle our way into wholeness without first acknowledging where we feel broken.

The embers are still small, still fragile. But they're real. And they're spreading.

ALL BRANCHES, NO ROOTS.

So let's return to that tree we talked about—the one that must sink its roots deep into dark soil before it can reach toward the light.

I've been the wrong kind of tree more times than I can count. "How are you, Lee?" "Oh, great!" I say, branches reaching confidently toward the sun while my roots barely scratch the surface. All growth upward, no growth downward. We all play this game, don't we? Racing toward the light, posting our wins, showcasing our branches heavy with achievement— while secretly feeling the wobble beneath us, knowing one good storm will expose how unsteady we really are.

For years, I thought I could cheat the system. Just keep growing upward. Read another self-help book. Try another morning routine. Manifest harder. Why dig into painful soil when you could just reach higher? Why examine old wounds when you could set new goals? I became an expert at looking successful while feeling hollow—a tree that photographs beautifully but would topple in the first real storm.

And life always sends that storm. It's almost like the universe has a way of testing whether you've done the real work or just performed it. In my own journey, every time I've tried to skip past the inner work— avoiding grief, numbing anxiety, distracting myself from shame—I've found myself toppling over when life's winds blew strong. The tallest redwoods have the deepest roots for a reason. We can rise only as high as our foundation is deep.

Lasting transformation happens when we balance reaching for the light with digging into the darkness. When we have the courage to examine our traumas, face our fears, and acknowledge our shadows—that's when we build foundations strong enough to support genuine growth. That's when we become like those ancient oaks that withstand centuries of storms because their roots run as deep as their branches reach high.

WHAT TREES HAVE ALWAYS KNOWN

So the tree we've been contemplating—with its roots reaching deep into earth while branches reach for light—it's been showing us the whole truth all along. We just had to learn to see it.

The Hero's Journey from Chapter 1 encoded this same wisdom. That moment when every hero must descend—when Jonah gets swallowed by the whale, when Inanna descends to face her dark sister, when Luke enters the cave on Dagobah? The hero's underworld IS the tree's dark soil. The dragon's lair, the belly of the beast, the labyrinth—these aren't detours from growth. They're where growth happens. Just as roots must push through darkness to find nutrients, the hero must descend into psychological depths to find treasure.

This is why trees dominate every mythology. Yggdrasil doesn't just reach toward Asgard—its roots plunge through corpse-shore Náströnd into the well of wisdom. Buddha didn't find enlightenment by climbing the Bodhi tree but by sitting beneath it, grounded. Even Eden gave us two trees—knowledge and life—as if to say from the beginning: consciousness and vitality both grow from the same dark soil.

What we call "depth work" in modern psychology, our ancestors simply called necessary. The tree has always known: you can only grow as high as you're willing to dig deep.

Those three evolutionary stages we traced—from atoms achieving stability to molecules forming bonds to systems creating cooperation— they map perfectly onto both the tree's wisdom and the hero's path.

The hero descending into darkness? That's Stage 1 viability work, establishing internal stability by integrating what we've avoided. It's roots pushing through soil, finding foundation. Finding mentors and allies? Stage 2 compatible bonding—the mycorrhizal networks that connect forest root systems, sharing nutrients and information. Returning with gifts for the community? Stage 3 cooperation—the tree that gives oxygen, shelter, fruit, a whole ecosystem of mutual benefit.

The pattern is fractal, repeating at every scale. From cosmic to cellular to personal, it's the same dance of stability, connection, and service.

WHAT THAT RESTLESS FEELING REALLY IS

Which brings us back to that bone-deep restlessness that started this whole exploration.

Remember Neo staring through his monitor at the beginning of this chapter? That soul-dissolving certainty that you're meant for more? Now we know what it is: the same force that taught atoms to bond, that pushes plants toward light, that spent 13.8 billion years turning stardust into consciousness. It's evolution itself, knocking at your door.

That 2 a.m. restlessness isn't a flaw in your programming—it's the program working perfectly. When you lie awake wondering "Is this all there is?"—that's not ingratitude or weakness. That's the universe saying you're ready for your next stage of growth.

Your discontent is cosmic. Your yearning is evolutionary. The itch you can't scratch is the same force that builds galaxies now trying to build something through you.

The universe has been preparing for your growth since the Big Bang. Every star that formed, every atom that bonded, every creature that learned to cooperate—all of it has led to this moment where you sit reading these words, feeling that familiar hunger for more.

This restlessness arrives precisely when you're ready. Maybe you've found stability in one area and now feel pulled toward deeper connections. Maybe you've found your people and sense a call to serve something greater. Or maybe you're being called to circle back, to sink your roots deeper before reaching higher.

The question isn't whether you'll evolve—that's as inevitable as gravity. The question is: will you work with this force consciously, or be dragged forward by your suffering?

What stage calls to you now? Where do you need to establish viability —what roots need strengthening? Who are your compatible bonds—what connections await? What larger purpose might you serve once your foundation is solid?

That restless feeling isn't telling you something's wrong. It's telling you something's ready to be born. The force that builds galaxies is building something through you.

The tree has been showing us all along: growth requires both light and darkness, both ascending and descending, both the visible triumph and the invisible work.

All you have to do is say yes to both.

————

CHAPTER 2 SUMMARY

So, Chapter 2 took us from Neo's cubicle existential crisis to discovering we're literally made of stardust—and that restlessness you feel? It's the same force that built galaxies now building you. We traced this cosmic itch through three stages everything follows: getting your shit together (viability), finding your weird tribe (bonding), and doing something that actually matters (cooperation). Plus that time I got paid to read self-help books at 18? Peak capitalism meets personal development.

KEY LEARNINGS:

- Your existential crisis is evolution tapping you on the shoulder
- The universe has been getting its act together for 13.8 billion years—you're just the latest project
- That self-help book addiction isn't fixing you because it's all branches, no roots
- Can't skip stages: you need internal stability before meaningful connection
- That Sunday night dread? Cosmic growing pains, mate
- Trees knew all along: you can only grow as high as your roots go deep

KEY TAKEAWAYS:

- Your dissatisfaction isn't a bug—it's the feature that drives all growth
- From atoms to civilizations, same pattern: survive, connect, contribute
- Toxic positivity can keep us stuck in the hallway, never entering the rooms of deeper work
- Understanding you're part of something bigger makes the struggle worthwhile
- The Hero's Journey descent = the tree's roots = your inner work (it's all the same pattern)

Reflective Questions:

1. Which stage has you right now—still sorting yourself out, desperately seeking your people, or hearing that call to serve something bigger?
2. What are you avoiding by reaching for another self-help book instead of sitting with the uncomfortable darkness where real growth happens?

WHY HAVING EVERYTHING CAN STILL LEAVE YOU FEELING EMPTY

I remember my first encounter with the term "shadow work" at a breathwork session in Mexico. When the facilitator suggested I needed to "do my shadow work" after we finished our intense breathing exercises, I nodded politely while thinking, *"What the hell is that?"* I thought it was some kind of shadow boxing activity like capoeira (that Brazilian martial art where they dance-fight on beaches). Was I supposed to physically battle my demons or what?

Turns out, shadow work isn't about physical combat—it's about having the courage to face the parts of ourselves we've hidden away or disowned. Those aspects we've banished to the shadowy regions of our inner world. Remember that tree metaphor from Chapter 2—how we need deep roots in dark soil before we can grow tall? Well, shadow work is what happens down in that darkness. It's the psychological equivalent of sending roots into the hidden parts of ourselves we'd rather ignore.

Think about it this way: we all have aspects of our personality that we've learned are "unacceptable"—maybe anger, vulnerability, selfishness, or neediness. Rather than embracing, working with, and accepting these natural parts of ourselves, we often push them into the shadows—sometimes consciously suppressing them, other times unconsciously repressing them—pretending they don't exist. But this is the thing about shadows—

just because you can't see them doesn't mean they're not there. They don't disappear; they go into hiding underground, where they can quietly influence our behavior in ways we often don't recognize.

You know those people who drive you absolutely nuts for reasons you can't quite explain? The ones whose behavior hits a nerve? That's often your shadow at work. The qualities that provoke the strongest reactions in us tend to be the very ones we've disowned in ourselves—though we rarely make that connection in the moment. The person whose neediness drives you crazy might be reflecting your own unacknowledged need for attention. The colleague whose arrogance bothers you could be mirroring your own hidden pride. These aren't coincidences—they're invitations to reclaim the parts of yourself you've rejected.

Shadow work is the process of bringing these hidden aspects back into the light—not to act them out destructively, but to *integrate* them consciously. It's about becoming whole rather than just appearing good. And this integration is absolutely essential for any genuine psychological growth, whether we're talking about meeting our basic human needs or pursuing deeper transformation.

Shadow work ties directly into what psychologist Abraham Maslow called self-actualization—the process of becoming *who* we truly are rather than who we *think* we should be. Unfortunately though, things can get a bit confusing in our culture: when most people hear "self-actualization," they picture it as the classic Western ladder of success. Career advancement, financial achievement, social status, personal accomplishments—climbing step by step toward becoming your "best self." Many people mistake this conventional ladder of success for what Maslow actually meant by self-actualization.

This misunderstanding leads to that familiar problem: you can have everything society defines as success yet still feel empty inside. Remember that CEO from Chapter 2 who'd read every self-help book but still felt like he was "playing a role rather than living his life"? He'd climbed what he thought was the ladder to self-actualization, but without doing the foundational work of facing his hidden aspects—his shadow—he remained fundamentally disconnected from himself, and wasn't able to truly stand tall.

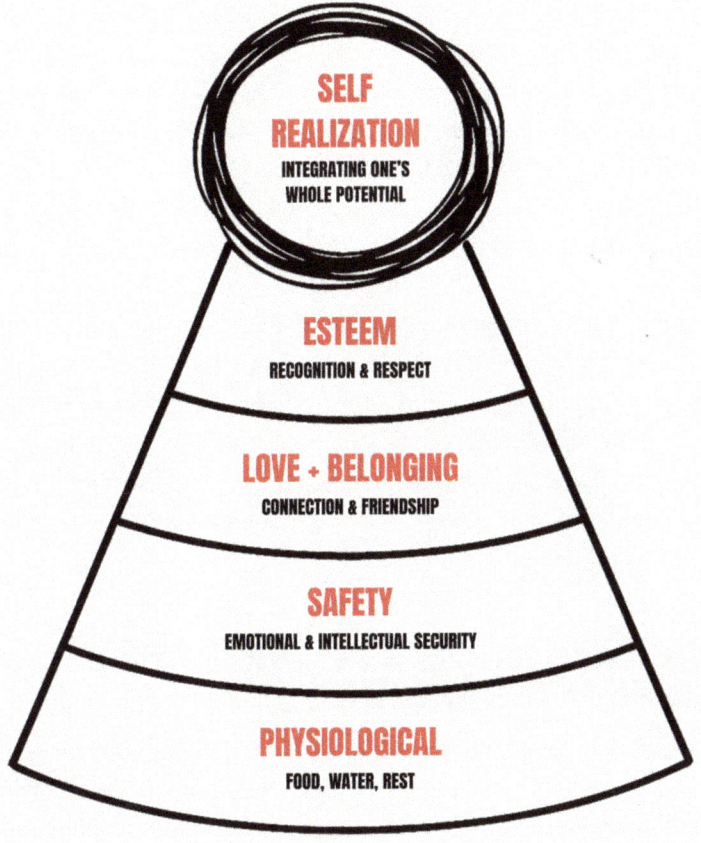

Figure 3.1: Maslow's Hierarchy of Needs. *Maslow's famous pyramid—turns out you can't ponder life's meaning when you're hungry. The hierarchy shows why basic needs come first, and why having everything you "should" want can still leave you empty if your growth needs aren't met.*

True self-actualization isn't about reaching the top of society's prede-termined success metrics. It's about authentically becoming yourself—which means you can't get there while significant parts of yourself remain hidden in the shadows, quietly undermining your foundation.

This is where Maslow's hierarchy of needs becomes such a powerful framework for understanding this deeper work. It's the practical work of facing our shadows that makes authentic growth possible.

You've probably seen the pyramid diagram somewhere—it maps out five fundamental human needs. They stack up from the most basic to the most advanced: physiological needs, safety needs, love and belonging needs, esteem needs, and finally, self-actualization at the top. The idea is that these needs are what drive our behavior and shape what motivates us and what we're aiming for in life.

For us modern heroes, understanding Maslow's hierarchy provides that crucial wisdom—a map showing which needs must be addressed before we can reach our fullest potential.

Maslow recognized what many of us discover the hard way: we can't skip steps on this journey. Just as you wouldn't try to build the top floor of a house before laying the foundation, we can't fully pursue self-actualiza-tion when we're worried about our basic security. And this is where shadow work becomes essential—because often, it's our unacknowledged wounds and fears that secretly sabotage our foundation, no matter how stable things appear on the surface.

MASLOW'S HIERARCHY OF NEEDS: A FRAMEWORK FOR UNDERSTANDING HUMAN MOTIVATION

So let's look at how Maslow actually mapped this out with his framework —the one everyone's seen as that pyramid diagram. It maps out five funda-mental human needs that drive our behavior and shape what we're aiming for in life. Starting from the bottom, they are:

- Physiological needs: water, air, food, homeostasis, and sex
- Safety needs: shelter, clothing, routine, and familiarity
- Love and belonging needs: connection to others and affection

- Esteem needs: external esteem (respect from others, reputation) and internal esteem (self-respect, accomplishment)
- Self-actualization needs: self-growth and realizing our full potential

Basic Needs: The Foundation of Survival and Well-Being

Basic needs, which include physiological and safety needs, are essential for survival and well-being. Think of them as the ground floor of a house—not the most exciting part perhaps, but try building the upper stories without it. Maslow referred to these as "deficiency needs" because when they aren't met, we can experience anxiety and fear. Once these needs are satisfied, though, they no longer dominate our consciousness.

Meeting basic needs gives us a temporary sense of happiness, as the brain releases dopamine, the pleasure chemical. But, this happiness can often be fleeting, quickly replaced by anxiety and fear about meeting future needs. Even when today's needs are met, we start worrying about tomorrow's—will I have enough money next month? What if I lose my job? This creates an exhausting pattern: feel anxious about needs → meet them → feel briefly relieved → immediately start worrying about meeting them again → back to anxiety.

I notice this in myself when I'm overtired or hungry—suddenly my capacity for compassionate interaction goes out the window, and I'm focused solely on the immediate need. Or when I feel financially insecure, my creative work suffers. These aren't character flaws—they're natural responses to unmet basic needs. This constant worry about future needs can make it challenging to focus on growth, as we might be preoccupied with ensuring tomorrow's security even when today's is handled.

But there's a catch: this pattern can also trap us. We end up constantly worried about meeting basic needs, even when they're actually met. Plus, all that anxiety about survival stops us from taking risks or pursuing growth. Makes sense from an evolutionary standpoint—our caveman brain figures it's better to stay alive than to pursue our dreams of becoming a poet. Our deficiency needs will always take precedence over our growth needs, which is why addressing and satisfying our basic needs comes before pursuing higher levels of development. Put simply: it's hard to ponder the meaning of life when you're worried about making rent.

Growth Needs: The Path to Self-Actualization and Alignment with the True Self

Just as that tree needs both strong roots and reaching branches to thrive, humans require both basic security and higher growth to feel complete. This balance forms the core of Abraham Maslow's hierarchy of needs, where our journey toward self-actualization depends on addressing both foundational stability and reaching toward our highest potential.

This isn't just a rich guy problem either—it's a human problem. I've sat with men from all walks of life in group councils—not just executives, but teachers, tradesmen, artists, retired military, stay-at-home dads. Doesn't matter their profession or paycheck. When they feel safe enough to drop the masks, the same confession emerges: 'I have everything I should want, but I feel nothing.' These aren't lazy or ungrateful men—they're human beings who've secured their basic needs but haven't addressed their growth needs. Their souls are hungry.

Growth needs are about feeling like you're actually living your life instead of just going through the motions of some role society handed you. Maslow referred to these as "being" needs—a way of being in the world with minimal fear and anxiety, allowing us to feel a deep sense of alignment with our authentic nature.

The weird thing about growth needs though, is the more you feed them, the hungrier they get. The goal is making this alignment with our soul permanent—living a life driven by our values and purpose rather than just ticking boxes society handed us. That's when life can stop feeling empty despite having all the "right" stuff.

You know that feeling on Sunday evenings—the dread that settles in before another workweek begins? That's often a signal that your growth needs aren't being met, even if your basic needs are well-covered. You might have a job that pays well and offers security (meeting basic needs), but doesn't allow you to express your creativity or make a difference (growth needs). That misalignment creates a nagging sense of dissatisfaction that no amount of material success can resolve.

When our soul is in alignment, we experience a deep sense that our life has both meaning and significance. The ability to make a difference in the world creates feelings of significance, while a lack of autonomy or the sense that our life has no meaning can leave us feeling empty and unfulfilled. Finding meaning and making a difference are crucial for satisfying our growth needs.

Maslow eloquently captures this relationship between our different needs:

"Man's higher nature rests on his lower nature, needing it as a foundation...The best way to develop this higher nature is to fulfill and gratify the lower nature first."

— ABRAHAM MASLOW

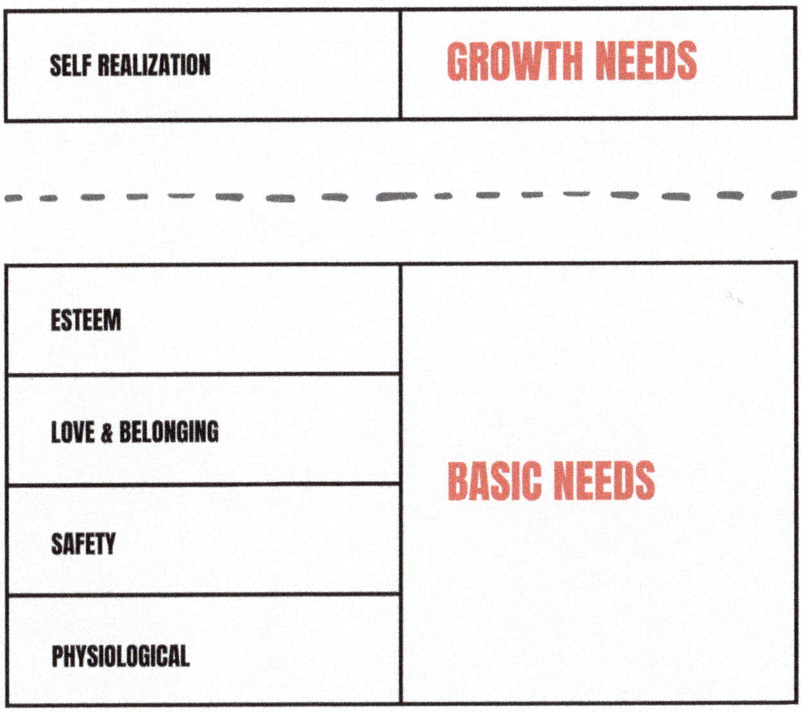

SELF REALIZATION	**GROWTH NEEDS**

ESTEEM	
LOVE & BELONGING	**BASIC NEEDS**
SAFETY	
PHYSIOLOGICAL	

Figure 3.2: Basic Needs vs. Growth Needs. Maslow's famous pyramid—turns out you can't ponder life's meaning when you're hungry.

Have you ever achieved something you thought would make you happy, only to feel a strange emptiness afterward? That's often a sign that you've satisfied a deficiency need but not a growth need.

When any of these needs aren't being met—whether it's basic survival stuff or deeper growth stuff—you feel it. Your whole system goes into alert mode. And here's the key: once you've got the foundation sorted, that's when the real adventure begins. That's when your soul starts tapping you on the shoulder, asking "Right then, what are we actually here for?"

That Tree metaphor we keep talking about? This is exactly what it looks like in practice. Maslow's hierarchy works the same way. Your basic needs—food, safety, shelter—they're like the roots. You've got to get those sorted before you can focus on the branches—love, self-respect, actually becoming who you're meant to be. Think about it: a tree with dodgy roots isn't going to waste energy on pretty leaves. It's too busy trying not to fall over.

I love how everyday stories can help us understand complex psychological concepts, and *Stranger Things* does this brilliantly. The show's journey from monsters-in-the-woods terror to meaningful connection offers a perfect lens for understanding Maslow's hierarchy.

Remember when we first met the kids in Hawkins? Their ordinary world gets flipped upside down (literally), and suddenly they're scrambling just to stay alive. Demogorgons hunting them, shadowy government types chasing them—their focus narrows to pure survival, the bottom of Maslow's pyramid. It's fight or flight, no room for existential questions when something's trying to eat you.

But watch what happens as the series unfolds. Once they catch their breath from immediate danger, their focus shifts. The "Party" they form isn't just a practical monster-fighting squad—it becomes family. These kids, some outsiders and misfits, create belonging for each other. I see this in workshops all the time; once people feel physically safe, their hunger for connection emerges like it was there all along (which it was).

By later seasons, you can spot esteem needs emerging. Eleven struggling to understand her worth beyond her powers. Will searching for identity after being "that kid who disappeared." Even Steve Harrington—remember his journey from superficial popular guy at school to the reluctant, but reliable, guardian? That's what growth toward self-actualization looks like, and it rarely happens in a vacuum. His perceived needs are completely transformed because of the people around him.

What hits home for me about *Stranger Things* is how it shows that we don't climb Maslow's pyramid alone. Each character supports the others' development. When Mike tells Eleven "You're not a monster," he's helping meet her belonging needs. When the group validates Will's experiences, they're addressing his esteem needs. The modern Hero's Journey isn't a solo trek up a mountain—it's more like a group expedition where we take turns carrying each other's backpacks.

The thing is, knowing where you are on this hierarchy is only half the battle. The real work comes in recognizing what's actually needed at each level—and being honest about which needs are genuinely unmet versus which boxes we're just checking because society told us to.

When we've checked all the boxes at the lower levels of Maslow's hierarchy yet still feel that strange emptiness, we're hearing something important. Without alignment to something beyond ourselves, our achievements often feel hollow despite outward success.

But before we dive deeper into this rabbit hole, maybe give yourself some *leeway* here and ask: Which level of the hierarchy resonates with what you're living through right now? What needs the most immediate attention, and what one small action could you take today to address needs at that level?

THE HERO'S CAVERN: INTEGRATION THROUGH GUIDED DARKNESS

Every hero carries wounds from their past that shape their journey. My own story is no different. Like Luke Skywalker's missing hand or *Harry Potter's* lightning scar, my wounds became both a vulnerability and a source of strength. I experienced firsthand how early events that breach our sense of security can shape our beliefs and fears, creating obstacles on our path to personal growth.

During formative years, away from my family's protective circle, I faced a situation that left marks no one could see but that I felt every day. Nothing Hollywood-dramatic—but it was a single moment that compromised the trust and safety most children take for granted. For years, I carried the emotional scars of this early incident, unconsciously allowing it to shape my beliefs about myself and the world around me. Struggling with trust issues, fear of abandonment, and a general sense that the world was not a safe place, it wasn't until I began actively working on my personal growth and self-awareness that I found the strength to confront this early trauma and embark on the journey of healing.

Look, I'm not trying to turn this into some sob story about my past. But here's what I've learned the hard way: if you don't deal with your old wounds, they deal with you. They become the invisible puppeteers pulling your strings, making your decisions, and you're walking around thinking you're in charge when really, you're just acting out patterns you don't even recognize.

And here's what nobody tells you about healing: it doesn't happen overnight or in a straight line. For me, it was a stumbling journey of two steps forward, one step back—therapy sessions where I'd have break-throughs followed by weeks of resisting the very insights I'd gained. But gradually, with the support of trusted friends and mentors who made me feel heard and seen, I began cultivating an inner sense of safety that no external circumstance could completely shatter. And in hindsight, I can see how each painful step was actually moving me forward on my Hero's Journey, though it rarely felt heroic in the moment.

Through this healing process, I discovered exactly what Maslow meant about not being able to skip levels. My unresolved childhood trauma—those unmet safety needs from years ago—had been quietly sabotaging every attempt to reach higher levels of the hierarchy. I couldn't truly connect with others (love and belonging) or develop authentic self-worth (esteem) while part of me still felt fundamentally unsafe in the world. The wounds had to be addressed at their root level first.

Understanding Maslow's framework on paper is one thing. But what happens when we actually put ourselves in situations that force confrontation with our deepest fears? What lies on the other side of that darkness? Rather than just theorizing about this, let me share an experience that showed me—in ways both beautiful and terrifying—what these psychological principles look like when they play out in real life. What I didn't know at the time was how my own experience with abandonment would prepare me to guide another man through his deepest wound.

Years later, I found myself at a men's intensive wilderness retreat. Like many who had come to this remote location, I was seeking something beyond what I could articulate—a deeper understanding of myself, perhaps, or answers to questions I hadn't yet formed into words. The setting itself felt designed for transformation: surrounded by dense forest, misty hills visible in the distance, and a silence that city life rarely allows.

Our group was diverse—men from different backgrounds, ages, and life experiences, all gathered in this wilderness for a week of intensive personal work. For the first few days, we engaged in a carefully designed sequence of group sessions, physical challenges, and contemplative practices. The safety container built slowly but steadily, allowing layers of social armor to be set aside as we moved deeper into authentic connection.

Among our group was a man we nicknamed "Joey Gold." The name had emerged naturally in those first days, a recognition of his genuine heart and generous spirit that shone through despite the personal struggles he carried. Joey was in his mid-thirties, with laugh lines around his eyes that deepened when he smiled, which was often—even as he wrestled with painful parts of his story.

As our work together intensified, Joey began sharing more about his relationship with his father—or more accurately, the absence of that relationship. His father had abandoned the family when Joey was eight, disappearing so completely that Joey had spent decades wondering if he was even alive. This abandonment had left a wound that Joey had tried to numb with alcohol, a coping mechanism that was now threatening his marriage and relationship with his own children.

A few days into our retreat, following a particularly emotional morning session where Joey had finally expressed the grief he'd been carrying since childhood, our group gathered in a secluded clearing for afternoon integration work. The midday sunlight filtered through leaves, aptly creating patches of light and shadow that danced as the breeze moved through the canopy above.

Joey sat slightly apart from the circle, his face still bearing the aftereffects of the morning's emotional release. Though physically present, his eyes had that distant look of someone processing something serious. The facilitating elder, a man of quiet wisdom earned through decades of guiding men through inner wilderness, had been observing Joey with quiet attention.

As our session continued, the facilitator quietly approached me where I sat on a fallen log at the edge of the clearing. He settled beside me, his movements deliberate and unhurried.

"I need to ask something important of you," he said, his voice low enough that only I could hear.

Something in his tone made me pay close attention. This wasn't a casual request coming.

"I want you to take Joey into the cave."

I looked around, confused. "Cave?"

He then gestured toward what I had assumed was just another part of the rock face bordering our clearing. Now that I looked more carefully, I could see a dark opening partially hidden by undergrowth—an entrance I'd completely missed despite having sat in this very spot multiple times over the past days.

He explained what he was asking me to do. I would lead Joey deep into the cave in complete darkness. Once we were deep enough—though he gave no specific measure of distance or time—I was to leave Joey there alone in that absolute blackness before finding my way back out. Later, I would return to him and bring him back.

"How far into the cave do I go?" I asked, the gravity of the responsibility beginning to register.

"You'll know," he said simply.

My stomach tightened as I realized what he was really asking: to take a man already wrestling with abandonment issues, lead him into complete darkness, and then leave him there. This wasn't some assigned role in a workshop exercise—this was being asked to deliberately trigger someone's deepest wound at what might be their most vulnerable moment.

"Why me?" I asked, genuinely curious about his choice.

The facilitator's eyes held mine steadily. "You have something Joey needs right now—a balance of strength and compassion. You won't leave him out of carelessness, and you won't rescue him out of fear."

Despite my apprehension, I found myself accepting this responsibility. Something deeper than my conscious mind recognized the significance of what was being requested.

Our group then gathered at the mouth of the cave. Unlike me, Joey had not been prepared for what was about to happen. When he was asked if he wanted to go into the cave with me, I could see immediate fear flash across his face. Joey, as I would later learn, had always been afraid of the dark, and the prospect of entering a cave intensified that fear significantly. Yet when asked who he would trust to lead him through this experience, he pointed to me without hesitation.

The cave entrance was unassuming—a gap in the rock face partially hidden by undergrowth, as if the ancient rock were reluctant to reveal this passage to its depths. A cool current of air flowed outward, carrying the scent of stone and earth. All the members of our group formed a ceremonial circle at the entrance, their presence creating a container for what was about to unfold.

"I'm with you," I assured Joey as I prepared to lead him into the darkness, the weight of responsibility settling over me. What made this especially daunting was knowing I would need to memorize every twist and turn in our path through touch alone in complete darkness, with no clear indication of how far we should go.

Entering the cave, I went first, with Joey right behind me. The daylight quickly disappeared behind us, and we were soon surrounded by a darkness so absolute it felt almost tangible. The temperature dropped noticeably, and sounds changed—our breathing and footsteps taking on a hollow quality as they echoed off invisible walls. The cave narrowed, forcing us to our hands and knees. The cool, damp earth beneath my palms, the musty scent of rock sediment, and Joey's increasingly rapid breathing behind me became my only anchors in the void.

With each turn we navigated—left at what felt like a stalactite formation, right where the ceiling dropped suddenly, straight past a narrow corridor—I committed our path to memory with an intensity born of knowing someone else's well-being depended on it. The darkness wasn't just around us; it pressed against us, an almost living presence challenging our resolve with each forward movement.

As we continued deeper, I found myself in the strange position of having to make a crucial judgment call with no external reference points. How would I know when we had gone "deep enough"? Minutes stretched in the darkness, and with each passing moment, the question grew more pressing.

Finally, we reached a space that felt somehow different, and I simply knew we had arrived where we needed to be.

The space was just large enough for us to maneuver, and I explained to Joey that we needed to switch positions so that I could find the way back out. As the reality of what was happening dawned on him—that I would be leaving him here alone—his reaction was immediate and visceral.

"No, please don't leave me here," he pleaded, his voice breaking in the darkness. "Please don't go."

The sound echoed slightly, amplifying his fear.

"You're coming back for me, right?" he asked, his voice small and vulnerable in a way that struck directly at my heart.

"I'll come back for you," I assured him, trying to project a confidence I wasn't entirely feeling. "I promise."

Hesitantly, I turned away, each step a battle against my instinct to protect. The sound of his muffled sobs followed me through the narrow passages as I concentrated fiercely on retracing our path. One wrong turn could leave us both lost in the caves depths.

The sunlight was almost shocking when I finally emerged, my eyes having adjusted completely to the darkness. But what happened next caught me completely off guard. As I rejoined the waiting group, an unexpected wave of emotion crashed over me. I found myself overcome, and broke down as the full weight of what I had just done hit me.

In leaving Joey in that darkness, I had stepped into his father's shoes. I had enacted abandonment—and the pain of it was almost unbearable. How could anyone do this to their child? How could Joey's father have walked away, knowing the devastation it would cause? The experience had unexpectedly transformed into a life-changing lesson for me as well, showing me the deep impact of abandonment from the other side. Though I couldn't have known it then, this was also preparation for my own next stage of life—fatherhood—teaching me about the sacred responsibility of never abandoning those who depend on you.

When the time came to retrieve Joey, another elderly participant from our group, John, insisted on joining me, despite his advanced years and the physically demanding nature of the cave journey. This man had recently lost his adult son to tragedy, yet here he was, determined to help bring another man safely back from darkness. His quiet insistence on participating added another dimension to what was unfolding—three men of different ages, coming together in a shared act of care and responsibility.

Together, we navigated back through the maze of absolute darkness on hands and knees, calling Joey's name as we approached. The sound of something striking stone reached us before we found him—a rhythmic tapping that grew louder as we drew closer. We discovered Joey huddled in the darkness, clutching a small rock he had been using to beat against the walls—his desperate attempt to fill the terrible silence with something, anything.

When we reached him, even in the complete darkness, his relief was palpable. The three of us found ourselves in a cathartic embrace in that lightless void—elder, guide, and initiate. Joey's body shook with emotion as he realized we had actually returned for him as promised. This was perhaps the most powerful part of the experience—not just the confrontation with darkness and abandonment, but the healing counterpoint of return and reliability. Unlike his father, we had come back. The dark had been balanced with light, absence with presence, wounding with healing. In that moment of reunion, something healed in each of us that went beyond the original purpose of the journey.

The journey back through the tight passages required the same careful navigation, all of us crawling on hands and knees through the darkness. When we finally emerged from the cave, the contrast between Joey's expression going in and coming out was striking—exhaustion lined his face, but behind it shone a clarity I hadn't seen before.

Later that evening after some tranquil processing by the campfire, Joey presented me with two treasures: the rock he had clutched in the darkness and a cherished baseball card from his childhood collection. As he placed them in my hands, he explained how he could feel **how** his experience was transforming him and showed me gratitude for the role I played in coming back for him. Yes, he had faced the terror of abandonment in its most visceral form—but more importantly, he had experienced its healing opposite: the return of those who promised to come back. This completion of the abandonment cycle—where the story doesn't end with being left alone but continues with being found again—had shifted something fundamental in his understanding of himself.

I sat with these gifts long after the ceremony ended, turning them over in my hands, feeling the weight of the experience settle into something rich and lasting.

That night, I couldn't have articulated what exactly had happened in theoretical terms. I just knew we'd touched something ancient and powerful—a pattern of descent and return that felt woven into the very structure of transformation itself. Years later, when I encountered formal psychological frameworks that explained what I'd witnessed, they only confirmed what I had felt intuitively that day: that our deepest growth often requires us to move through our greatest fears rather than around them, and that sometimes the most intense healing comes from experiencing not just the wound, but its resolution—not just the abandonment, but the return.

What Joey and I had both experienced in that cave was Maslow's hierarchy in action—the movement from basic survival fears to something far more meaningful. Growth needs are driven by a powerful inner calling. When we align with a higher level of consciousness, we infuse our lives with meaning and significance, creating a sense of fulfillment and purpose. Conversely, without meaning and significance, we may feel that our lives lack direction.

In that cave, Joey experienced his lowest moment—complete abandonment in darkness—but this confrontation with his deepest fear created the conditions for his most significant growth. This pattern, where breakdown precedes breakthrough, shows up consistently in human development.

The feeling of significance arises when we recognize our ability to make a difference in the world, whether it be to our family, friends, colleagues, humanity, or the planet as a whole. Finding meaning and making a difference are integral to satisfying our growth needs—discovering purpose and contributing to something greater than ourselves is crucial for feeling fulfilled and content with our lives.

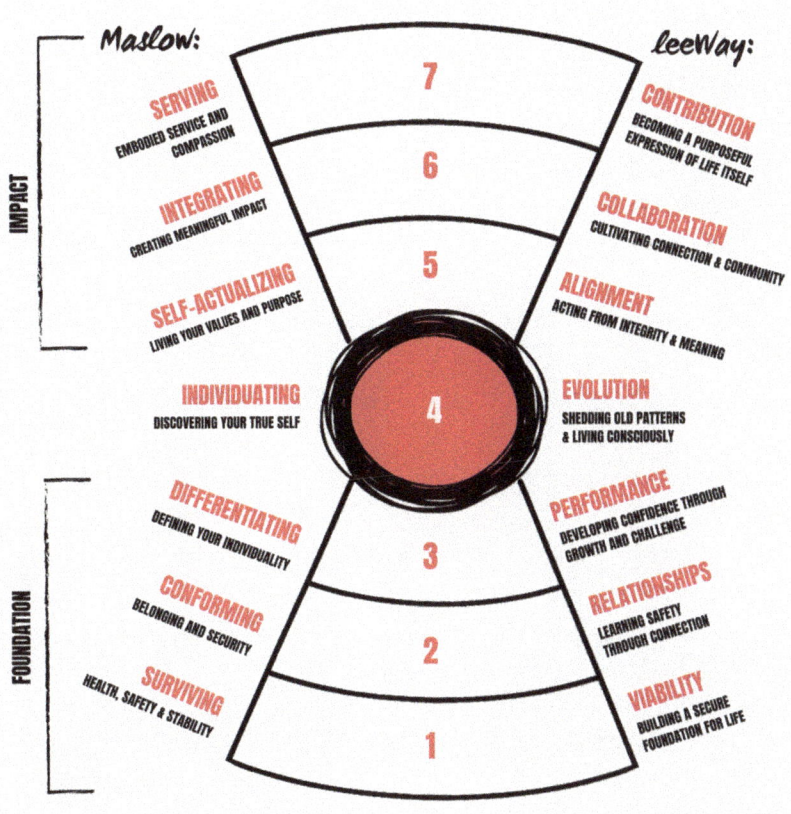

SEVEN LEVELS OF
CONSCIOUSNESS

Maslow:

IMPACT

SERVING
EMBODIED SERVICE AND COMPASSION

INTEGRATING
CREATING MEANINGFUL IMPACT

SELF-ACTUALIZING
LIVING YOUR VALUES AND PURPOSE

INDIVIDUATING
DISCOVERING YOUR TRUE SELF

FOUNDATION

DIFFERENTIATING
DEFINING YOUR INDIVIDUALITY

CONFORMING
BELONGING AND SECURITY

SURVIVING
HEALTH, SAFETY & STABILITY

leeWay:

CONTRIBUTION
BECOMING A PURPOSEFUL EXPRESSION OF LIFE ITSELF

COLLABORATION
CULTIVATING CONNECTION & COMMUNITY

ALIGNMENT
ACTING FROM INTEGRITY & MEANING

EVOLUTION
SHEDDING OLD PATTERNS & LIVING CONSCIOUSLY

PERFORMANCE
DEVELOPING CONFIDENCE THROUGH GROWTH AND CHALLENGE

RELATIONSHIPS
LEARNING SAFETY THROUGH CONNECTION

VIABILITY
BUILDING A SECURE FOUNDATION FOR LIFE

7 6 5 4 3 2 1

MODERN HERO

Figure 3.3: Seven Levels of Consciousness. *Richard Barrett's model answers the question: "What happens after self-actualization?" The left side shows Maslow's original levels (Foundation), while the right reveals the territory beyond—where personal growth transforms into purposeful contribution.*

THE BARRETT "SEVEN LEVELS OF CONSCIOUSNESS" MODEL: EXPANDING MASLOW'S HIERARCHY

When I reflect on what happened with Joey in that cave, I see a journey that moves beyond Maslow's hierarchy into expanded territory. Joey had his basic needs met at our retreat, but the cave experience pushed him toward something deeper—a confrontation with identity, purpose, and meaning that transcended self-actualization.

So let me back up a second. Remember Maslow's hierarchy we just explored? Well, Richard Barrett, a British consciousness researcher who spent decades studying human development, looked at it and thought, 'That's great, but what happens after self-actualization?' His model adds these additional levels that, honestly, speak to something I've felt but couldn't name—that yearning for meaning that goes beyond just "being your best self." It's like he mapped out what happens when personal growth transforms into something bigger than just our individual journey.

This model introduces several key changes, including:

- Renaming the levels as "levels of consciousness" rather than "needs"
- Combining Maslow's "safety and belonging" stages into a single "survival" level
- Dividing Maslow's basic needs into "ego needs" and "growth needs"
- Adding four additional levels beyond self-actualization that focus on deeper aspects of the Self

In Joey's journey through the cave, we can see a movement from the lower levels of Barrett's model toward the higher ones. His initial terror spoke to survival concerns (Level 1), while his plea "You're coming back for me, right?" revealed his relationship needs (Level 2). The transformation that occurred represented a shift toward the upper levels—toward finding meaning beyond his trauma.

These additional levels explore self-expression, alignment, self-actualization, and the desire to make a difference in the world through service and contribution. They include:

1. **Evolution and transformation:** At this level, we become aware of the classic existential question, "Who are we? And why are we here?" We begin to question the true nature of our being and the meaning we attach to our lives. Here, we gain enough distance from the social environment that has conditioned our beliefs and values to make our own choices, becoming the authors of our own lives and developing our own voices.

2. **Self-Expression, Alignment & Self-Actualizing:** This level of consciousness involves discovering our soul's purpose and aligning the beliefs of our ego with our soul values. Our ego and soul become fully integrated, creating a soul-infused personality.

3. **Integrating, making a difference:** We begin to discover and develop the deeper aspects of our soul, cultivating an intuitive sense of knowing that goes beyond reasoning and starts to guide our decision-making. Our soul's purpose of making a difference in the world is fully activated at this level. We realize that our ability to collaborate with others who share a similar purpose significantly enhances the impact we can make.

4. **Service and contribution:** At this level of consciousness, the quest to make a difference becomes a way of life. We naturally operate with humility, compassion, and selfless service, comfortable with uncertainty and able to tap into the deepest wells of wisdom. We become increasingly aware of feelings of 'oneness' with all that is.

I witnessed a glimpse of these higher levels in John, the elder who joined me to retrieve Joey from the cave. Having recently lost his son, he could have remained trapped in grief. Instead, he channeled his pain into service, perhaps unconsciously, insisting on helping another "son" find his way out of darkness. This was Level 4 of Barrett's model in action—where contribution becomes a way of life and suffering is transformed into compassion.

While the cave experience shows this evolution of consciousness in raw, immediate form, we can also see it brilliantly portrayed in *The Lion King*.

Simba begins his journey fleeing from trauma and guilt—the loss of his father and his perceived role in it. He buries himself in Barrett's lower levels of consciousness with "Hakuna Matata," focusing only on immediate pleasure and survival, avoiding any deeper meaning or responsibility. Like many of us running from pain, he creates a life that looks carefree but is actually a sophisticated avoidance system.

What makes this story such a perfect illustration of Barrett's model is how Simba must confront progressively deeper truths. Nala's arrival cracks open his defensive shell (relationship awakening). Rafiki's wisdom—"The past can hurt, but you can either run from it or learn from it"—forces self-confrontation. But it's Mufasa's spirit declaring "Remember who you are" that pushes Simba toward his deepest reckoning with identity and purpose.

Joey's cave experience shares this theme of running from abandonment only to be forced into direct confrontation with it. Like Simba couldn't escape his father's death by fleeing to the jungle, Joey couldn't escape his father's abandonment by avoiding the darkness. Both had to face their deepest wound to transform.

The final confrontation with Scar represents moving into Barrett's highest levels—Simba doesn't return for personal glory but to restore balance to the Pride Lands. His transformation from self-focused survival to serving the greater good shows consciousness evolution in action.

I can't help but see parallels between what happened with the three of us in that cave—Joey, myself, and John—and Simba's journey. We all discovered the same truth: consciousness evolution isn't a solo expedition. Simba needed Nala to remind him of connection, Rafiki to crack open his defenses, and his father's spirit to awaken his true identity. Similarly, Joey needed companions willing to enter the darkness with him—both to guide him there and to return for him. This mirrors what I witnessed: transformation requires both the courage to face our depths and companions who believe in our capacity to emerge whole.

As we've seen through both Maslow's hierarchy and Barrett's expanded model, the journey toward wholeness requires integrating all these levels

—from basic survival through transcendent service. Joey's transformation in that dark cave, Simba's return to Pride Rock, my own journey from TV shopping network tea boy to seeking something more meaningful—they all follow this same ascending pattern. Which brings us back to that ancient symbol that's been weaving through our exploration: the Tree of Life.

THE TREE OF LIFE: A METAPHOR FOR INTERNAL STABILITY AND EXTERNAL EQUILIBRIUM

The tree metaphor that's been weaving through our journey becomes particularly powerful when we consider the ancient symbol of the Tree of Life, which appears across cultures worldwide. This symbol perfectly illustrates a pattern we'll see repeatedly throughout this book—regardless of which framework we explore, whether Campbell's Hero's Journey, Maslow's hierarchy, or Barrett's model of consciousness, the same fundamental principle applies: growth requires both depth and height, both roots and branches, both darkness and light.

Barrett's model maps beautifully onto this ancient symbol. The lower levels represent our roots reaching into darkness—ego needs, survival, relationship. The upper levels are our branches stretching toward light—self-expression, service, contribution. And right there in the middle? That's where the magic happens—where ego and soul integrate.

The cave journey embodied this perfectly. The descent into absolute darkness forced Joey to confront his deepest wound of abandonment, while forcing me to experience the other side—the terrible weight of being the one who walks away. The transformation came not from escaping that darkness but from integrating it. When we returned for him—unlike his father—something healed in both of us, creating more solid foundations for growth.

According to Barrett, when our ego needs align with our soul's purpose, we hit that sweet spot of internal stability. Add in external equilibrium—when our physical needs align with our environment—and suddenly we're in flow, operating at peak performance.

But who exactly is experiencing this flow? Who's doing all this balancing between ego and soul? In the next chapter, we'll meet the full cast of characters living in your psyche according to Carl Jung—the parts of you that help, the parts that sabotage, and the mysterious Self that's orchestrating the whole show. But first, let's recap what we've discovered about the psychology of human needs and motivations.

———

CHAPTER 3 SUMMARY

Well, Chapter 3 dove deep into what makes us modern heroes tick—and surprise, it's messy. Starting with Maslow (can't self-actualize on an empty stomach, sorry), we discovered why those self-help books gathering dust aren't working. Then came the heavy stuff: early trauma, shadow work, and that cave experience with Joey that still haunts me. Barrett showed us there's life beyond self-actualization—actual service to others. Who knew?

KEY LEARNINGS:

- Those shiny self-help books skip the dark stuff that actually matters
- Shadow work isn't optional—it's the price of admission to real growth
- You're not broken for having trauma; you're human
- The Tree of Life nailed it: deep roots in darkness, branches in light

KEY TAKEAWAYS:

- Basic needs first, enlightenment later—Maslow wasn't kidding
- What you avoid owns you; what you face transforms you
- Modern culture's positivity obsession is making us sicker
- True fulfillment = personal growth + actually helping others

Reflective Question: What dark corner of your psyche are you desperately avoiding that probably holds your next breakthrough?

"We must be willing to let go of the life we planned
so as to have the life that is waiting for us."

– Joseph Campbell

MAPPING THE UNCONSCIOUS AND THE SOUL WITH CARL JUNG

The cave experience with Joey kept haunting me long after we'd returned from that wilderness retreat. I'd find myself revisiting it in quiet moments, sensing there were deeper layers I hadn't quite grasped yet. What had really happened in that darkness when I left him there? When he handed me that rock and baseball card, what was he actually giving me? Not long after, I stumbled across Carl Jung's work and it was like finding the missing manual for everything I'd just experienced.

See, Jung wasn't just mapping stages of growth like Maslow or Barrett —he was mapping the actual territories of our inner world. Those hidden forces that might make us do things we don't understand. The parts of ourselves we can't see but that run the show anyway. Reading his work, I finally had language for what had happened in that cave.

Quick backstory on Jung for those who don't know him. Picture the early 1900s, psychology is just getting started, and there's this Swiss psychologist working with Freud—yeah, the "everything is about sex and your mother" guy. They're close colleagues for a while, master and protégé, until Jung starts having ideas that make Freud uncomfortable.

While Freud's focused on repressed sexual desires, Jung's exploring these wild ideas—that we all share some kind of deeper mental inheritance, that coincidences might actually mean something, that we're on some kind of soul journey toward becoming whole. Freud thinks Jung's lost the plot, and Jung thinks Freud's missing the bigger picture. Their breakup was significant—like a professional divorce that split the field in two.

The scientific establishment largely dismissed Jung after that. Too mystical, they said. Too spiritual. You can't measure meaningful coincidences in a lab. So his work got labeled "Jungian theory" rather than mainstream psychology, while Freud became the father of psychoanalysis.

But the thing is—science has limits. We can measure brain activity, but can we measure the experience of love? We can track neurons firing, but can we capture what it feels like to have a profound insight? Jung was willing to venture beyond what could be proven in a lab because he understood that human experience includes phenomena that science doesn't yet have tools to measure. And honestly? Good on him. Every major breakthrough in human understanding started with someone willing to explore beyond the accepted boundaries of their time.

Besides, Jung's ideas are everywhere now. The Myers-Briggs personality test? Based on Jung's work. The concept of introverts and extroverts? That's Jung. All that talk about "finding yourself" or "shadow work" in modern therapy? Jung's influence again. His fingerprints are all over modern psychology and spirituality, even when people don't realize where it came from.

One of Jung's major contributions was mapping out what he called the psyche. Now, "psyche" originally meant soul or spirit in Greek—the essence of who you are beyond just your physical body. By Jung's time, scientists had basically stripped it down to just mean "mind." But Jung wasn't satisfied with that. He wanted to map the whole thing—not just our conscious thoughts, but all the hidden stuff underneath, not just our individual minds but the patterns we all seem to share as humans.

CONSCIOUSNESS: A JUNGIAN PERSPECTIVE

Most of us think we know what consciousness is—it's being awake, aware, thinking. It's what's happening right now as you read these words. But Jung showed us that what we call consciousness is just a tiny fraction of what's actually going on in our psyche.

Figure 4.1: Jungian Model of the Psyche. Human consciousness according to Jung. Notice how the ego sits at the surface while the Self resides at the core—we think we're driving, but there's a deeper intelligence orchestrating the whole show. The shadow and anima/animus operate between personal and collective layers, showing how our individual wounds connect to universal patterns.

Think of an iceberg. That small part above water? That's your consciousness—everything you're aware of right now. Your thoughts about this book, what you had for breakfast, that meeting tomorrow you're dreading. But underneath lies massive territories of the unconscious, running programs you don't even know exist, influencing your thoughts and behaviors in ways you rarely recognize.

Jung mapped out this hidden architecture of the psyche in fascinating detail. At the surface, we've got consciousness with the ego at its center (your sense of "I") and the persona (the masks you wear for different situations). Just below lurks the personal unconscious—all your forgotten memories and suppressed experiences. Deeper still lies the collective unconscious—a shared psychological inheritance of all humanity. Within these depths, Jung identified powerful forces: the shadow (all the parts of yourself you've rejected), the anima and animus (your inner feminine or masculine), and various archetypes that show up in every culture's myths and dreams. At the very core lies what Jung called the Self—not your everyday ego-self, but the totality of who you are, conscious and unconscious combined. (Don't worry if this sounds abstract right now—we'll explore what this actually means when we're ready to approach it.)

[See Figure 4.1: Jung's Map of the Psyche]

Sound complex? It is. But don't worry—we're going to explore each part of this map in detail, starting with the piece you're probably most familiar with but might understand the least: the ego.

THE EGO: A DOUBLE-EDGED SWORD

Most people think the ego is just about being arrogant or controlling. But here's what I learned the hard way—it's actually laying a crucial role in our psyche as mediator between our inner unconscious world and external reality. It forms during early childhood as a means of organizing and understanding our experiences, and basically, the ego's job is to make sure our basic needs for survival, safety, and security are met.

Remember that moment I emerged from that cave into sunlight? That was a powerful ego experience. My carefully constructed self-image as a "good guy who helps others" crashed headfirst into the reality that I had just deliberately caused someone pain. My ego was suddenly caught between two contradictory realities—protector and abandoner—and boom that unexpected emotional breakdown.

While the ego's desire for order and structure is essential, it's equally important to recognize the inherent complexity and fluidity of the world around us. The ego loves to put things in neat little boxes, organizing our messy reality into tidy categories it can manage. But life rarely fits into those boxes, does it? The world operates more like those intricate fractal patterns found in nature, and a more holistic view may prove more accurate and fulfilling in the long run.

Evolution-wise, the ego's pretty important. It's shaped by our experiences and helps us navigate the world. Think of it as a filter, prioritizing information relevant to our survival and well-being, acting like a filter for what we perceive and remember. This helps us maintain a sense of self and make decisions that promote our basic needs.

You've probably heard people talk about the "reptilian brain"—this idea that deep in our skull lurks this ancient lizard part that's all about survival basics: fighting, fleeing, feeding, and fornication. And yeah, there's truth to this. Those primitive brain structures we share with reptiles—parts of the brain stem, cerebellum, and basal ganglia—do play a crucial role in our automatic survival responses. Our amygdala and hypothalamus can trigger immediate fight-or-flight reactions when we perceive danger, often before our conscious mind has time to think.

But here's where pop psychology gets it wrong—they portray these brain regions as operating in isolation—as if there's a separate "reptile brain" that occasionally hijacks our more rational human brain. The reality is more integrated. These ancient brain structures don't operate independently; they're deeply interconnected with our more evolved brain regions. Our ego emerges from this complex interplay between primitive survival mechanisms and higher-order functions like self-awareness, planning, and emotional regulation.

What's interesting, is how we cycle through different levels of consciousness based on which needs are being threatened or fulfilled at any given moment. Remember Maslow's hierarchy of needs and Barrett's seven levels of consciousness we discussed earlier? When our basic survival needs are threatened, those ancient brain regions focused on immediate safety do take precedence—that's why even the calmest person can react with startling aggression when genuinely threatened. As our basic needs get met, our more evolved brain regions can start running our responses, allowing for greater emotional intelligence and eventually higher-order thinking.

This whole ego-as-mediator thing? I got a crash course in it when I left Joey in that cave. As I mentioned earlier, I had been entrusted by the facilitator with guiding Joey through this intense healing experience—deliberately leaving him in the darkness as part of a transformative process, then returning for him later. When I emerged from the cave into sunlight after leaving him there as instructed, I broke down sobbing—something that caught me completely off guard. In that moment, my ego was performing its most basic function: trying to make sense of two things that didn't fit together.

Here's what was happening inside me: I've always seen myself as someone who takes care of people, who stays with them when they're afraid, who doesn't walk away when they're in need. This isn't just some casual idea about myself—it's at the core of who I believe I am. But what had I just done? I had walked away from Joey while he called out to me, begging me not to leave him alone in the darkness. Yes, I was doing exactly what I was supposed to do as part of this healing journey. Yes, I knew I would return for him. But in that raw moment, the sound of his voice fading behind me as I crawled away through the darkness felt like a betrayal of everything I stood for. My actions and my self-image crashed into each other, and neither one could simply give way.

What hit me was basically cognitive dissonance—that uncomfortable mental tension that occurs when our actions contradict our deeply-held beliefs about ourselves. Even though I rationally understood I was helping Joey through a necessary process, emotionally I felt like I was violating my core value of being someone who doesn't abandon others. This clash between my actions and my self-image created such intense psychological discomfort that it manifested physically in those unexpected tears. The mind doesn't care about our rational justifications—it responds to the raw disconnect between who we think we are and what we see ourselves doing.

The power of this moment lay partly in its timing. I'd met someone special—a woman who had completely upended my understanding of what connection could feel like. Naturally, I'd been quietly thinking about what it would be like to build a life with her, about what it might mean to become a husband, and perhaps someday a father. These weren't just idle thoughts but a deep contemplation about the kind of man I wanted to be in those roles.

Then came Joey's voice in that cave, pleading: "Please don't leave me!" Those words seemed to echo not just through the stone passages but through time itself—connecting to that primal fear we all carry of being left alone when we need someone most. The sound of his muffled sobs forced me to confront what abandonment really means. Suddenly, I wasn't just experiencing Joey's abandonment; I was facing the full weight of what it means to be someone who walks away. My ego couldn't hold these contradictions: that I was simultaneously being cruel and kind, hurtful and healing, abandoning and returning. The tension between these opposites literally broke me open. Those tears weren't just emotion—they were the sound of my ego temporarily surrendering control when it couldn't make these pieces fit together.

See, the ego, at its core, is desperately trying to maintain a coherent story of who we are. When our actions don't match that story, even when those actions are necessary and ultimately helpful, the emotional conflict can hit us physically. My body responded with tears before my mind could even put together what was happening. This is the ego trying to bridge our inner world of values and our outer world of actions—and what happens when that bridge temporarily collapses.

Now usually, we handle cognitive dissonance in one of three ways: we change our beliefs to match our actions, we justify our actions through new beliefs, or we deny/minimize what we've done. But sometimes, when we actually just allow ourselves to fully experience the dissonance rather than rushing to resolve it, something transformative can happen. The discomfort becomes a doorway to deeper understanding and growth.

What's wild is how transformative this ego crisis became. By experiencing what it felt like to "abandon" someone, even in this structured, therapeutic context, I suddenly understood something crucial about what Joey's father had done, and the sacred responsibility of never truly abandoning those who depend on you. This painful contradiction didn't just break me down—it clarified what truly mattered to me. The gap between immediate action and deeper intention, gave me crystal clarity about who I wanted to become. The very next day, with the cave experience still raw in my mind, I knew with absolute certainty that I wanted to spend my life with the woman I loved, to build a family with her, to commit fully to becoming the man I aspired to be. Just a few weeks later, I proposed to her with a conviction and clarity I'd never experienced before. That ego breakdown, painful as it was, was the catalyst for one of the most important decisions of my life.

But while the ego's focus on survival is essential, it can sometimes lead us astray. When it perceives threats, even minor ones, it can trigger negative emotions like anxiety or impatience. This can cause us to react impulsively or focus on short-term gains over long-term goals.

I learned this the hard way at a pool party several years back. The memory still makes me wince—my stomach churning whenever I think about it.

There was this guy who'd been causing trouble throughout the day, getting increasingly intoxicated and confrontational with various guests. I'd been keeping my distance, but later in the evening, he approached our group and got into an altercation with one of the girls I was with. When he suddenly lunged toward her, raising his hand, something ancient, instinctive and primal just... switched on inside me.

Before my thinking brain could catch up—before I could consider words or de-escalation or literally any other option—I'd stepped forward and thrown a punch that connected with devastating precision. The guy went down hard. The sound of it—that dull thud of body meeting earth—silenced everything for a moment, before being replaced by something worse: the piercing screams of the girls in our group.

I remember standing there, my knuckles stinging, hands shaking as the reality hit, suddenly aware of every eye on me. The party had gone dead silent. Even the music seemed to have stopped, though maybe that was just my perception narrowing to this single, horrible moment.

Then I heard it.

At first, I couldn't process what I was hearing. The sound coming from the ground where he lay didn't match anything I'd expected. No angry curses. No threats of retaliation. No macho posturing about getting back up and finishing this. Instead, what reached my ears was a sound that would echo in my nightmares for years to come. The man, sprawled on the concrete, was crying for his mother. Actually crying for her. 'Mom... mommy...' over and over, in a voice that had transformed from aggressive adult to frightened child in the span of a single punch.

My friends—the same people I'd supposedly been "protecting"—rushed to help him up, carrying him away while shooting uncertain glances back at me.

In that moment, standing alone while the crowd parted around me like I was contaminated, the full weight of what I'd done crashed down. This wasn't some righteous defense; it was an assault that could have ended catastrophically. What if he'd hit his head on the concrete patio as he fell? What if he'd suffered brain damage? What if he'd died? I was milliseconds and inches away from potentially becoming a manslaughter case, from throwing away my entire life and devastating his family—all because my ego couldn't tolerate the discomfort of a tense situation.

And yet... what if I'd done nothing? What if he'd struck my friend instead? What if his aggression had escalated and someone else had been seriously hurt? This is the kind of brutal moral math that keeps you up at night. The situation had no clean answer, no obvious right choice that guaranteed everyone's safety. There existed a legitimate threat that needed addressing—just perhaps not in the way I'd addressed it.

The thing that messed with my head most was the ambiguity. It wasn't a simple case of me acting badly; it was a complex situation where intervention of some kind might have been necessary. But my ego had seized on this legitimate concern and used it to bypass any thoughtful consideration of how to intervene effectively. It jumped straight to the most primitive, violent solution available, skipping over all the potential intermediate steps: stepping between them, firmly telling him to back off, calling for help from others, creating distance.

The legal consequences alone were terrifying—assault charges, lawsuits, jail time—but somehow it was that sound, that grown man crying for his mother, that burrowed deepest into my psyche. It stripped away any pretense that what I'd done was heroic. I hadn't stopped a threat; I'd created trauma. For him, for the witnesses, and ultimately for myself.

Yeah, I'd "protected" the women—or at least that's the story I desperately wanted to believe as I walked away, my stomach twisted into nause-
ating knots, my hand trembling slightly. But the truth crawled underneath
my skin, impossible to ignore: What the hell had just happened? I'd gone
from concerned bystander to violent aggressor in the span of heartbeats.
My ego had spotted a threat and gone straight into action mode, skipping
right over the part where I might've, you know, paused for even half a
second.

Later that night, alone with a glass of whiskey I didn't really want, I sat
on my balcony wrestling with this impossible question: what was the right
thing to have done? Was there a perfect solution that would have kept
everyone safe while causing no harm? I didn't know. I still don't. But what
I did know was that my response hadn't come from careful moral deliberation—it had erupted from something far more primal, far less conscious.
That was the part I couldn't reconcile with my self-image as a thoughtful,
ethical person.

What terrified me most wasn't that I'd hit someone—it was how automatic, how unconscious the whole thing had been. Like some hidden
program had executed without my permission. I hadn't chosen violence;
violence had chosen me, using my body as its instrument. And my ego,
ever the clever storyteller, was already spinning justifications: He deserved
it. They needed protection. What else could you have done?

But underneath those convenient narratives, a harder truth waited: I
hadn't acted from wisdom or even conscious choice. I'd reacted from a
wound, from programming, from habit. And now I had to face what that
revealed about who I really was beneath my carefully constructed self-
image as the "good guy."

This incident didn't just haunt me as an isolated event—it cracked
open a door to other confrontations throughout my life that I'd never fully
processed. Suddenly, I was seeing patterns everywhere: that bar fight I'd
written off as "standing up for myself," the heated argument with my
brother that escalated to fighting, even the way I'd intimidate people in
business when I felt cornered. What I'd previously framed as "not letting
people walk all over me" now appeared in a different light. The pool party
punch—not the good kind— became a flashpoint that forced me to
examine a lifetime of moments where my ego had chosen confrontation

over communication, dominance over dialogue. As I dug deeper into these memories, I had to be brutally honest with myself about each one. There was no lumping them all together with a neat label like "overreactions" or "moments of weakness." Each required its own uncomfortable reckoning: What was I actually feeling in that moment? What did I tell myself was happening? What story was I creating about who I was and who the other person was? The gaps between my idealized self-image and my actual behavior when threatened were painful to acknowledge.

Upon reflection, I can see the ghostly echoes of my boxing tent days in Australia. Those experiences gave me something valuable—confidence, resilience, a certain kind of strength. But they also left behind a shadow— this comfort with confrontation that isn't always healthy. When you've spent weeks getting punched in the face for a living, throwing a punch doesn't seem like crossing a line; it's just comfortable.

The boxing tent taught me I could survive physical conflict, that I wouldn't shatter if hit. But what it didn't teach me was discernment— knowing when confrontation is necessary and when it creates more harm than good. I carried the physical memories of those fights in my muscles, ready to spring into action, without fully processing their deeper impact on my psyche.

Turns out the road to hell really is paved with good intentions. I meant well—who wouldn't want to protect people getting threatened?—but my reaction just added another layer of violence to the mix. And here's the best bit: this wasn't a one-off. This same pattern kept showing up in my life. I'd jump in to "help," all heart and impulse, and somehow make things messier. Like that time I got pulled into a domestic situation thinking I could fix things, and... well, let's just say I didn't exactly bring peace to the valley.

It took me way too long to see how my ego was fooling me into thinking I was being heroic when actually I was just feeding its need to control situations. The ego hates feeling helpless, so it convinces us that quick, decisive action—even violence—is sometimes necessary. And maybe sometimes it is. But my ego wasn't exactly consulting with the wiser parts of me before launching into Superman mode.

Understanding what happened at that party took years, and learning to handle my ego's reactivity took even longer. The journey wasn't linear. I'd like to say I had an immediate awakening and never threw another impulsive punch, but the truth is messier. There were more mistakes, more moments where my ego hijacked my better judgment, each followed by deeper regret and stronger resolve.

The real breakthrough came unexpectedly. I'd been attending a men's gathering and one of the elders there—a soft-spoken man in his seventies with kind eyes—offered to drive me to the airport. As we drove through the long stretches of highway, I found myself sharing my pool party punch story. Something about his quiet presence made it easy to talk. When I finished, he was silent for a long moment, just nodding slowly.

"You know," he finally said, his voice almost lost beneath the hum of tires on asphalt, "I spent three years in prison when I was younger for nearly killing a man in a bar fight." I turned to look at him—this gentle elder who taught meditation and spoke of compassion—trying to reconcile this revelation with the man I thought I knew.

"Your ego isn't your enemy," he continued, hands steady on the wheel. "It's like a good guard dog that wasn't properly trained. It's doing exactly what it thinks will keep you safe." He glanced over at me. "It heard a noise, thought there was an intruder, and it attacked. That doesn't make it bad—just untrained."

That reframing changed everything. Instead of fighting my ego, I started to work with it—to train it, understand it, and even appreciate its intentions while redirecting its methods. Simple practices began to create space between stimulus and reaction: a deliberate breath when I felt that familiar heat rising, a mental note when my ego began spinning self-protective stories, regular meditation that strengthened my capacity to observe these patterns without immediately acting on them.

Those boxing tent fights had taught me I could survive a confrontation, but they hadn't taught me the more subtle art of knowing when to avoid one altogether. My body remembered the rush of adrenaline, the split-second decisions, the raw immediacy of physical conflict. What my body hadn't learned was the wisdom to pause, to breathe, to consider whether my action might create more suffering than it prevented.

Understanding the ego's influence has been crucial for my personal growth. By recognizing these automatic responses, I've learned to choose more consciously. I've practiced stepping back, assessing situations calmly, and making choices aligned with my deeper values rather than my ego's immediate impulses. This continues to allow me to live a more fulfilling and meaningful life—though I'm still very much a work in progress.

Speaking of ego gone wrong, the Greek myth of Narcissus perfectly captures what happens when the ego runs wild. A strikingly handsome young man, Narcissus became fatally enamored with his own reflection. So captivated was he by his image in a pool that he could not look away, ultimately wasting away in this obsession and perishing.

The myth warns us about the thin line between healthy self-appreciation and destructive self-absorption. Narcissus' story illustrates how some level of positive ego regard is necessary to value our own gifts and qualities. But, the tale highlights the dangers of an ego run rampant—losing perspective, ignoring the needs of others, and ultimately self-destruction.

After years of my ego running the show—making all the decisions without bothering to check with me first—I've picked up a few things that sometimes help. When I'm getting irritated or annoyed—not in a split-second crisis where you need to protect someone, but in everyday moments where I actually have time to think—I try to flip the script. Instead of letting my ego blame everything and everybody else like it loves to do, I'll attempt to ask myself: "What's my part in this?" Sometimes I remember to do this, sometimes I don't. But when I do, it forces me to pause before my ego's protective instincts completely take over.

Sometimes it's as simple as looking at my son—instant perspective on what actually matters. Other times I need the reality check of my men's group or mentors who won't let me get away with my usual ego tricks and call me on my bullshit with some unfiltered direct feedback. I don't respond brilliantly to feedback—not many of us do, do we? My initial reaction is often defensive, sometimes even a bit confrontational. But once that settles, I usually find they were right. That's why I purposely try to surround myself with people I genuinely trust and respect—it's the only way I'll actually hear the hard truths and grow from them. These reality checks from the right people are priceless for keeping my ego in check.

The tools aren't magic, and I still mess up plenty. But that guard dog the elder talked about? It's still there, still protective, still ready. The difference is now it sometimes checks with me before it attacks. We're learning to work together, though it's definitely a work in progress.

THE PERSONAL UNCONSCIOUS: A RESERVOIR OF HIDDEN INFLUENCES

"There are certain events of which we have not consciously taken note; they have remained, so to speak, below the threshold of consciousness. They have happened, but they have been absorbed subliminally."

— *MAN AND HIS SYMBOLS,* CARL JUNG

Remember how I said consciousness was just the tip of the iceberg? Well, right below the surface—before we even get to the really deep stuff— there's this whole layer Jung called the personal unconscious. The personal unconscious, as Jung mapped it, contains everything from our individual life experiences that we're no longer consciously aware of. While Freud focused almost exclusively on repressed sexual desires and forbidden urges, Jung saw something broader—forgotten experiences, overlooked perceptions, and memories we've pushed away because they were too painful or didn't fit our self-image.

What makes Jung's insight particularly powerful is recognizing that this unconscious material isn't just sitting there passively. When you have an emotional reaction that seems way out of proportion to what's happening, when you keep repeating the same self-sabotaging patterns, when certain dreams feel mysteriously significant—that's often your personal unconscious making itself known.

Here's how I finally got my head around this concept. You know that one drawer in your kitchen—the junk drawer? That chaotic catch-all where you toss the stuff you don't quite know what to do with but can't bring yourself to throw away. Mine's an archaeological dig of good intentions gone wrong. Mystery keys that probably opened something important once. Instruction manuals for appliances I haven't owned in years. Takeout menus from restaurants that probably closed years ago, and at least three phone chargers for phones that became extinct before anyone had even heard of TikTok.

We all have this drawer. We stuff things in, push it shut, and go about our day. But eventually, it gets so crammed that you can barely close it. Need to find something specific? Good luck. And inevitably, when you have people over and need that one thing, the whole drawer explodes in an avalanche of undealt-with chaos.

That's exactly how our personal unconscious works. Those embarrassing memories, unexpressed emotions, denied impulses, and forgotten experiences don't disappear when we push them out of conscious awareness. They just get stuffed into our psychological junk drawer, continuing to influence us from behind the scenes. And just like that kitchen drawer eventually demands attention when it won't close anymore, our unconscious material finds ways to make itself known—often at the most inconvenient moments.

Christopher Nolan's *Inception* offers one of the best illustrations I've seen of how this actually plays out. In the film, Cobb (Leonardo DiCaprio) is haunted by projections of his deceased wife Mal during his dream missions. What's brilliant is how perfectly this captures three key aspects of Jung's personal unconscious:

First, it shows how the personal unconscious contains emotionally charged material we've pushed away. Cobb's guilt about his role in Mal's death is too painful to face consciously, so he's relegated it to his unconscious—but it won't stay put.

Second, it demonstrates how unconscious material influences us even when we're unaware of it. Mal's appearances consistently sabotage Cobb's missions and relationships, despite his conscious intention to succeed. He can't figure out why he keeps undermining himself because he can't see what's actually driving it.

Third, it reveals how the personal unconscious communicates through symbolic forms. Mal doesn't appear as a rational thought about guilt or a simple memory. She manifests as a complex character with her own agenda, which is exactly how our unconscious material tends to show up —in dreams, slips of the tongue, or behaviors we can't quite explain.

There's also that brilliant moment when Ariadne is learning dream architecture and Cobb explains: "We create and perceive our world simultaneously." That's Jung in a nutshell—we project our unconscious material outward, then experience it as if it's coming from outside ourselves.

The real breakthrough in the film comes when Cobb finally acknowledges what he's been avoiding. He has to face his guilt, integrate it, rather than let it control him from the shadows. This is exactly Jung's approach—

making the unconscious conscious transforms our relationship with these hidden parts of ourselves.

Like finally organizing that kitchen drawer, bringing awareness to our personal unconscious changes everything. What once controlled us from the shadows becomes something we can consciously engage with and understand. The patterns start to make sense. The mysterious emotional reactions become less mysterious.

So maybe it's time to open that drawer and see what's really in there.

PERSONA

The ego doesn't just deal with internal conflicts—it's also constantly managing how we show up in the world. When society tells us certain feelings or behaviors aren't acceptable, the ego creates what Jung called the "persona." The term comes from ancient Roman theater, where actors wore masks to play different characters. We do the same thing, just without the props.

This mask, though, actually serves a real purpose. It helps us navigate social expectations, maintain appearances, and avoid the judgment or rejection that comes with being too raw, too real, too much ourselves in the wrong contexts. The persona allows us to function in communal life without constantly shocking or pushing everyone away.

Jung described it as "that which in reality one is not, but which oneself as well as others think one is." It's the professional you at the office party, the confident you on a first date, the together-parent you at school pickup. These masks help us navigate social situations, and oh boy, do we need them. The problem though, can come when we wear them so long that we forget they're masks at all.

The real work is learning when to take the mask off and actually look at what's underneath. Not always comfortable, but that's where the good stuff lives.

Think about social media—it's basically persona on steroids. Those perfectly curated Instagram feeds showing only the wins, the vacations, the moments when the lighting was just right? I'll admit it: I've definitely spent ten minutes staging a photo to look "effortlessly casual." The really sneaky part is how the lines blur. Post enough filtered versions of our lives, and we might start believing that's actually who we are. The performance becomes so automatic we can forget we're performing.

Jim Carrey's *The Mask* might be the most literal exploration of Jung's persona concept ever put on film. Think about it—mild-mannered Stanley Ipkiss literally puts on a mask that unleashes all the repressed parts of his personality. Everything he's too scared or socially conditioned to express comes exploding out in cartoonish extremes. It's Jung's theory with a green face and zoot suit. The mask doesn't create a new person—it reveals what was already there, just buried under layers of social conditioning and fear. "Somebody stop me!" isn't just a catchphrase; it's the cry of someone whose unconscious material has suddenly taken the wheel.

The Wolf of Wall Street also shows exactly where over-identifying with our persona can lead. Jordan Belfort gets so high on his own persona—the successful broker, the big shot, the guy who's winning at capitalism—that he completely loses touch with any authentic self underneath. By the time he's deep in his spiral of excess and lobbing money off his yacht, the mask has completely taken over. Same thing in *The Great Gatsby*. Jay Gatsby builds this elaborate persona of the mysterious millionaire, throws these legendary parties, all to impress a woman who knew him before the mask. The tragedy isn't just that it doesn't work—it's that he's forgotten who he was without it.

These stories hit hard because we all do this to some degree. We craft our professional selves, our social media selves, our first-date selves, and sometimes we get so good at the performance we forget it's a performance. The mask becomes comfortable. Familiar. Taking it off starts to feel more frightening than keeping it on.

And what's really messed up about over-identifying with our personas is that we can start making choices that go against our values and goals, just to keep the performance going. We might screw over a colleague to maintain our "successful professional" mask. We'll stay in relationships that make us miserable because admitting failure doesn't fit our "has it all together" persona. We end up pushing away the people who might actually see us—really see us—because letting them close would mean dropping the act.

The loneliness that comes from this can be brutal. We can be surrounded by people and feel completely unknown because nobody's actually connecting with us—they're connecting with our performance. It's like being trapped in a play where we can never break character, even when the theater's empty. That emptiness people talk about? That sense that something's missing even when life looks perfect on paper? That's often what happens when the mask stays on too long. We achieve everything our persona was designed to achieve and feel... nothing. Because it wasn't really us who achieved it.

So how do we keep our personas from taking over? I've had to develop some practices to catch myself when I'm getting too attached to my various masks.

First, I've created what I call "persona-free zones"—relationships and spaces where the performance stops. Again, my oldest friend is the gold standard here. He knew me before I had any professional identity worth performing, and he has this beautiful refusal to be impressed by any of my accumulated titles or achievements. When I'm with him, there's literally no point in putting on a show. He'd just laugh and call me out on it. That kind of relationship is grounding, and medicine for the soul.

My monthly men's circles have become another sanctuary. What makes them extra powerful is that we intentionally don't know what most of us do for work. Someone might be a billionaire for all we know, another might be unemployed—we actively avoid finding out. If someone starts talking about their career or dropping status markers, the group gently gently steers the conversation back to what matters: the human being beneath the social masks.

I've come to cherish this circle of trust where we're known for our hearts, not our résumés. The freedom of connecting without the weight of others' expectations based on what you do has been a game-changer for me. We relate as humans first, witnessing each other's struggles and celebrations without the filters that professional contexts demand.

Second, I regularly gut-check myself with this question: "What am I afraid would happen if people saw the unfiltered me right now?" The answer usually reveals exactly what the persona is protecting. Sometimes it's necessary professional boundaries. Often it's just fear of being judged for being human.

This can get especially tricky in business situations. I've made authenticity in professional settings something of a personal mission, but let me tell you—it comes with costs. I've watched rooms go silent when I name emotions in a board meeting. I've lost deals because I refused to play political games that felt fundamentally dishonest and against my values. I've been labeled "too intense," "too direct," "emotional," "an overthinker," or "unprofessional" for speaking truth in environments built on polite corporate theatre.

For me, I've learned that authenticity in business often comes with a cost, but pretending weighs even heavier on the soul. And let's be honest —capitalism rewards the persona over the person most of the time. There are still boardrooms where vulnerability is weakness, where admitting uncertainty is career suicide, where the language of KPIs and quarterly targets leaves no room for complicated humanity.

And in that same spirit of vulnerability, here's an honest truth: sometimes I cave. Why? Because sometimes my resistance to wearing that persona crashes head-on into those basic needs at the bottom of Maslow's pyramid we discussed earlier. Those needs don't magically disappear just because we're on a journey of authenticity. When they feel threatened— the mortgage, the kids' college funds, basic financial security—I find myself reaching for the mask and betraying my authentic self. "This isn't selling out," I remind myself, "it's ensuring survival needs are met so I can pursue higher-level growth in other areas of my life." Temporarily, of course.

Even with all this talk about authenticity, I still adjust parts of myself depending on where I am. Not lying or pretending to be someone else— more like turning the volume up or down on different parts of who I actually am. There's a difference between adapting thoughtfully and completely abandoning yourself. Dialing down my intensity in a stuffy boardroom? Sure. Pretending I'm someone else entirely? That's where I draw the line.

To manage this tension, I've developed some micro-practices throughout my workday. Sometimes I'll take a 20-minute power nap using the old "bell falling" technique—holding something that drops and wakes me as I drift off. Other times it's guided meditations or binaural beats between meetings. These reset moments help me remember who I am beneath whatever mask the situation seems to demand.

I've also learned to track the physical sensations that signal I'm performing rather than being. For me, it's this specific tightness in my chest, like wearing a shirt that's a size too small. My breathing gets shallow. My voice shifts to a register that isn't quite mine. These body signals often alert me before my mind catches on.

The goal isn't to eliminate personas—we need them to function in society. It's about staying conscious of when we're wearing them and making sure we can still take them off. As Jung put it:

"Fundamentally, the persona is nothing real: it is a compromise between the individual and society as to what a man should appear to be. He takes a name, earns a title, represents an office, he is this or that. In a certain sense all this is real, yet in relation to the essential individuality of the person concerned it is only a secondary reality, a product of compromise, in making which others often have a greater share than he. The persona is a semblance, a two-dimensional reality."

The masks serve a purpose. Just remember there's a face underneath.

COMPLEXES: THE SUBPERSONALITIES OF THE PSYCHE

You know that moment when you're in an argument and suddenly you hear your mother's voice coming out of your mouth? Or when you swear you'll never be like your dad, then catch yourself doing exactly his disappointed head-shake? That's a complex hijacking your personality. Jung called these things the "subpersonalities of the psyche," but really they're like psychological possession—parts of you that grab the wheel and start driving while you're still figuring out what the hell just happened.

Jung put it this way: "When we say a person has a complex we mean he is strongly preoccupied by something that he can hardly think about anything else. In modern parlance, he has a 'hangup.' A strong complex is easily noticed by others, although the person himself may not be aware of it." - *A Primer of Jungian Psychology*.

Everyone else sees it. You're the only one who doesn't. It's like having spinach in your teeth at a party—obvious to everyone but invisible in your own mirror.

Here's where Freud and Jung had another one of their academic disagreements. Freud, predictably, blamed everything on childhood trauma—as if every complex was just mummy not hugging you enough or daddy being too mean. Everything boiled down to some primal scene where little you got psychologically messed up.

Jung looked at that and said, 'Okay, sure, but what about all the weird stuff humans have been doing since before we could write it down?' He believed complexes tap into something way deeper—something he called the 'collective unconscious'—an underground river of patterns and instincts that every human who ever lived somehow shares.

All those myths about heroes and monsters? The gods we keep inventing? The same damn dreams showing up across cultures that never met? That's the collective unconscious bleeding through. And exactly where Joseph Campbell found the patterns for his Hero's Journey.

Honestly? They're both right in my view. Of course your childhood messes you up in specific, personal ways—that's just basic math. But Jung's onto something with the deeper, universal themes that transcend individual experience.

Why else would we all have the same nightmares about being naked in public? Why do completely different cultures keep inventing the same stories about floods and serpents and wise old mentors? There's something underneath the personal trauma, something older and mysterious that we're all swimming in.

We're all walking around with these patterns running our lives. In my case, I can trace the whole damn timeline. That desperate need to be the "best" soccer player, the "premier talent"? That wasn't about trophies. It morphed into this endless hunger for acknowledgment, for someone to see me and say 'Yes, you matter.'

Then it dressed itself up in fancier clothes—became this need to save everyone, guide everyone, be everyone's wise mentor. Hell, I dragged Joey through a cave because of it. I'm writing this book because of it! The savior complex is just the achievement complex wearing a spiritual costume.

But here's the head-scratcher—even when you see your complexes clearly, even when you can name them as I just did, like old enemies, they're not necessarily bad. This desperate need for recognition? It's also what makes me bust a gut to actually be helpful. It drives me to lead well because I need people to think I'm worth following.

That savior complex? Sometimes it actually saves people. Our complexes aren't always negative character flaws to amputate—they're rocket fuel that can either blow you up or get you to orbit. The trick is pointing them in the right direction for growth.

But I still fall for the same old traps. These complexes are like whack-a-mole—you think you've handled them, then BAM, there they are in a new costume. Imposter syndrome hits and suddenly I'm convinced everyone's about to figure out I'm just three kids in a trenchcoat pretending to be an adult.

Or I'm in a business meeting and someone else makes a good point, and this primal thing in me wants to make a better point, win the invisible contest no one else knows we're having.

Business environments are, again, my kryptonite. They're basically complex playgrounds—everyone pretending their spreadsheets matter more than their souls, measuring success in metrics that have sweet FA to do with being human.

One world rewards you for being a shark; the other for being a dolphin. I'm constantly trying to master walking in both these worlds at the same time. It's one of the biggest challenges I live through on a daily basis.

And just when you think you've evolved past your old patterns—surprise!—there's your achievement complex wearing a new suit, speaking fluent corporate while your soul quietly dies in the conference room. Some days I nail it. Most days I feel like I'm at my wits' end.

No amount of therapy or plant medicine or meditation retreats makes these patterns disappear. They just get sneakier.

These complexes aren't personality quirks—they're full-blown psychological fortresses built around our deepest wounds and greatest gifts. They're going to express themselves whether you like it or not, seeking expression throughout our lives in ways that can either limit or enrich our development—depending on our willingness to recognize and engage with them consciously.

Jung knew you can't kill these things—that's like trying to surgically remove your own history. The work is making friends with your demons, bringing them to the negotiating table instead of letting them run guerrilla warfare from your unconscious.

Once they're in relationship with your conscious mind, they lose their power to drive you blindly. So the only question is whether they'll run your life from the shadows or become conscious allies in your growth.

Unfortunately, this process of dragging complexes into consciousness usually requires other people to call us on our shit. By definition, we can't see our own blind spots—that's the whole point of blind spots. We need other people to hold up the mirror, and trust me, we'll hate them for it.

Our ego will scramble for every possible excuse: they're projecting, they don't really know us, they're jealous, they're the ones with the problem. That immediate defensive rage that flares up when someone names our pattern? That burning need to explain why they're wrong? That's not wisdom defending itself—that's our complex protecting its hiding place. Most of the time.

I learned this the hard way during a men's intensive retreat when the group confronted me with what they called my 'second wave of ego.' See, I thought I was crushing it at this retreat. I'd shared vulnerably about my relationships, shed real tears during ceremony, felt like I was really doing the work.

Then came the evening of the "fire council"—where each man receives unfiltered observations from the group.

When my turn came, their words knocked the wind right out of me. One by one, they described a version of me I'd been completely blind to:

"Lee, you use words like a fucking shield," said one man. "You're so goddam articulate and profound, but I never feel like I'm reaching the real YOU in all those perfect words."

"Your energy dominates the space," observed another. "It's like a spotlight that's too bright, leaving no room for shadow—yours or ours."

The hardest one came from the elder of the group: "You speak entirely from your head, not your heart. You're so busy analyzing the experience that you're not actually having it."

Jesus. I wanted to crawl into that fire pit and disappear.

One guy said I was like someone "kicking the ball on their own in the corner"—physically present but completely disconnected. Another nailed it: "You're eating the menu rather than the meal."

But the worst came from one guy who really didn't pull punches. "You're masturbating with words while the rest of us are trying to make love to life."

Yeah... you can imagine how long those words stayed with me for.

I sat there, fighting my natural defensive with all my might, but intuitively recognizing the truth in their words. Here was my soccer complex, decades later—still positioning myself as the "premier talent," still using intellectual prowess to maintain distance and control, still performing rather than connecting.

So let me unpack what was really happening here, because this is exactly how complexes operate—mine was doing its familiar dance right there in that circle.

Remember how I mentioned my childhood drive to be the "best" at soccer? It wasn't just ambition. It was survival. Being exceptional meant coaches noticed me, teammates needed me, parents praised me. I existed most fully when performing at the highest level.

When my soccer career ended, the complex didn't vanish—it just found new playing fields. If I couldn't dominate with footwork, I'd dominate with words and ideas. Different game, same strategy: be so competent, so articulate, so intellectually impressive that no one could dismiss or abandon me.

What those men saw—what I couldn't—was this complex in full operation. Someone shares a vulnerable story? I respond with perfectly crafted analysis. Emotions rise in the group? I offer eloquent frameworks for understanding.

I thought I was helping, but I was actually maintaining control. Every insight, every well-turned phrase was another defensive move—keeping the ball in my possession.

The complex even had physical manifestations I'd never noticed. I'd literally lean back slightly, creating physical distance while my words created psychological distance. My hands would move in certain gestures, as if orchestrating the conversation to my own rhythm.

And here's what's tricky about complexes: they're brilliant at self-justification. Mine had rationalizations locked and loaded: "I'm helping people understand their experiences." "Someone needs to bring clarity here." "I'm contributing my gifts."

All partially true, which made them perfect covers for what was really happening—a scared part of me desperately maintaining control to avoid the messiness of genuine emotional connection.

The "kicking the ball in the corner" metaphor was devastating in its accuracy. Just like young Lee was more interested in showing off his skills rather than passing to teammates, adult Lee was hoarding the intellectual "ball"—performing solo when connection required collaboration.

This is pure Jung—complexes as semi-autonomous subpersonalities with their own agendas. My competence complex had one mission: never be caught without answers, never appear inadequate, never fumble for words. It would hijack my consciousness the moment my intellectual standing felt threatened.

The paradox crushed me. This complex—whatever its original purpose—was now actively preventing the very connection I claimed to want. Whether it formed to ensure I mattered, to guarantee I'd never be overlooked, or simply to survive in a competitive world, it had become a barrier to real connection.

By always having insights, I never had needs. By maintaining intellectual superiority, I avoided the equality required for real relationship. By speaking from my head, I protected my heart from actual contact.

Random, I know, but I couldn't help but think of *Star Trek* in those immediate moments after the men's feedback. I was basically Spock with a messiah complex. You know Spock, right? Dude spends the entire original series acting like emotions are beneath him, like they're some primitive human weakness he's evolved beyond.

"Highly illogical," he says, while everyone else is actually living their lives. But the whole point of his character arc is that he's terrified of feelings because they're too intense, too uncontrollable. That Vulcan logic isn't wisdom—it's armor.

And there I was, pulling the same move, hiding behind articulate analysis while pretending it was enlightenment. At least Spock had the excuse of being half-alien. What was mine?

Months later, I finally had a bit of a breakthrough on this whole hiding-behind-words thing—and ironically, it happened without words at all. I came across a Rothko painting, one of those color field pieces he's famous for, and felt this immediate, inexplicable pull. Two distinct fields of red, one above the other. The upper field darker, the lower glowing with vibrant intensity.

Now, I wasn't a stranger to art. I'd dated artists, spent countless hours in museums, knew all the clichés—'Don't analyze it, just feel it.' I'd nodded along to that wisdom a hundred times while secretly dissecting every brushstroke in my head.

But this time was different.

I wasn't trying to be different—that's the thing. I just... couldn't think my way into this painting. It wouldn't let me. The two fields were essentially the same red, but man, what a difference.

The upper field was muted—all that potential color held back, like my thinking mind with its careful constructions and measured responses. The lower field? Same red, but alive. Vibrant. Pulsing with the energy that was always there, just... freed.

Looking at those two reds, something in me recognized my own journey. The upper field felt like my mental thinking with good intentions of the heart—all those intellectual offerings I'd made from a safe distance. The lower felt like what I longed for—the full embodiment of the heart itself, the same energy but unleashed, unguarded.

This wasn't analysis—it was recognition. The painting was doing to me what I'd been unable to do for myself. Moving me from my head to somewhere deeper. The medium was the message, and for once, I actually got it without having to think about getting it.

And yes—here I am now, using words to describe the wordless. I get the irony. But I've learned that this is often how the mind works—it re-enters the scene after the heart's had its moment, trying to shape the feeling into something shareable. The difference now is that I know that's what I'm doing.

I actually ended up buying a print of that Rothko. It hangs in my home now—a visual reminder of the journey from head to heart. When I catch myself intellectualizing to maintain distance, I try to spend time with those two fields of red, letting them guide me back to heart wisdom rather than clever mental machinations. The painting doesn't "mean" something —it simply is, inviting me to simply be.

Those men at the retreat gave me a gift I didn't appreciate until I met my wife. Their feedback about my word-shields suddenly became practical wisdom. When she'd share something difficult, that fresh awareness would remind me: she doesn't need solutions, she needs to be heard. This simple understanding—that most people want support, not strategies—changed everything.

Had I met her before that retreat, I probably would have analyzed us right out of a relationship. But with that awareness still fresh, I could actually show up for her instead of performing for her. My intellectualizing wasn't a flaw—it had protected me when I needed protection. Now I'm learning when to set it aside.

THE COLLECTIVE UNCONSCIOUS: A SHARED ANCESTRAL HERITAGE

Ever wonder why every human culture seems to know certain things without being taught? We all fear the dark, even in our safe modern homes. Cultures separated by oceans tell identical flood myths—Noah, Gilgamesh, Manu. Dragons appear in stories from Wales to China despite no contact between these civilizations. That's always blagged my head a little bit.

Way before I'd heard of Jung's collective unconscious, I was this kid obsessively drawing spirals in the margins of my notebooks. I couldn't help myself. There was something deeply satisfying about watching that pattern unfold—starting from a tiny center point and spiraling outward into something bigger. I had no idea then that I was tapping into one of humanity's oldest symbols, the same pattern that shows up everywhere from prehistoric caves to Celtic stones to Maori tattoos. Cultures that never knew each other existed, all drawing the same spiral.

As a kid, I also had this weird pull toward fire. Don't worry, I wasn't some little pyromaniac plotting to torch the neighborhood or anything. But I'd often just lose myself staring at campfires or candle flames, completely mesmerized. Something about that flickering light, the way those flames danced and swayed, never the same pattern twice—it just got me. And the crackling sounds of a real wood fire? Hypnotizing. Back then I thought I was just spacing out, gazing into the flames like any kid might. But looking back, I recognize it as something way more primal—like my DNA was remembering something my conscious mind couldn't even access yet.

On reflection, many years later I realized—I wasn't just some pyromaniac kid. I may have been tapping into the most fundamental archetype in human experience. It's the discovery that literally made us human. For hundreds of thousands of years, every single night, our ancestors gathered around those flames. Warmth, protection, cooked food, storytelling—fire gave us all of it. Think about that. We've spent more time as a species staring into fires than doing basically anything else except sleeping. That's generations upon generations of programming.

Jung suggested this ancient relationship isn't just cultural memory—it's encoded into our bodies. So when I feel that magnetic pull toward a campfire, when I can't help but zone out watching those flames dance, I might be connecting with 400,000 years of human experience. My fascination isn't unique or random. It might be the echo of millions of ancestors who knew in their bones that fire meant survival—the difference between freezing and warmth, between raw meat and cooked food, between predator and protector.

These mysterious childhood experiences finally made sense when I discovered the psychological framework that could explain them.

Long before Campbell mapped the Hero's Journey across world mythologies, Jung was noticing something remarkable in his therapy practice. He kept seeing the same symbols, the same myths, the same deep patterns showing up in patients who'd never met. People from completely different backgrounds having identical archetypal dreams. When I eventually encountered Jung's work, it was like finding the instruction manual for all my childhood experiences. See, Jung wasn't satisfied with just mapping consciousness and the personal unconscious. He proposed something more profound—a third layer he called the collective unconscious.

So what exactly is this collective unconscious? Picture consciousness like geological layers. At the surface, you've got your conscious mind—everything you're aware of right now, your thoughts, that meeting tomorrow, what you had for breakfast. Just beneath that lies your personal unconscious—your own repository of forgotten memories, that embarrassing moment from third grade, all the complexes and patterns that are uniquely yours.

But Jung discovered something deeper. Underneath all our personal material, there's a layer that connects every human who's ever lived—a shared psychological inheritance that has nothing to do with your individual life story. You don't develop the collective unconscious; you're born with it, like your eye color or being right-handed. It's the deepest stratum of the psyche, containing what Jung called our "archaic heritage"—essentially humanity's psychological DNA.

Here's another way to think about it: if your conscious mind is the tip of the iceberg above water, and your personal unconscious is the ice below the surface, then the collective unconscious is the ocean itself. Every human iceberg floats in the same water. And this ocean contains hundreds of thousands of years of human experience—every pattern that helped us survive, every symbol that carried meaning, every fear and hope that got hardwired into our species.

And here's a bit of a mindbender: we don't just inherit grandma's nose or dad's metabolism. We inherit the whole psychological package. Those fears that kept our ancestors from becoming predator food? Still there. The symbols that helped them navigate reality? Downloaded. The stories they told around those ancient fires to make sense of existence? All still running in our deepest programming.

Jung kept having these revelatory moments with his patients. People from totally different worlds—different cultures, religions, no overlap— were having the same dreams, the same visions, the same deep patterns emerging. Someone who'd never read Greek mythology would dream about being devoured by a monster—echoing Kronos devouring his children. Another person with zero exposure to Buddhism would describe visions matching ancient Eastern texts. In his eyes, this wasn't coincidence.

It was evidence of something bigger. We're all drawing from the same well of human experience, and not because we learned it or absorbed it from our culture. We're born with access to it. Jung called the contents of this collective unconscious "archetypes"—universal patterns that appear wherever humans exist. Same symbols, same stories, same characters, same situations, just dressed in local clothing.

Most of the time, we're oblivious to this collective layer—it runs in the background like an operating system we never see. But Jung noticed that during crisis, major stress, or life upheaval, we can suddenly get access. It can break through in various ways: those gut instincts that guide us without thinking, insights that arrive fully formed, mysterious attractions to certain symbols, dreams that feel too significant to be random mental noise, or ancient fears that defy logic. These might not be personal quirks —they could be humanity's shared patterns playing through our individual lives.

I feel like that's exactly what was happening with my fire fascination. My connection to fire wasn't just personal—I was resonating with possibly the deepest archetype we carry, the one that literally shaped our evolution and social structures. And those spirals I couldn't stop drawing? It might be a reach, but the spiral shows up everywhere in nature—galaxies, shells, hurricanes, DNA itself. Ancient cultures from Ireland to Australia carved them into sacred stones, seeing them as symbols of life's cycles and the journey of consciousness. Maybe I was unconsciously tapping into a pattern that speaks to something fundamental about how energy moves through the universe. No one taught me spirals were meaningful—that knowledge seemed to be already installed.

So how do we know when we're accessing this deeper layer rather than just having random thoughts? Well, sometimes it announces itself through dreams so vivid and symbolically rich that they stay with you for years.

I had such a dream years ago. And it still haunts me to this day. It started in my childhood bedroom—everything exactly as I remembered it, safe and familiar, until something in the air changed. The toys on my shelf began to move. Books flapped open and closed. Furniture creaked and leaned toward me. Suddenly all these ordinary objects were alive and trying to smother and consume me. In a desperate attempt to fight them off I threw myself on top of them, frantically trying to hold them down. But then, they slowly began to merge and transform beneath me, into an old—and I mean old—hag type woman. But here's the embarrassing part —despite being impossibly old, with skin like weathered leather and eyes that held millennia, she was somehow irresistibly seductive. (Yeah, I know —Freud would have a field day with this one.) She beckoned me to her bed with fingers that were both withered and graceful, her voice both raspy and honeyed. It was like the Evil Queen from *Snow White*—that same impossible duality of decay and desire. Somehow I knew—this wasn't about sex or intimacy. She wanted to devour me.

The instant I resisted, the room vanished, and suddenly I was in an underground castle, dark stone corridors stretching in every direction. Soldiers in old armor pursued me through the halls, their footsteps echoing behind me. In the deepest part of the castle, I came face to face with a princess dressed in pure white. Without warning, she lunged at me with a blade. We struggled. I got the knife away from her and stabbed her with it, even twisting it to make sure she was finished. Her white dress turned red.

Then another woman appeared—calmer, wiser somehow. She looked at the dying princess and said simply: "We could heal her instead of letting her die." Those words changed everything. Somehow I instantly understood that compassion was the only way to transform an enemy into an ally—that this was the message being conveyed. That message has never left me.

Years later, when I studied Jung's work, I was shocked to discover that this dream—which I'd had with zero knowledge of Jungian psychology—was a textbook example of his archetypal patterns. In his collective consciousness framework, that childhood bedroom represented my personal history, my starting point. Those animated objects trying to consume me were classic "autonomous complexes"—parts of the psyche that can take on their own life. The old seductive hag? Jung would call this the "shape-shifting feminine" or the dark aspect of the Great Mother - representing how the nurturing feminine can also be devouring. The beautiful but ancient woman embodies the dual nature of the unconscious itself: alluring but potentially consuming. Descending into that underground castle was entering the collective unconscious itself. And that white princess I tried to destroy? She represented what Jung called the anima—feminine aspects we need to work with, not eliminate. My dream ally understood: transformation requires compassion, not violence.

But how did my unconscious mind spontaneously generate this perfect sequence of universal symbols? I hadn't read this anywhere, hadn't seen it in films. It emerged from that collective reservoir Jung mapped, like my psyche was running software I didn't know was installed. If that's not evidence we're all carrying these patterns, I don't know what is.

Skeptical? Completely fair. I get it. But here's where science enters the conversation and things get pretty interesting.

See, Jung's theory, once dismissed as too mystical, might actually have serious scientific support. Think about it—we already accept that diseases run in families through DNA. We know evolution hardwires survival instincts without question. So why is it strange to think we might also inherit our ancestors' psychological experiences? Their traumas, their triumphs, their deepest fears and hard-won wisdom—all potentially passed down like psychological heirlooms.

Recent studies are revealing something remarkable: our ancestors' experiences aren't just family stories—they might be literally encoded in our biology. Scientists call this "transgenerational epigenetic inheritance," which essentially means that trauma, resilience, and significant life experiences can leave biological markers that get passed to future generations.

When researchers studied Holocaust survivors and their children, they found the parents' trauma had actually altered specific genes, and those changes were inherited by their kids. Similar patterns appeared in Indigenous populations who'd faced historical trauma, even in laboratory mice passing stress responses to their offspring. It's as if our ancestors' most significant experiences—both traumatic and transformative—get written into our biology, influencing how we respond to the world before we're even born.

Consider this: if your grandmother survived a famine, her body didn't just remember—it adapted at the biological level to handle scarcity better. Those adaptations might have been passed to you through your DNA. So when you feel anxiety about wasting food, or your metabolism seems primed for scarcity that isn't coming—that could be your grandmother's survival programming still running in your system. Her lived experience might have become your inherited biology.

This cutting-edge research is basically giving Jung a posthumous high-five. The guy might have been right—we don't just get dad's eyes or mom's smile. We might inherit the whole psychological package: emotional patterns, trauma responses, survival strategies that kept our bloodline going when things got rough.

The bottom line: our ancestors' lives aren't just dusty old stories—they're alive in us right now, actively shaping who we are today and how we move through the world. That wartime trauma your great-grandmother endured? The grit and resilience your grandfather developed through the Depression? These aren't just family stories to pass down for reunions. They might be literally encoded in your cells, running the show when you don't even realize it. Why you freak out or are triggered by certain things, what makes you feel safe, how you handle stress—all of it could be your ancestors' experiences playing out through your nervous system. It's humbling as hell, but also kind of beautiful. We might not be alone in our struggles—we could be carrying our ancestors with us, their wisdom and wounds potentially woven into our DNA. Kind of comforting huh?

ARCHETYPES: THE UNIVERSAL PATTERNS OF THE PSYCHE

"For the sake of mental stability and even physiological health, the unconscious and the conscious must be integrally connected and thus move on parallel lines. If they are split apart or "dissociated," psychological disturbance follows."

— CARL JUNG, *MAN AND HIS SYMBOLS*

So Jung had this wild idea about archetypes—basically these universal patterns hardwired into every human's collective unconscious. They're like psychological templates we all inherit, popping up everywhere as symbols, images, themes in our stories, art, you name it. Jung mapped out the big ones: the mother, birth, death, rebirth, power, the hero, the child. He also figured there's probably as many archetypes as there are typical life situations.

These archetypal patterns aren't just ancient history though—Jung's framework suggests they're alive in our modern storytelling too, often in ways we don't always consciously recognize.

Every man and his dog seems to use *Star Wars* to explain Campbell's Hero's Journey, and fair enough—Luke's transformation from farm boy to Jedi brilliantly depicts that mythic structure through external adventure: quest, villain, victory. It's a powerful story, no question. But *Star Trek*? That show often explored something else entirely, something that aligns perfectly with Jung's framework. It wasn't about defeating Death Stars; it was about encountering the unknown aspects of consciousness itself. The best episodes—the ones that stuck with me—focused on the internal landscape where archetypes actually live, diving into what felt like Jung's collective unconscious, that shared reservoir of human experience we're all connected to. That's the key difference between Campbell and Jung—one maps the outer adventure, the other explores the inner territory. *Star Wars* and *Star Trek* mirror this exact split.

For the record, I've always been a Trekkie. But here's what fascinates me about the contrast: *Star Wars* presents the Force as having a light side and a dark side—external energies you choose between. You're either with the Jedi or seduced by the dark side, and the story typically ends with good defeating evil. Clear choices, satisfying resolution. Jung's framework suggests something more nuanced: we don't just choose between light and shadow—we contain both. And the goal isn't to eliminate one or favor the other, but to bring them into consciousness—to get them working together. The work is to face our darkness, not reject it—to understand and integrate it as part of becoming whole.

Luke's arc is about resisting the dark. Jung's path is about embracing it —recognizing that our darkness isn't evil to be destroyed, but material to be worked with. That's why Spock feels more Jungian to me. He's not trying to purge his human emotions or surrender fully to Vulcan logic. He's constantly navigating the tension between the two—finding strength not in choosing sides, but in learning to hold both.

Star Trek rarely dealt in simple good-versus-evil stories. Those strange alien encounters—energy beings, shape-shifters, reality-bending entities—weren't just sci-fi weirdness. They were metaphors for the parts of human consciousness we haven't fully faced. The show kept circling a deeper question: What if the real final frontier isn't outer space—but the uncharted territory within ourselves?

Take Q—if you know, you know. This omnipotent trickster would just pop onto the Enterprise bridge in a flash of light, usually when Picard was having a decent day, and proceed to challenge everything the crew believed. He could literally rewrite reality with a snap, but instead of conquering, he played cosmic games that forced growth. Imagine someone with godlike powers who uses them primarily to provoke existential crises. Pure Trickster energy.

This Trickster archetype appears across every culture. Loki shape-shifts and challenges the Norse gods. Coyote breaks rules in Native American tales to teach hard lessons. Even Yoda has trickster elements, making Luke balance on one hand while lifting spacecraft. They're all variations on the same theme—the force that disrupts comfort zones and catalyzes transformation. Yoda guides through patient wisdom; Q pushes through chaos and confrontation. Different methods, same archetypal function.

But *Star Trek* wasn't just the Q show—it was an archetypal buffet. You had your Wise Elders in those alien councils, dropping ancient wisdom between commercial breaks. Then there's the Shadow stuff, which got really dark. The Borg? That's our nightmare of losing ourselves to the collective, becoming another cog in some massive machine—basically everyone's fear of corporate culture taken to its logical extreme. The Klingons? They're all the warrior rage we've suppressed in order to function in polite society, walking around with their aggression on full display while we pretend we don't want to flip tables sometimes.

As a little Trekkie kid back then, I obviously didn't have Jung's vocabulary. I just sensed these encounters touched something deeper than entertainment—they were exploring what it means to be human through the metaphor of the alien "other." When I discovered Jung's work years later, it felt like finding the theoretical framework for territories I'd already been exploring through imagination.

Of course, these archetypal patterns extend way beyond sci-fi. The "wise old man" or "wise old woman"—what Jung called the sage archetype —shows up everywhere we tell stories about transformation. Gandalf arrives at precisely the right moment with the wisdom that saves the day. Obi-Wan continues guiding Luke even after death, his voice echoing through the Force when it's needed most. Dumbledore somehow always knows exactly what Harry needs to hear, even when his advice seems impossibly cryptic at the time. They're all channeling the same archetypal energy—that wise elder who appears at the crucial moment to help us navigate the unknown. Different robes, different worlds, but the same essential function in the human psyche.

But what I realized later through Jung's work is that these shadow encounters aren't random nightmares—they're initiations. The old woman wasn't just trying to destroy me. She was testing whether I had the strength to resist being consumed by the unconscious itself. When I fought her off instead of surrendering to that strange seduction, I was declaring my right to exist as an individual rather than dissolve back into the unconscious. Her seductive yet deadly nature was teaching something essential: trust your instincts when something feels dangerous, regardless of how alluring it appears. Jung saw these terrifying moments as necessary psychological passages—where we assert ourselves as conscious beings rather than remain driven by unconscious patterns.

This is classic Jung—every archetype's got a light side and a dark side, like psychological mood lighting. The same energy that gives you protective Gandalf can flip and become the witch in the woods who might just eat children. Our task isn't to avoid these darker encounters but to recognize them as part of our psychological education and to integrate the wisdom they offer. The shadow teaches different lessons than the light—usually harder ones—but both are necessary for wholeness.

But here's where Jung pushed the boundaries—he proposed that these archetypal patterns aren't just psychological curiosities. They evolved right alongside our ability to walk upright and use tools. While our bodies were learning to survive in the physical world, our psyches were developing their own survival equipment. And Jung was adamant about one thing: if you don't face this unconscious material and integrate it, you remain fragmented—no clear sense of identity, no real purpose. You're basically walking around as a psychological jigsaw puzzle with half the pieces missing, fragments pretending to be a whole person.

In Jung's framework, these archetypes don't just live in stories—they appear in real life, especially during major transitions. Lost your job? The trickster might emerge to shake things up further. Grieving someone? A wise elder figure often appears in unexpected ways. These archetypal energies seem to surface when our usual patterns aren't working anymore. Chapter 5 explores how trickster energy specifically disrupts our comfortable routines and forces growth we didn't know we needed.

After years of working with these ideas myself, here's what became clear for me: archetypal encounters aren't just interesting psychology or clever literary analysis. I've come to see them as gateways to deeper work. These patterns from the collective unconscious can prepare us for individuation—that process where we stop running on autopilot and start consciously integrating the different parts of ourselves.

So, have you ever had a dream that stayed with you for years? Met someone who triggered something you couldn't quite name? Maybe noticed the same symbol appearing repeatedly in your life? I've come to see these as invitations from the collective unconscious—signals that we might be ready for the next stage of development. Not the external hero's journey of *Star Wars*, but the internal adventure Jung mapped out. Which brings us to individuation itself—where ancient patterns meet conscious effort in the work of becoming integrated human beings.

THE INDIVIDUATION PROCESS: THE JOURNEY TO WHOLENESS

"I use the term 'individuation' to denote the process by which a person becomes a psychological 'individual,' that is, a separate, indivisible unity or 'whole'"

— CARL JUNG

So we've mapped out the collective unconscious—that shared storehouse of human experience holding all those ancient patterns and archetypes. We've seen how these forces show up in our dreams, our relationships, our life transitions. But recognizing these patterns is just the first step. The real work is learning how to integrate them—to consciously bring them into our awareness instead of being unconsciously driven by them.

This is what Jung called individuation—the journey of becoming who we actually are, not who we've been conditioned to be. It's the larger process I've been describing throughout this book: facing the shadow, recognizing the persona, bringing together those fragmented parts into something whole.

Integration is the actual work—the messy, ongoing effort of bringing unconscious material into conscious awareness. Every time we recognize a projection or face a shadow aspect, that's integration. Individuation is the lifelong journey that all this integration serves. We can't just intellectually understand we have a shadow; we need to actually integrate those rejected parts. Same with our persona—recognizing we wear masks isn't enough. We have to figure out how to be authentic while still functioning in society.

We've all been there—that Sunday night dread creeping in before another week of the grind. That nagging voice asking "Is this it?" even when our LinkedIn profile looks impressive and our life checks all the boxes society handed us. We've got the job, the relationship, maybe the house, but something essential feels missing. Like we're living someone else's life, or worse, a watered-down version of our own.

Jung was fascinated by these feelings of incompleteness—like parts of ourselves have broken off. But he didn't see them as problems to fix. He saw them as the psyche's navigation system, constantly orienting us toward wholeness. In Jung's view, those uncomfortable feelings aren't flaws—they're signals pointing toward who we're meant to become.

Jung's approach? Don't avoid the unconscious—engage with it head-on. Dive into our dreams like they're encrypted messages from our deeper self (because they are). Make art, write, dance—whatever gets the unconscious material surface. Sit with ourselves long enough to actually hear what's going on beneath the surface noise. It's through this active engagement that the magic happens: we start to understand not just who we think we are, but who we actually are and why we're here.

At its core, Individuation is the process of expanding our consciousness—healing the fragmented parts of the conscious and unconscious mind so they work in harmony instead of conflict. All those scattered pieces of ourselves—the parts we show, the parts we hide, the parts we don't yet know exist—finally recognize they belong to the same person. The internal war ends because there's no 'other side' to fight.

Jung made a crucial distinction that most people miss: our Ego and our Self are not the same thing. Our Ego is like our operating system—it keeps us functional, manages daily responsibilities, pays the bills, maintains our identity, helps us navigate social situations. It's absolutely necessary for navigating reality and meeting our basic needs.

But the Self? That's the entire system, not just the programs we're running. It includes everything—our conscious awareness, our unconscious depths, potentials we haven't discovered yet. The Self is our complete blueprint, the full version of us that's been there all along, waiting for us to grow into it.

In the first half of life, we're usually focused on building a strong Ego foundation. Jung called it "ego differentiation"—essentially figuring out where we end and the world begins, then establishing ourselves in the outside world, establishing our identity, and securing our basic survival needs. But because our ego is so busy trying to survive, looking out for threats and climbing social or career ladders, our inner world can become neglected and forgotten—like that gym membership we keep paying for but never use. Then somewhere around midlife—though it can happen earlier if life kicks our arse hard enough—we feel this pull inward. That neglected inner world starts knocking louder, demanding attention. That's individuation calling our name.

Until this shift happens, our identity—no matter how solid it feels—is basically a house built on partial foundation. We're operating on Ego alone, unaware of the vast unconscious territories and higher potentials within us. It's like thinking we know our house completely while never realizing there's an entire basement and attic we've never explored.

Sometimes, life events can completely blindside us or maybe even threaten and hurt the ego personality we've developed for ourselves to protect us. Divorce, death, job loss, illness—events that don't just shake our world but turn it completely upside down. That carefully constructed ego personality, that protective armor we've been wearing, can suddenly crack wide open. And here's the plot twist: that's often exactly what needs to happen. The breakdown becomes the breakthrough. When our masks shatter and we're standing there raw and vulnerable, that's when the deeper Self has space to emerge. Suddenly we're asking the real questions: "Who am I when I'm not playing my roles? What's left when all my identities are stripped away?"

Jung learned this the hard way after his difficult breakup with Freud sent him into his own psychological crisis. But instead of just seeing neuroses as mental illness to be cured, Jung had this radical insight: these psychological crises are actually our psyche screaming that something's blocking our natural growth. Our psychological crisis isn't the illness—it's our psyche's healthy response to being blocked. Like fever isn't the disease, it's our body fighting back. The real individuation work isn't about regressing to some pre-ego infant state. It's about having the courage to let our conscious Ego actually meet and integrate all those split-off parts—our persona (the masks we wear), our shadow (everything we've pushed into the psychological basement), and all we've been avoiding. This isn't comfortable work. It means examining parts of ourselves we've spent a lifetime avoiding. But it's the only way to heal the inner fractures and let our complete Self finally emerge and show up to the party.

So, now let's get into the meat of Jung's individuation map—the actual journey of becoming who we really are instead of who we've been programmed to be. Jung identified four major encounters we'll face on this path, but don't expect them to line up neatly like levels in a video game. They're more like recurring boss battles that show up whenever we're ready (or not) for the next round of growth. Each encounter requires us to face a different hidden aspect of ourselves, to stop running from the parts we've disowned, and to finally integrate all of who we are. Fair warning: this isn't a weekend workshop kind of transformation. It's the work of a lifetime.

Stage One: Confronting the Shadow

So here's where the real work starts—that gut-wrenching moment when we finally turn the spotlight on ourselves and see all the destructive patterns we've been running for years. This first stage, what Jung called confession and catharsis, means we have to take a hard look at ourselves and accept what we find. No more pointing fingers, no more deflecting. It's about taking responsibility for our growth and facing those darker aspects we've been avoiding. Basically, it's time to own our shit.

Take addiction—we can't heal until we admit we're the ones reaching for that bottle, that needle, that whatever-it-is that numbs us out. Or trauma—we have to somehow make peace with the fact that what happened happened, and no amount of wishing will unhappen it. This self-confrontation? It's brutal. Sometimes it'll make us feel like we're losing our minds for a while. But the thing is—that temporary neurosis is often the price of admission for real change. Sometimes, we have to lose ourselves, to find our Self.

And right at the center of this whole process? We meet our shadow—all that unconscious material we've repressed so deep we forgot it was there.

The shadow is basically everything about us that we've decided is too ugly, too shameful, too messed up to let anyone see—including ourselves. It's where we exile our scariest desires, our darkest impulses, all the parts that don't fit the "good person" image we're trying so hard to maintain. Society told us these parts were unacceptable, so we buried them alive, thinking that would keep us safe and loved.

Here's something that might sound familiar: whatever drives us crazy about other people? That's usually our own rejected stuff staring back at us. Me? I get really pissed off by people who cling to toxic relationships, folks who wear fake personas like they're auditioning for their own lives, conversation dominators who turn every topic into their personal monologue, and anyone walking around with unearned arrogance.

So it was a tough pill to swallow when I'd been the guy who lived through every single one of those behaviors. I stayed way too long in relationships that were harming me, performed versions of myself I thought people wanted to see and dominated conversations because I needed to be the smartest person in the room. Yeah. I was that guy. But our shadows are clever like that—they use other people as mirrors. When something makes us disproportionately angry, when we're ready to lose it over someone else's behavior, that's usually our own shadow waving a red flag saying 'Yo, remember me?'

The sweetest, most gentle souls among us? They might find a savage beast in their shadow, all teeth and rage. The super-rational, always-logical types? Their shadow might be a wild rebel who wants to burn the spreadsheets and dance naked in the rain. The key thing is–these shadow parts aren't all bad news. Jung believed the shadow doesn't just hold our darkness or shame. It also contains parts of ourselves we've rejected that are actually vital—our power, our creativity, our passion. Maybe someone once told us we were "too much," so we buried the boldest, most alive parts of ourselves to stay safe or be accepted. Later Jungians referred to this as the "gold in the shadow"—the idea that reclaiming our shadow isn't just about facing our demons, but retrieving the treasure we left behind.

Jung figured out that our shadow is like a houseguest who never actually leaves. And projecting it onto others, especially those who are different from us, is its main defense mechanism. "They're the problem, not me." Next thing we know, we're scapegoating entire groups, creating conflicts, even justifying violence—all because we couldn't face our own shadow.

It's also common for our shadow to show up in our dreams. And when it does, they can get pretty interesting. According to Jung's dream analysis, the shadow often appears as someone of our same gender—maybe that sibling who always triggered us, a stranger acting out our repressed impulses, or some mythological figure embodying our denied power. Jung noticed it sometimes shows up as our complete opposite too—if we're the super responsible type, our shadow might be the party animal trashing the hotel room and throwing TV's out of the window in our dreams.

Now here's where it gets tricky. As we start this shadow work, our ego goes into full protection mode. Remember, the ego thinks it's helping—it's been our bodyguard for years, keeping us safe from anything that might harm us. So when the shadow starts emerging, the ego panics. It gets defensive, throws up walls. Sometimes it tries to shove the shadow even deeper down. Other times it plays the victim card: "This isn't me, this is everyone else's fault."

The scary thing about our shadows though, is that they're relentless. And if we don't face them, you can be damn sure they'll find a way out one way or another. Often in very ugly ways, too. Remember Zidane's headbutt in the 2006 World Cup final? (If not, YouTube it—it's worth the watch.) Here's one of my soccer idols, the epitome of grace and composure, in the biggest match of his life. Not just any final—his last game ever before retirement. A billion people watching. The fairy tale ending all lined up. Then Materazzi says something, hits exactly the wrong button, and BOOM—Zidane's shadow takes over. All that repressed aggression, all that controlled pride, years of keeping it together—gone in one headbutt. His final image as a player? Not lifting the World Cup, but that lonely walk past the trophy after a red card.

This Zidane moment? It's like a masterclass in how the ego-shadow dance plays out. For years, Zidane's ego had built this identity—football's poet, all elegance and artistry, rarely losing his cool. And this wasn't just PR spin; he genuinely was that player most of the time. His ego worked hard protecting this image, making sure nothing tarnished the legend of the composed maestro.

But, for those familiar with the beautiful game, there were warning signs. Little flashes of temper throughout his career, moments where the mask slipped. But we all overlooked them, didn't we? The football world,

Zidane himself, everyone preferred the story of the elegant artist who transcended the rough side of the game. Those glimpses of his shadow? We filed them under "competitive spirit" and moved on.

Then came that final, and whatever Materazzi said, it created the perfect storm. No next game to make it right, no chance for redemption—just this moment, with everything on the line. The ego that had been holding everything back for so long just... gave way.

I've been there on the pitch myself. Usually football's where we get to channel that competitive intensity in a healthy way, right? But sometimes someone knows exactly which button to push, says exactly the thing that bypasses all our control mechanisms. Next thing we know, we're doing something insane while our rational mind watches in horror.

For Zidane, years of stuffed-down aggression and wounded pride chose the absolute worst moment to explode. The shadow didn't just peek out—it kicked the door down and took over the whole show.

This is exactly why the ego's protection strategy can backfire. By trying to keep us "safe" from our shadow, it's actually unknowingly building a pressure cooker. If Zidane had made peace with his aggressive side earlier—acknowledged it, worked with it, given it some room to breathe—maybe it wouldn't have needed to take over in front of a billion people. But when we keep pushing things down, they don't disappear. They just wait for the worst possible moment to emerge. Or even worse, erupt.

So just remember, our shadows will get their moment, one way or another. It's like water finding cracks—persistent, patient, inevitable. The more we deny it, the stronger it gets, feeding on our resistance. All that repression turns into resentment, then anger, then those explosive moments that can destroy our relationships and sense of Self.

Stage Two: Working with the Persona

So we've started getting cozy with our shadow—great. But now Jung throws another curveball at us: the persona. If the shadow represents what we've rejected about ourselves, the persona is what we've constructed to show the world—our carefully crafted social mask. And here's where things get tricky: we face two major temptations that can derail us. First, we can project all our disowned parts onto others instead of owning them.

Second, we can keep suppressing our authentic self just to maintain the performance.

That first temptation—projection—gets extra tricky when we're defending our personas. We've already seen how we project our shadows onto others, but when our carefully crafted mask is threatened? The projection goes into overdrive. Someone calls out our inauthenticity, and instead of examining our persona, we attack their "jealousy" or "negativity." We'll do anything to avoid seeing that we're the ones wearing the mask.

Sometimes the persona defense can get even more extreme. When our constructed identity feels seriously threatened, our ego might split off parts of itself entirely, creating internal fragmentation. Or it slips into victim mode—suddenly we're not fake, we're just "misunderstood." The ego gets remarkably creative when protecting the performance we've invested so much in maintaining.

The second temptation's equally compelling—we keep pushing our authentic self further down to maintain our persona's smooth operation. We're essentially lying to ourselves, pretending whole parts of our personality don't exist. The result? A life built on self-deception, where we're constantly performing instead of living.

My twenties were basically one long borrowed persona experiment. I was doing a bad cover band version of people I admired who seemed to have figured out this whole "success" thing. You know that theatrical mask we discussed earlier? Mine was cobbled together from pieces of other people's performances. Not exactly authentic.

Looking back now, I realize those "successful" people I was imitating? They were likely putting on their own desperate performances, wearing whatever masks they thought would get them ahead. Coming from working-class roots, I had limited access to 'successful' people. Their approach to success became my template, and I thought that imitating their persona was the ticket out.

The problem was, underneath all that borrowed confidence, I'm hardwired for authenticity and straight talk. This set up an internal war of tension that would've made Jung nod knowingly—textbook persona versus authentic self cage match. Ever tried writing with your wrong hand for hours? That's what living in someone else's persona feels like. Sure, we can manage it, but it's exhausting and never stops feeling fundamentally off.

This internal conflict peaked when I packed up and moved from the UK to Silicon Valley, chasing that shiny tech startup dream. I was absolutely convinced I could reinvent myself as a tech entrepreneur—my ego was working overtime on that delusion. In reality? Complete fish out of water, totally out of my depth. I was "hustling," "crushing it," throwing around buzzwords like confetti—meanwhile, every investor and potential partner could smell the bullshit from a mile away. When deals didn't materialize and connections fell flat, what did I do? Blamed Silicon Valley, naturally. "This place just isn't for me," I'd tell myself, instead of admitting I wasn't showing up authentically. The irony? Silicon Valley actually values authenticity more than most business environments. They trade in trust, not carefully crafted performances.

The turning point came when I started the vulnerable work of removing that mask. It was scary, letting people see the real me instead of my polished performance. But here's what surprised me—as the persona fell away, genuine connections started forming. People actually preferred the unfiltered version. One mentor particularly—highly successful by any measure—showed me something crucial through his own example. Here was someone at the top of his game who'd regularly admit when he didn't know something, spoke vulnerably about his failures, treated everyone with genuine warmth, and still commanded massive respect and success. He wasn't teaching authenticity; he was living it. Watching him operate shattered my belief that we had to choose between being real and being successful. No surprise then, that someone who embodied this integration of authenticity and achievement would later introduce me to the Hero's Journey framework we've been exploring together.

All that energy I'd been spending to maintain my false persona? I could finally redirect it toward actual creation and genuine connection. My shadow work revealed something important: ambition wasn't my problem —it was the inauthentic way I'd been expressing it that created the conflict. The parts of myself I'd been hiding? Turns out they were actually my superpowers all along. I just had to stop apologizing for them and let them emerge naturally.

This internal pressure doesn't just affect us individually—it ripples through our relationships and communities. Repressed emotions have a way of spreading, affecting everyone around us. Plus, when we're busy suppressing our shadows, we become vulnerable to toxic environments and people who can sense our unresolved issues and exploit them.

Look at Cinderella—perfect example. If she'd kept playing nice and suppressing her shadow (all that buried longing for freedom and self-expression), she'd still be scrubbing floors and talking to mice. We do this constantly—push down our shadows because facing them feels incredibly uncomfortable. In my experience, we're often just postponing the inevitable. The longer we resist, the more life has a funny way of forcing our shadows into the spotlight, usually when we're already dealing with major crisis, loss, or challenge. The timing? Always when you're already knee-deep in ordeal.

From what I've seen, keeping our shadows suppressed tends to create more than just self-deception—it can distort our entire sense of identity. While deflecting it onto others can prevent us from accepting it as a vital part of who we really are. Real growth, real individuation—it requires us to step up, look our shadow in the eye, and invite it to the table. Not as an enemy, but as a teacher carrying exactly the wisdom we need.

Our ego has four main strategies for dealing with persona and shadow: denial ("What shadow?"), projection ("That's your issue"), integration ("This is part of me"), and transformation ("Let's work with this"). We know the saying "You are your own worst enemy," but here's the insight—often that enemy is wearing the very mask we think protects us. When we first start catching glimpses of our personas, it's like seeing the Matrix code for the first time. We might get a flash of how fake we've been living, but full acceptance? That takes time. We usually start with "Okay, maybe I wear a mask sometimes" before we get to "Holy shit, I've been method acting my entire life."

If we want to make real progress on this individuation journey, we need awareness on both fronts—our shadows AND our personas. The parts we hide AND the parts we perform. Bringing shadow material into consciousness? Scary as hell, no sugar-coating it. But it's the only way we'll address what needs fixing and see beyond our BS social performances.

In my experience, avoiding shadow work or never questioning our personas is like rolling out the red carpet for ongoing chaos and imbalance. Remember that Tree of Life metaphor we explored? I've found that when I'm overly attached to my social masks or completely rejecting my shadows, I lose my footing—both my internal stability and external equilibrium go out the window. A tree cut off from its roots or decorated with plastic branches isn't really growing—and in my experience, neither are we when we live that way. I haven't been able to grow authentically while denying parts of myself. That's been my pattern anyway, and I hear similar stories from others on this path.

This individuation process essentially involves integrating—or marrying—our opposites: getting our dark and light sides to play nice, finding that sweet spot between being authentically ourselves and not getting shunned by society. When we achieve this integration, something magical can happen: we stop being slaves to our shadows, we use our personas like tools instead of prisons, our ego and psyche stop their death match and find harmony, and we might actually discover some inner peace. Imagine that.

Speaking of integration, this whole integration dance can feel intensely personal, like it's just our own private circus. But nope. Remember those archetypal patterns from the collective unconscious? Well, Jung noticed that when we're in the thick of shadow work and persona-peeling, these ancient patterns can start showing up uninvited—popping into our dreams, hijacking our thoughts, coloring our projections. It's like the collective unconscious sees us doing the work and goes, 'Oh, you're ready for the advanced course now.'

And as the deeper we dive into this work, the more mysterious it can become. We can start encountering figures in our dreams, recognizing patterns that feel much older than our personal history. It's like we're connecting with something ancient and collective. This is where Jung's work becomes truly remarkable—but that's territory for our next exploration.

Stage Three: Encountering the Anima/Animus

Stage three brings us face to face with some of the most mysterious forces Jung mapped: the anima and animus. For those of us who identify as male, this means encountering our inner feminine aspects. For women, it's about recognizing the masculine qualities within. But honestly? However we identify, we're all dealing with the same thing here: integrating our inner opposite—those complementary energies that can make us whole.

So we've been wrestling with our shadow—all those parts we rejected and stuffed in the psychological basement. But the anima and animus? They're something else entirely. These aren't an expression or manifestation of traits we buried because they were too ugly or shameful. No. They're qualities we never even got to develop in the first place. Why? Because someone, somewhere, decided they didn't fit with who we were "supposed" to be.

Here's how it usually goes: society traditionally encourages us to overdevelop certain traits that align with our assigned gender role, while leaving their counterparts completely dormant. Men, for example, get rewarded for being logical, tough, in control—while sensitivity and emotional awareness? Forget about it. Women get praised for nurturing and empathy—but assertiveness and independent thinking? Not so much. But, here's the kicker: we've all got both sets of qualities in us. Of course we do. But one half never got any sunlight, never got to grow. It's like having a garden where you only water half the plants.

And this splitting usually starts early. Really early. Traditionally, boys learn that tears equal weakness before they can even tie their shoes. 'Big boys don't cry.' 'Man up.' 'Don't be a sissy.' The message is clear: feelings are dangerous, vulnerability is failure. Girls? They get their own version: 'Be nice.' 'Don't be bossy.' 'That's not ladylike.' Assert yourself too much and suddenly you're 'difficult' or 'aggressive.' By the time we're adults, we've had decades of this conditioning.

Now, Jung wasn't saying this integration is about changing who we're attracted to or how we identify. That's not what this is about. It's about psychological wholeness. When men develop emotional intelligence, when women embrace their inner strength—they're not becoming less themselves. They're becoming more complete. It's not about switching sides; it's about having access to your full range.

Jung called the anima and animus our "soul images," and I view them as working like bridges—not just to our personal unconscious, but to something way deeper: that collective unconscious we've been exploring. See, while the shadow pulls us into our personal history and all that repressed material, the anima and animus? They're leading us into archetypal territory. They're like mediators between our everyday ego and that vast unknown. They help us gradually encounter forces that would otherwise completely overwhelm us.

Think of it this way: just like the persona acts as our social mask to protect us out in the world, these archetypes serve as a kind of inner protection. They help us recognize when we're projecting parts of ourselves onto others—you know, when we fall for the same type over and over, or when our reaction to someone is way bigger than what actually happened. According to Jung, these reactions are usually the anima or animus trying to show us our own missing pieces through other people.

The anima and animus aren't the destination—but they're damn powerful guides into the deeper dimensions of our Self.

So how do they usually show up compared to the shadow? While shadow material often confronts us directly through what repels us, the anima and animus work more indirectly—drawing us in through mysterious attractions and compelling dreams.

Dreams can become powerful teachers at this stage. Unlike shadow material that often appears as threatening figures or shameful scenarios, the anima and animus tend to be more... alluring. They show up as mysterious figures who seem to possess exactly what we're missing. Some of us might dream of wise women who speak in riddles but somehow know our deepest truths. Others might encounter powerful masculine figures who appear at crucial moments with exactly the guidance we need. Classic anima/animus appearances.

Jung noticed these figures often emerge during major life transitions—career changes, relationship crises, midlife passages. It's like the psyche knows we need access to our full toolkit for what's ahead, so it starts sending ambassadors from the undeveloped side. And here's what's fascinating: these dream figures often feel more real than regular dream characters. Many people wake up genuinely moved, sometimes even feeling in love with these internal figures.

But dreams are just one avenue. More often, the anima and animus hijack our waking life through projection. Remember how shadow projection makes us irrationally annoyed with people who embody our rejected traits? Well, anima/animus projection creates the opposite—irrational attraction, fascination, or idealization.

That person at the party who seems to glow with some indefinable quality? The one we can't stop thinking about even though we barely spoke? That's often anima/animus projection in action. We're not seeing them—we're seeing the qualities we never developed, dressed up in human form. They seem to complete us because, in a way, they're showing us our own completion.

The intensity of projection can be overwhelming. These aren't casual attractions—they're consuming, often obsessive. We think about them constantly, construct elaborate fantasies, feel like we'll die without them. This intensity makes sense when we realize what's at stake. We're not just attracted to a person—we're attracted to becoming whole. The anima or animus is showing us everything we could be if we developed those dormant qualities.

But what if the difference between projection and genuine love has less to do with finding someone who completes us, and more to do with finding someone who helps us see our own wholeness? What if real connection happens not when we find our "missing piece" in another, but when we're with someone who reflects back our complete self—shadow, light, anima/animus and all?

When we're caught up in projection, we stop seeing the actual person in front of us. Instead, we're obsessed with what we think they can give us —the qualities we never developed. And that's where relationships usually fall apart. No real person can be responsible for developing our missing qualities for us. They're not here to complete us or fix us. They're on their own journey, dealing with their own stuff. The work of individuation involves withdrawing these projections—recognizing that what we see in others actually belongs to us, then consciously developing those qualities within ourselves. It's not about losing the attraction or admiration; it's about recognizing its true source. When we can say 'That quality I'm so drawn to? That's actually mine to develop,' we begin the real work of becoming whole.

Time for some brutal honesty about my relationship history. Ever since I was a kid, I'd fall completely head over heels for girls—those all-consuming crushes that felt like life or death. By my twenties, this had evolved into something more sophisticated: I convinced myself I was naturally drawn to people who 'needed help.' Noble of me, right? But looking back now? The pattern is so obvious it's almost comical. I wasn't randomly finding these situations—I was unconsciously seeking them out, drawn to people I could "save" or "fix." Sure, we were mirrors for each other, both playing out our unconscious patterns, but I was too busy wearing my rescuer cape to notice I was the one who needed rescuing.

Then came a relationship that finally cracked me open to this truth. She'd had a challenging upbringing—the kind that leaves real scars. We were in those early dating days, actually vibing, getting closer, sharing those intimate conversations that make you feel like you've found your person. As she trusted me with pieces of her story, my ego was having a field day. There I was—peak twenties arrogance, zero self-awareness—ego fully inflated, unable to just let a beautiful moment be. Instead? My savior complex kicked in and I destroyed the magic with one spectacularly tone-deaf declaration: "You should be with me because I can help you!" Yep, I actually said that.

Her response? "Who the fuck are you to think you can rescue me? Maybe I'm the one who can rescue you."

Pure anima wisdom delivered like a knockout punch.

Her words cut through my ego like a hot knife through butter. This was textbook anima work—that feminine wisdom within me that I'd been ignoring, now showing up externally to drag me kicking and screaming toward growth. The anima doesn't mess around. She shows up as that challenging feminine force that basically says, "Nice try, buddy, but we're going deeper." For me, that meant facing the ugly truth: my whole savior schtick wasn't about helping anyone. It was about feeling important, avoiding my own mess by focusing on someone else's, using relationships as a spiritual bypass.

The relationship crashed and burned eventually, but not without more than its fair share of turmoil and painful lessons in humility first. My ego couldn't handle that level of truth, but apparently it could handle plenty of denial. Still, it was exactly the drawn-out disaster I needed to finally begin real individuation work. Sometimes relationships aren't meant to last—they're meant to transform us, like those crisis moments that force our shadows into the light. This one launched me into serious inner work, just took the scenic route through hell first.

The irony is, I'd actually had some advantages with anima integration from the start. Growing up, nobody told me boys don't cry. My parents— high school sweethearts who genuinely loved each other—showed me that emotional connection was just how people who love each other act. I had a close relationship with my mum, went through a boy band phase without shame, and learned that talking about feelings was as normal as talking about football.

But here's the shadow side of that gift: it made me cocky as hell. I knew I was loved, knew I'd always be okay no matter what, and that safety net made me arrogant. I took emotional connection for granted because it had always been there. While other men were desperately seeking what they'd never had, I was carelessly playing with what I'd always known.

What I see now is that most men are fighting an exhausting civil war with their own feminine aspects. All that projection onto women? That's the exiled anima desperately trying to get recognized. The real integration isn't about being the guy who cries versus the guy who doesn't—it's about having access to the full spectrum and the wisdom to know which tool fits which moment.

So what does this actually look like when we stop projecting and start integrating? For me, it meant recognizing that every woman I'd been obsessed with was carrying something I needed to develop in myself. Those "intuitive" women I kept falling for? That was my own intuition asking for attention. Their "emotional intelligence" that seemed so magical? I had that capacity too—I'd just never been given permission to develop it.

The real work started when I could catch myself mid-projection and actually pause. Instead of thinking "She's so amazing," I learned to ask, "What quality in her am I not letting myself express?" This shift changes everything. Suddenly you're not hunting for completion in others—you're excavating it from within.

The real shift happened when I met my wife. By then, I'd done enough of this work to recognize the difference between projection and genuine connection. Instead of being attracted to what I was missing, I was drawn to someone who could see and appreciate the wholeness I was developing.

She didn't carry my unlived life—she had her own. We weren't two halves making a whole; we were two whole people choosing to create something together.

This is what Jung meant about withdrawing projections. When you stop hunting for your missing pieces in others, you can actually see them. And when someone can mirror back all of you—not just your persona, not just what you project, but your shadows, your growth edges, your integrated aspects—that's when real love becomes possible. She could see my sensitivity not as something special or lacking, but just as part of who I was. And I could see her strength not as something I needed to borrow, but as her own beautiful expression.

Looking back, this is probably why our relationship actually worked when all my previous ones had crashed and burned. Before, I was falling in 'love' with projections and my idealized fantasy of what the perfect woman should be—desperate, consuming attractions that always ended in disappointment when the real person couldn't live up to my impossible expectations. But with her, I was seeing myself reflected back through her —my wholeness, not just my missing pieces. And she was seeing herself reflected through me. We became mirrors for each other's completeness rather than reminders of what we lacked. That's a completely different foundation. No wonder we could build something real on it.

I do, though, think that this kind of real seeing only works if you can tolerate seeing yourself. If I'd met her earlier, before I'd done any of this integration work, her clear reflection would have sent me running. And if she'd met that earlier version of me—all projection and savior complex— she would've run a mile too. When we dislike or can't accept parts of ourselves, the last thing we want is someone who can see us fully. Warts and all. We prefer someone who only sees our persona, or who reflects back our fantasies, not our reality.

The fact that we could both stand to truly see each other—and be seen in return—spoke to the work we'd each done separately before we met. Real intimacy requires being okay with being seen—shadows, flaws, undeveloped parts and all. The inner work has to come first, or we'll just keep choosing projection over truth.

Our ancestors understood this dance between masculine and feminine long before Jung gave it psychological language. They encoded these truths in the stories they told. In mythology, the animus shows up as those heroic blokes who are all action and determination—like Heracles, who got his divine strength from Zeus but was raised by his mortal mother. Classic masculine energy, right? All muscle and quests and slaying monsters.

The anima? She appears as characters like Ondine, this seductive water nymph who—get this—doesn't have a soul. Apparently she can only get one through a man's embrace. Talk about projection material, never mind dated patriarchy. These mythical women have this incredible power over men, using their allure to either transform them or completely wreck them. Bit like my dating history, actually.

Then there are the mermaids luring sailors underwater. The message seems to be: yeah, dive into those unconscious waters, find your inner treasure, but whatever you do, but be careful not to drown in the depths of your unconscious and remember to come up for air. Nobody wants to be the guy who got so lost exploring his feminine side that he forgot how to function in the real world.

The animus in folktales gets a little weird—it often shows up as "little people" like the Seven Dwarfs. These guys work underground, mining for gold, which Jung saw as the animus helping bring up valuable insights from the depths. Snow White needed all seven of them to keep her safe until she was ready for the prince. Make of that what you will.

But here's where mythology throws us a curveball. Take Athena—born from Zeus's head without a mother (yes, really), goddess of both wisdom and warfare, patron of crafts and strategy. She's undeniably feminine yet embodies what Jung would classify as "masculine" qualities. A bit confusing, I know.

What's interesting is how she helps heroes like Odysseus and Jason—not by doing the work for them, but by offering strategic wisdom. Jung thought her enemies represented the parts of our unconscious that have "gone wild" from neglect. Makes sense when you think about what happens to any part of us we ignore for too long.

My favorite Athena story? Her competition with Poseidon for Athens. He shows up all macho, strikes the ground with his trident—boom, salt water spring. Impressive but useless. Athena? She plants an olive tree. Food, oil, wood—actually helpful. She wins not through force but through wisdom and practical generosity. That's integration right there—not beating down the wild masculine energy, but offering something better.

For the ancient Greeks, Athena was just... Athena. They didn't stress about a goddess having both warrior strength and feminine wisdom. She showed what full integration looked like—not a woman trying to be masculine or denying her femininity, but someone who had access to the whole spectrum. Maybe our ancestors understood what we're just redis-covering: true power comes from integrating both energies, not from staying in one lane.

Still, most mythological traditions use the marriage of masculine and feminine as the symbol for psychological wholeness. The sacred marriage, the divine union—it's all pointing to the same thing: integrating conscious and unconscious, masculine and feminine, into one complete Self.

But perhaps the best illustration is Beauty and the Beast. The Beast has to integrate his anima—find his capacity for tenderness and vulnerability instead of just roaring at everyone. Belle needs to integrate her animus—stop just being the caretaker and find her own strength and agency. Neither one "fixes" the other. They both do their own work, and that mutual growth is what breaks the spell. Now that's a relationship model I can get behind.

These patterns don't just live in fairy tales—they show up in our actual dreams, often when we least expect it. Jung was obsessed with cataloging how these figures appear, and honestly, once you know what to look for, it's kind of wild how consistent they are.

They usually show up as the opposite gender—anima as feminine figures for men, animus as masculine for women. Classic yin and yang territory. But here's where it gets interesting: they have their favorite disguises. The animus loves showing up as eagles (all about that higher perspective), bulls or lions (raw power anyone?), or those obvious phallic symbols like towers. The anima? She's more into mysterious cats, caves (the whole womb-space thing), or ships that somehow help you sail through emotional storms without completely losing it.

It's easy to dismiss our strange dreams as meaningless static, but some-times they arrive as messengers during life's pivotal transitions. These aren't random firings of sleeping neurons—they're the psyche's way of processing big change, often through imagery so disturbing it breaks through our waking defenses.

I experienced one such dream during a period of intense personal transformation. It began innocuously—with a phone call from an ex-girlfriend, checking in on how the dog we'd shared was doing. As I spoke, the scene shifted—as dreams do—and suddenly, I was at her door.

She was inside, getting ready for something. She mentioned she'd been waiting hours for her "housemate." There was tension in her voice—familiar, tired anxiety. And then *he* appeared.

A dwarf. Old, short, bearded, impeccably dressed. He wore a tailored suit, leaned on a cane, and had an almost theatrical presence about him. On his feet were gold slippers—soft, luxurious, ceremonial. Not something you'd wear outside. He looked like someone who once held real power but now mostly performed the role. There was politeness to him, almost ritualistic, but I sensed something volatile simmering underneath that composed exterior.

He belonged to her world—her housemate in the dream, but more than that. He felt like a guardian of her psychic space, a figure I no longer had access to. Yet here he was, acknowledging me with peculiar hospitality.

This dwarf represents exactly what we've been exploring—a manifestation of what Jung called the animus archetype, one of those "little people" from the collective unconscious. Like the dwarfs in Snow White who work underground bringing up gold, this figure had emerged from that shared reservoir of human experience with something valuable—insight about a relationship I needed to finally release.

He asked me about cars, then proudly showed me his own—a big 1970s American muscle car with matte paint. But his favorite part was the license plate. It read: "Plan it, save it, pommit." The first two words made sense, but "pommit"? Like the riddling dwarfs of folklore, he'd given me something cryptic to puzzle over. Those words lodged themselves deep in my consciousness—not because I understood them, but because they felt like a key to something I wasn't quite ready to unlock.

Then the mood shifted. We noticed commotion in the street—a fight between two families, white and Māori. Children, women, dogs caught in the middle. Chaos that felt primal, tribal.

What happened next was violent. Very violent.

One man was brutally punched, dragged into the street, and beaten to death. I didn't see the final blow, but I heard it—the gargling, choking, crack of bone. The body became unrecognizable. Torn apart, brain and entrails exposed. And his dog—his loyal companion—was being held there, forced to watch. Straining against the leash, desperate to reach his owner.

The crowd began retreating—shame and fear taking over. But a few kept going, kept hitting even after life had left him. That's when I noticed the blood flowing toward my car—the vehicle I'd arrived in but hadn't really seen until that moment. If I didn't move soon, that blood would reach it.

I woke up in shock.

But beneath the shock was a strange, powerful clarity: that man in the street was me. Not the me sitting here now, but the version of me who had existed in that relationship with my former partner. The one who stayed long after he should have left. The version who tried to be strong, supportive, indispensable—who bore too much not out of love, but out of loneliness and a desperate need to belong.

Time has shown me I was telling myself I stayed out of "love." And maybe there was love, yes. But not the right kind. There was something deeper and more desperate—a need to belong, to be needed, to fill an aching gap of fear and isolation in an unfamiliar land I'd recently moved to. When genuine connection didn't happen naturally, I began trying to force it, crafting stories about being the protector, the savior—anything to satisfy my ego's need to feel worthy.

I took it on myself to carry someone else's pain, to be the dependable one, the rescuer. It destroyed me.

That version of me—the one who tried desperately to hold something broken together—was the one who got torn apart in the process. I'd constructed a role that felt noble, but it cost me my instincts, self-respect, and sense of who I really was.

And that blood? It wasn't just blood—it was the past itself. And the car it was flowing toward represented my future, my path forward. The man I was becoming, the new relationship I was building, everything I was creating with the woman who would become my wife.

I was terrified that if I didn't properly bury that broken part of myself, he would follow me. The fear that all that built-up damage would spill into the good things I'd finally found.

And the dog in the dream? That was my instinct—the part that knew this relationship was hurting me. But I'd leashed it, made it watch and suffer in silence.

The dwarf in gold slippers felt like a guardian of her world, someone whose job was to say, "You've had your time here. Now it's time to go." Not hostile, not kind—just ceremonial. The unpredictable authority of someone escorting you out when your part of the story is finished.

Those gold slippers represented something that looked valuable but kept you stuck—comfort, familiarity, but no longer right. That version of life wasn't painful anymore, just stale. Safe. Finished.

On reflection, I now see him as a symbol of closure itself.

So to that version of myself, I say: "You did what you thought you had to do. You tried to love, protect, and help—though really, you were trying to love, protect, and help yourself. Your time is done. You don't need to carry that weight anymore."

I let him go. I let him rest.

If you've ever clung to something that was slowly destroying you because the unknown felt worse—you understand this. At some point, you have to put that version of yourself to rest. Otherwise, the blood of the past keeps seeping into the life you're trying to build. Bury what needs burying. Get back in your car. Drive forward—not to escape, but to finally move on.

This dream gave me a real education in Jung's anima/animus concepts. That dwarf with his gold slippers? Classic animus figure—the wise but volatile masculine energy that emerges from the unconscious during major transitions. Just like Jung described, this encounter happened during significant upheaval, marking the end of an old cycle and beginning of something new.

By recognizing this figure and actually listening to his cryptic wisdom, I could make the shift I needed—releasing a self-image that was blocking my path forward.

You know what's both humbling and fascinating about this entire experience? I'd already proven to myself I could survive alone years before on that Australian beach where Danny and I parted ways. I'd panicked initially, terrified of continuing without my anchor. But I did continue—and I thrived. I built friendships, found work, created a life on my own terms. I'd already walked through that particular fire and emerged stronger.

Yet here I was, years later in this relationship, with the same core fears wearing different clothes. My ego had gotten more sophisticated, disguising my need for security and belonging as noble purposes—being the rescuer, the protector, the one who stays. The Hero's Journey hadn't failed me; I'd just discovered what every hero eventually figures out: the work's never done. We spiral through the same territory at deeper levels, meeting familiar demons in new costumes.

That's why Campbell drew it as a circle, not a straight line. Growth isn't some destination we reach and settle into. It's a practice we return to, again and again, as life keeps presenting new versions of old challenges.

Stage Four: Approaching the Self

By now we've figured out this work doesn't get easier. If anything, it gets weirder. The thing is—we've wrestled with our shadows, caught ourselves performing behind those social masks, maybe even had those trippy dreams about mysterious figures that Jung would've had a field day with. But honestly? What comes next is the most challenging phase (at least for me!)—what Jung called the Self. This isn't our everyday ego-self who pays bills and doomscrolls at 2 AM, but something far more expansive and mysterious. It's the *you* that exists beyond all your roles, masks, and identities. And approaching it? That's not a weekend workshop deal—it's a long haul that'll probably turn our whole worldview inside out.

One of the most powerful ways we can begin to approach the Self is through what Jung called the "mana personality"—moments when a deeper wisdom emerges from within us. We've all been there, right? That situation where the perfect words just fall out of our mouth, or we know exactly what to do without any logical reason. Like wisdom is flowing through us from some mysterious wellspring within?

During this stage, we may begin to encounter archetypal figures of wisdom—the wise old man, the crone, the sage who knows all the secrets.

But remember, these archetypes aren't just external mentors, they're actually our own inner wisdom trying to wake up and get our attention. The crone? She's the fierce truth-teller who's done pretending and cuts straight through our BS. The sage? He's that patient, been-there-done-that energy that knows the long game. A valuable guide as we navigate the challenges and changes we experience while integrating the unconscious and conscious aspects of our psyche.

Here's where things get really interesting—and potentially confusing. When we meet these wise figures—whether they show up in dreams, meditation, or as that mentor who drops truth bombs—we're actually connecting with those deeper parts of ourselves. We just almost never recognize it as our own at first.

I learned this firsthand during a difficult period when a mentor shared this cryptic wisdom:

"If you want to hunt a lion, go into a herd and bleed, then walk with a limp."

This advice lodged itself in my consciousness like a splinter I couldn't remove and carrying a weight I couldn't grasp at first. Then one day, during another challenging period of life, the penny dropped.

I realized their rich wisdom: to achieve something truly significant—to hunt the lion, the ultimate prize—we've got to be willing to be vulnerable first. We have to walk right into the challenging territory (the herd), let our wounds show (bleed), and own our battle scars (walk with a limp). This isn't weakness—it's the most courageous thing we can do. Real achievement doesn't come from looking invincible. It comes from being brave enough to let people see us struggle, fail, and get back up with a limp. That limp? It's not holding us back—it's proof we didn't quit when things got difficult.

For years, I thought this was all my mentor's genius. It didn't occur to me that recognizing the depth in those words meant something was awakening in me too. That resonance I felt? That was my own wisdom recognizing itself in the mirror, like "Oh shit, there I am.

Our mana personality shows up through all kinds of strange channels as we get closer to the Self. We can get those intuitive insights that make no logical sense—just knowing exactly what to say or do, no explanation available. Dreams where some wise figure shares knowledge that proves invaluable weeks later. Those creative flow states where insights pour through us like we're channeling something bigger. Synchronicities that are so perfect they feel orchestrated by a part of us that knows the script. And those meditation moments when the most complex problems suddenly resolve themselves, like someone just pulled the right thread.

We've all had those moments—sudden insights that drop in from nowhere but feel absolutely true. Not random thoughts—these are glimpses of our own deeper wisdom trying to get our make itself known

We see this pattern everywhere in our culture and the stories we love. Look at *Star Wars*—Luke spends the entire saga thinking Obi-Wan and Yoda are the only ones who understand the Force. It takes him the whole trilogy to realize he's got that same wisdom inside him, that he can be a Jedi Master by trusting his own knowing. Same thing in *The Matrix*. Neo thinks Morpheus is this all-knowing master, but eventually has to realize he's got the same reality-bending ability. The wisdom was in him all along —he just needed to stop projecting and start accessing it.

The journey from projection to integration usually follows a pretty predictable path when approaching the Self. First, we're convinced all the wisdom lives in other people—those teachers and guides who've got what we desperately lack. Then we start recognizing something in us resonating when they speak—like a tuning fork finding its matching frequency. Gradually, we learn to consciously engage with our own deeper knowing, trusting those inner voices and insights. Finally, we come to embody this wisdom without inflation or false humility, understanding that it flows through us rather than from us.

Years after receiving that lion-hunting wisdom, I found myself in a moment where someone needed help and these words just... arrived. Multi-layered, profound, carrying weight I couldn't have manufactured. Revelation moment: I wasn't repeating my old mentor. I was tapping into something that had always been there, waiting. I'd just needed to see it in someone else first, like training wheels for recognizing my own depth.

As our mana personality becomes more accessible, we face two major pitfalls. First is under-identification—staying stuck in the belief that wisdom only lives in other people. This keeps us on the hamster wheel of endless seeking, always chasing the next guru, the next workshop, the next book that'll finally give us the secret. We stay addicted to external authorities, perpetually convinced we're one insight away from enlightenment. Meanwhile, our own inner authority sits there gathering dust.

The second pitfall is over-identification or inflation—getting so intoxicated with our own wisdom that we think we're uniquely special. Suddenly we're the chosen one, the enlightened being who's transcended all that messy human stuff. This inflation turns us into those difficult spiritual narcissists who can't take feedback because obviously everyone else just isn't evolved enough to understand. We stop doing the basic human work—relationships, responsibilities, continuing to grow—because we've convinced ourselves we've graduated from life's lessons.

The sweet spot involves recognizing this wisdom as our own while maintaining humility about it. We understand that wisdom flows through us rather than from us, that we're part of something larger while still being our unique, specific selves. We can tap into our deeper knowing without mistaking it for our entire identity. It's like being a skilled musician—we're not the music itself, but we know how to let it play through us.

Through various practices—be it meditation, breathwork, dreams, or ceremonial experiences with plant medicines—I've had a few pretty wild experiences with my own mana personality that, to be honest, totally changed my understanding of consciousness and reality. Often receiving intense, what I can only describe as "downloads"—information I had no conscious way of knowing. In those expanded states, I connected with what felt like ancient wisdom residing within me—not hallucination, but genuine encounters with parts of myself I didn't know existed.

These weren't just interesting psychological phenomena—they were critical turning points in my individuation process, moments when my mana personality was making itself known in increasingly direct and powerful ways. But here's what I've learned: the real work isn't in having extraordinary experiences. It's in bringing the wisdom gained from them back to ordinary life, actually living it when we're doing everyday tasks or dealing with mundane challenges. Getting attached to the peak experiences is just another ego trap. And I've been guilty of it, more than I'd like to admit.

Experiencing our mana personality—that flow of inner wisdom—is actually the Self offering us a gift: a preview of what's possible. Think of it this way: The Self (our complete, integrated wholeness) can't just show up all at once—it would overwhelm our ego completely. So instead, it sends an ambassador first—the mana personality. Through these experiences of powerful wisdom flowing through us, we get a taste of what it's like to be connected to something larger than our everyday ego—our ordinary sense of self. It's the Self saying: 'This wisdom, this flow, this connection to something deeper? This is my gift to you, showing a glimpse of what's available when all your parts are integrated. This is what you're moving toward.'

And look, becoming whole doesn't mean we need to be perfect. It means living in our genuine authenticity—being able to be both strong and vulnerable, wise and still learning, confident and uncertain, to make mistakes and keep growing, all at the same time without feeling like we're falling apart. The Self isn't some flawless, enlightened version of us. It's the *us* who can finally hold all the contradicting parts of ourselves and say, 'Yeah, this is me—all of it.'

But the mana personality is just the preview. To reach that wholeness it's showing us, we need to integrate all our contradicting parts—bringing our shadows into consciousness, dropping our false personas, integrating our inner masculine/feminine. The mana personality is the Self's invitation to keep going, showing us what wholeness feels like so we know what we're working toward.

As we approach the Self, we might start to notice some peculiar things happening. Remember how we talked about being strong and vulnerable at the same time, wise yet still learning? That capacity seems to settle in, and other shifts might follow. An inner authority may develop that doesn't need anyone's approval to feel real. That exhausting need to prove ourselves? It might start fading, along with some of those personas we've been maintaining. We might find ourselves surprisingly comfortable with not knowing, with mystery, with questions that don't have clear answers. And meaning? It might start emerging from within instead of being something we chase in the outside world. Though honestly, everyone's journey probably looks different—these are just some patterns that seem to show up.

When we start deepening our relationship with the Self, we begin recognizing the difference between living by everyone else's script and actually writing our own, even if our handwriting's a bit messy. And this is where it gets tricky—something I personally wrestle with every day. Because the closer we get to our authentic light, the more aware we become of our shadow. And the brighter that authentic, inner light shines, the bigger our shadow becomes. Life gets both easier and harder. Easier because we're not juggling multiple false versions of ourselves or desperately seeking approval. Harder because we're now fully aware of how contradictory and mysterious existence is, and we can't pretend otherwise.

We might notice synchronicities popping up everywhere, too—not because the universe suddenly started caring about our personal story, but because we're finally tuned into patterns that were always there. Our creativity might emerge from some deeper, more authentic place. Our relationships might shift as we stop performing and start genuinely showing up. This journey toward the Self isn't about becoming some special enlightened being who transcends human messiness—though that is an ego trap to beware of. It's about becoming fully, authentically human— owning our light and our shadow, our strength and our vulnerability, what we know and all that we'll never figure out.

The journey toward the Self never ends—there's no graduation ceremony where Jung's ghost hands us a certificate saying "Congrats, you've individuated!" Instead, we just get better at living from our depths, responding to life from our authentic center instead of our reactive patterns or the identities we borrowed from others.

I guess what I'm really saying is this: As we stumble forward on this path, let's pay attention to those moments when we feel most authentically ourselves—not the performed version, not the "should be" version, just... us. Raw and real. Those moments? They're the Self waving at us, saying "Hey, want to live from here more often?" That deep, unique, mysterious center that nobody else has—that's home base.

But approaching the Self is just that—an approach. The glimpses of our own wisdom, those moments of feeling whole, recognizing when we're projecting onto others? That's just us getting close enough to the Self to realize it exists. Like finally noticing there's been this wise part of us trying to get our attention this whole time. And once we've felt that? Once we've had a taste of what it's like when all the different aspects of ourselves work together instead of against each other? Well, the cat's out of the bag—we can't exactly pretend we don't know it's there anymore. But knowing it's there and actually living from that place? That's a whole different ball game.

Which brings us to the real work—integration. Because let me tell you, there are some serious ways to mess this up. And I've probably tried most of them.

The Final Stage: Integration and the Realization of the Self

"Know thyself"

These two words, carved into the Temple of Apollo at Delphi over 2,500 years ago, might be humanity's oldest homework assignment—and we're still working on it. Deceptively simple, these two words have been challenging philosophers, seekers, and people like us for generations. But what does it actually mean to know ourselves?

Look, if we've made it this far together—through all that ego wrestling, shadow work, anima/animus territory—all those psychological landscapes we've been mapping—then maybe we're ready to finally understand what's been at the center of it all along. The Self. We've been building toward this since we first mapped the psyche, approaching it through shadow work, personas, and those mana personality moments. Now it's time to understand what we've been working toward all along. This final piece that ties everything together.

I've been wrestling with how to explain this for years, and I'll be straight with you—trying to describe the Self is like a fish giving a TED talk about water. We're swimming in it, breathing it, basically marinating in it 24/7, but somehow it stays invisible to our everyday awareness. Funny how the most essential stuff is usually hiding in plain sight, isn't it?

But perhaps the best approach is through experience rather than explanation. Think about those rare moments when everything in your life seemed perfectly aligned—when your actions, thoughts, feelings, and deepest values all pointed in the same direction. You know those moments I'm talking about, right? Those glimpses of wholeness? That's what the ancient directive "Know Thyself" is really pointing toward—not as occasional flashes but as a way of being. I've caught these fleeting moments in nature, in creative flow states, and in deep connections with others. They're like signposts pointing toward what's possible when we bring all parts of ourselves into harmony.

But how do we move from occasional glimpses to lasting integration? How do we translate this ancient philosophical directive into a practical path we can actually follow? How do we take this ancient wisdom and turn it into something we can actually use in our messy, modern lives? For thousands of years, seekers have been chasing this answer—heading off to monasteries, holing up in meditation caves, enrolling in mystery schools. The problem was, the instructions usually came wrapped in so much metaphor and ritual that only the most dedicated souls who could commit their whole lives figured them out.

This is where Jung becomes our hero. He built a psychological bridge between ancient wisdom and our modern understanding. He didn't just philosophize about knowing ourselves—he actually mapped the psyche and marked a trail that any one of us could actually follow, without having to abandon our regular lives and become hermits in a cave. Where mystics talked about the soul's journey in riddles, Jung gave us individuation in plain(ish) language. Where spiritual traditions dangled enlightenment like a carrot we might never reach, Jung showed us the Self as something already within us, waiting to be uncovered—not a distant goal but an ever-deepening relationship.

Jung transformed this ancient wisdom into something we can actually work with. Imagine all the different parts of you—the stuff you show the world, the stuff you hide, even the stuff you don't know exists—finally sitting down for dinner together instead of throwing food at each other. That ancient Greek inscription "Know Thyself"? Jung basically turned it from a philosophical fortune cookie into an actual GPS we can follow. Though fair warning: the journey's still a bit like assembling IKEA furniture after losing half the instructions and your allen key.

Individuation is our journey of actively—and yeah, sometimes painfully—getting to know all these different aspects of ourselves. We're talking about facing the parts we pretend don't exist (hello, Shadow), making friends with our inner opposite (the Anima/Animus), recognizing the universal patterns within us (archetypes), and somehow weaving our whole messy personal history into something that makes sense.

The Self—and honestly, I'm still figuring this out alongside you—is what emerges when we've really done that deep dive into self-knowledge. It's not just knowing about our parts like items on a grocery list; it's actually knowing them, accepting them (even the weird ones), and somehow getting them all to play nice together—integrating them into a harmonious whole.

In this final stage of individuation, we encounter the archetype of the Self—not as some distant ideal, but as the living center that organizes our whole psyche. Unlike the ego, which only knows our conscious identity, the Self includes all of who we are—conscious and unconscious combined.

The Self isn't just our ego—that's only the captain steering our ship through daily life. The Self? That's the whole damn ship, plus the ocean we're sailing on, plus those mysterious stars we're navigating by. It's everything we are, everything we've been, everything we might become—all rolled into one. Think of it as the blueprint we came with, the unified whole that emerges when we've finally got all our parts working together instead of staging mutinies.

Our Tree of Life symbol really comes alive again here. Those roots digging down? That's us descending into the unconscious, doing our shadow work in the dark where nobody's watching. The branches reaching up? That's us bringing all that underground material into the light, integrating it into who we consciously are. Jung's showing us something beautiful here: we've got to keep growing in both directions—deeper into that rich, dark soil of the unconscious while stretching toward the light of awareness. Both movements are essential for staying vital and whole.

It's like those Infinity Stones from Marvel. When they're scattered across the universe, each one controls a different aspect of existence—time, space, reality, mind, power, soul. We can think of these as parts of our own psyche: Space Stone? That's how we handle relationships and boundaries (or don't). Reality Stone? Our perception and the stories we tell ourselves about what's "real." Power Stone? Our ability to actually take action instead of just thinking about it. Mind Stone? Our intellect and understanding. Time Stone? How we're haunted by our past or anxious about our future. Soul Stone? The deep stuff—our core values, what actually matters when everything else burns away.

But when these stones unite in the Infinity Gauntlet, they don't just add up—they create something entirely new that can reshape reality itself. The Self works the same way. When all our parts—conscious and unconscious, shadow and persona, masculine and feminine—finally stop fighting and start collaborating, we don't get a neat sum. We get something that transcends the equation entirely.

It's like the difference between musicians playing their parts correctly versus that rare moment when they merge with the music and something transcendent comes through. Something none of them could access alone. That's the Self—not our psychological pieces finally getting along, but a deeper intelligence that emerges when we create the right conditions. It was always there, waiting for us to integrate enough to let it express itself through us

Remember Neo's journey in *The Matrix*? He starts as Thomas Anderson, another programmer living a mundane life, wondering if this is all there is. After taking the red pill, he enters training—downloading skills, pushing limits, classic self-improvement. We've all been on some version of this journey.

But the pivotal moment comes when Agent Smith shoots him and Neo rises again. He doesn't return faster or stronger—he returns seeing differently. The bullets don't stop because he's faster—they stop because he's operating outside the Matrix's rules entirely. He's seeing the code itself. That's transformation beyond mere improvement.

This captures what I've experienced when we encounter the Self. Neo didn't just level up within the Matrix—he transcended the entire system. The rules that used to define him? They don't apply anymore. He's not 'Thomas Anderson with maxed-out stats.' He's glimpsed what exists beyond the game itself, operating from a different level of awareness entirely. That's what connecting with the Self can feel like—we're no longer bound by the old programming.

Think about what Neo had to go through to reach this moment—all those fights he lost, the painful training, discovering his whole life was a lie, watching friends die, even dying himself. Sound familiar? We've been on our own version of this journey—facing our shadows in the cave of our psyche, getting our arses kicked by our own complexes, realizing our personas were as fake as the Matrix itself. Like Neo, we had to "die" to who we thought we were. And just like Neo, there's something waiting on the other side of that death that can change everything.

This is what Jung discovered, and what we can discover too: when we're brave enough to let go of who we thought we were, we finally connect with the Self and discover what wholeness actually feels like. We gain access to the full spectrum of being human. Yeah, sadness hits deeper, grief lands harder. But here's what Jung didn't emphasize enough —when we're integrated with our true Self, when we're operating from wholeness rather than fragments, we can hold these depths without drowning. And something even more meaningful happens.

Because we're no longer numbing the difficult emotions, the beautiful ones can finally reach us too. Joy becomes something we feel in our bones, not just our thoughts. Love transforms from that desperate grasping into something real and sustaining. Peace isn't the absence of storms—it's discovering we have roots deep enough to weather them. We might find a happiness that has room for sadness, a strength that includes vulnerability, a contentment that doesn't need everything to be perfect.

That nagging "is this it?" feeling? It can finally quiet—not because life becomes easier, but because we're experiencing it fully instead of just going through the motions. We're not half-alive anymore. Decisions become clearer because we're operating from our whole Self, not just our frightened ego. Relationships deepen because we're showing up with everything we are, warts and all. And that creative spark that seemed dead and buried? It often comes roaring back like it was just waiting for us to stop filtering ourselves.

Jung mapped the psychology, but through my own journey, I've learned that individuation doesn't just make us more whole—it can make us feel alive in ways we'd forgotten were possible. Let me be clear: I'm not claiming that I've "arrived." Of course, my ego still hijacks me regularly, I keep discovering new shadows, and yes, I still catch myself performing old personas. But in those moments when I do connect to this wholeness, when the different parts of me work together instead of against each other? Something shifts. We're no longer fragmented, trying to manage life with only part of ourselves. When we operate from wholeness, we have access to all our resources—intuition and logic, strength and vulnerability, action and reflection.

This is individuation as I'm learning it: the never-ending adventure of becoming more fully human. Not perfect—far from it—but inching toward something more complete. Not walking around in perpetual bliss, but more awake and alive with each piece we integrate. It's like learning to play the full symphony of human experience—we're still learning instruments we didn't know we had, making plenty of mistakes while we figure out the harmonies. It turns out that's the modern hero's journey—not reaching some finish line where we're "done," but staying committed to becoming more authentic, more human, more ourselves.

If all this "becoming fully human" stuff sounds lovely on paper, let me tell you—the actual practice can feel like learning to tango with ourselves. Connecting with the Self means our ego—that part that's been running the show—has to loosen its grip without completely checking out. The ego doesn't disappear; it still handles all our practical functions. It just stops trying to run the whole show. Think of it as the difference between a panicked manager making every decision and that same manager executing a broader vision. Same skills, healthier relationship. It's a delicate dance—the ego learning to serve rather than dominate, while still keeping us functional in the world.

THE EXPERIENCE OF SELF-CONNECTION: SIGNS ALONG THE PATH

So what happens when we actually connect with the Self? Well, it's like our personality's center of gravity reorganizes—the ego's still there, it's just not calling the shots anymore. We might notice life feeling different in some key ways:

- **A Stronger Sense of Inner Wholeness and Peace:**
  Remember that feeling of being at war with ourselves? Different parts pulling in opposite directions like we're being drawn and quartered by our own psyche? That starts to fade. The internal "noise"—that constant background noise of self-criticism and second-guessing? Quietens down. We feel less fragmented,

more whole. There's a deep, quiet sense of peace and stability that isn't dependent on external circumstances.

- **Radical Self-Acceptance:** We start making peace with all our parts—the shiny bits we show off at parties and the shadow stuff we've been shoving in the basement since childhood. The strengths and the weaknesses, the parts we love and the parts that make us uncomfortable. These aren't flaws that need fixing. They're all part of being human. Once we stop wasting energy trying to hide parts of ourselves, we have so much more available for actually living.

- **Increased Authenticity:** Once we stop treating ourselves like we're fundamentally broken, something wild happens—we quit performing so damn hard. We feel less need to wear those exhausting masks or pretend we're someone we're not just to get people to like us. Our actions, thoughts, and feelings become more aligned with our inner truth. This authenticity feels liberating, though it inevitably disturbs others who preferred our performance, and we'll need to consciously navigate their resistance to our change.

- **Finding Our Center:** As we move closer to identifying with our true Self, we can experience what Jung called "greater internal stability and external equilibrium." Internal stability means our sense of worth no longer depends on external validation or circumstances. We're less reactive to criticism, less desperate for approval, and more anchored in our own inner knowing. External equilibrium happens when this inner stability shapes our outer world—we naturally create healthier boundaries, attract more authentic connections, and respond to challenges with greater wisdom and less drama.

- **Clearer Direction and Purpose:** When we connect with the Self, decision-making becomes clearer. Not because life gets simple, but because we tap into a deeper knowing. Those anxious thoughts about our life direction quiet down. We stop making choices based purely on external expectations. There's an inner knowing that's hard to describe—like finding our internal compass.

- **More Authentic Relationships:** Once we stop projecting our shit onto everyone else, we start seeing people for who they actually are instead of who we need them to be. Our relationships stop being these exhausting projects where we're either desperately needy or compulsively trying to fix everyone. I used to be the king of this—always trying to save people who didn't ask to be saved. Now? More genuine connection, less codependence. We can actually be with people instead of performing for them or trying to change them.
- **Enhanced Creativity and Flow States:** Being connected to the Self means more frequent flow states. With less internal conflict, there's more energy for creating.And when our conscious and unconscious minds stop fighting and start collaborating? That's when the magic happens. Intuition kicks in, spontaneity shows up, and suddenly we're in that zone where time disappears and everything just... flows.
- **Meaningful Synchronicities:** Okay, this one might sound a little woo-woo. As our inner world aligns with the Self, synchronicities start popping up everywhere. We're talking about those coincidences that are too weird to be coincidences —thinking about someone and they call, needing an answer and it shows up in the most random place, patterns that make us wonder if the universe has our phone number. Jung was obsessed with this stuff, and honestly? Once we start experiencing it regularly, it's hard to just write off as wishful thinking.

All these signs of Self-connection—the wholeness, the authenticity, the synchronicities—point to something fundamental: we're learning to hold opposites together. Which brings us to one of the most powerful symbols for understanding how the integrated Self actually works.

We've all seen that yin-yang symbol—black and white swirling together, each containing a dot of the other. Well, it turns out it's not just a cool tattoo design. This symbol perfectly captures the essence of Jung's Self as the integration of opposites. All those opposites we've been wrestling with—conscious and unconscious, light and shadow, masculine and feminine—aren't meant to battle. They're meant to balance.

See that curvy line between the black and white? That's the genius part. It's not some rigid wall—it flows, suggesting these energies are always in motion, always in relationship. And those little dots? Black in the white, white in the black? That's life telling us nothing's ever pure anything. We're not purely logical or purely emotional, purely strong or purely vulnerable. The integrated Self gets this—it can hold opposites without having an existential crisis every five minutes.

When we integrate both these yin and yang aspects, we essentially upgrade our psychological toolkit. We can switch between receptive and assertive without getting stuck in either mode. Need to analyze something? We can. Need to trust our gut? We can do that too. Structure when it helps, spontaneity when it's called for. It's like having the full Swiss Army knife instead of just one tool.

The Taoists had a word for this—Wu Wei, which translates to something like "effortless action" or "non-doing." When we've integrated these opposing forces, we no longer struggle against ourselves. Action becomes more fluid and natural, arising from our whole being rather than from the limited ego's striving.

I lived through this integration when I finally stopped trying to be either "corporate Lee" or "real Lee" and instead, began allowing both to exist simultaneously. The boardroom strategist and the emotional human. The logical thinker and the intuitive feeler—they weren't opposing identities. They were different aspects of the same person. Same dude, different settings. Once I stopped treating them like Jekyll and Hyde, I could bring whatever aspect was needed to each situation while staying whole and without feeling like a fraud. The relief was massive.

Paulo Coelho's *The Alchemist* captures this transformation process perfectly. If you haven't read it (and honestly, it's worth the hype), here's the gist: shepherd boy Santiago travels halfway around the world looking for treasure, only to find out it was buried in his backyard the whole time. Classic Hero's Journey move, right? But it's also exactly what happens with individuation—we go on this epic quest to find ourselves, only to realize we were carrying what we needed within us all along.

What's interesting is that this story reflects the same wisdom Jung found in an unexpected place—the ancient practice of actual alchemy. You know, that mysterious medieval practice where guys in robes tried to turn lead into gold. Sounds crazy, right? But what looked like failed chemistry to most people—attempts to turn lead into gold—Jung recognized as an important metaphor for psychological transformation. The lead isn't discarded; it's transformed through a process that mirrors our own inner work. When I first encountered this concept, it helped me understand my own journey: we don't eliminate our shadows and difficulties—we transform them into wisdom and strength.

That's exactly what happens in our own Hero's Journey, isn't it? We don't discard our shadows, wounds, or difficult parts—though sometimes I've wanted to! We work with them. We bring them into the light of awareness, dissolve old patterns that aren't serving us, separate what's useful from what's holding us back, and eventually bring everything back together in a new, more integrated way.

This is why I find both *The Alchemist* and actual alchemy so relevant to our conversation about the Self. They remind us that the "gold" we're seeking isn't something foreign we need to acquire—it's the transformed version of what we already possess. Just like Santiago had to journey far from home to eventually recognize the treasure that was waiting for him all along. He needed the whole adventure to become the person who could see what was always there.

I've done this dance more times than I can count—desperately searching "out there" for answers that were sitting in my own backyard, only to discover they were within me the whole time, just waiting for me to develop the eyes to see them. But I couldn't have skipped the journey. None of us can, really. The lead only becomes gold through the messy, often painful, sometimes ridiculous process of actually living it.

And yet, knowing the journey can't be skipped, I still catch myself in the seeking trap. Which raises an interesting question: What if all our seeking—reading books (including this one), attending workshops, following teachers—is actually part of the journey too? Maybe that's what Jung was getting at when he talked about the Self. Not something to achieve through seeking, but something we uncover by transforming what already is. Even our seeking, when we're ready, becomes part of the alchemy.

INTEGRATION PITFALLS: THE SHADOW SIDE OF APPROACHING THE SELF

Now, I realize I've been painting a pretty inspiring picture of this whole Self-integration journey. Time for some real talk about what can go wrong. As we approach the final stage of individuation—actually integrating the Self—we need to navigate some more serious psychological pitfalls. And trust me, I've encountered a few myself and learned the hard way. We've already explored different types of projection—shadow onto others, anima/animus onto partners, wisdom onto mentors.

But there's an even more dangerous projection that can happen when we bump into the Self's full power. Remember, the Self is everything—our complete wholeness, all of who we are rolled into one. And when we're not ready to own that much power? Well, there's a high chance we can project it outward in more extreme ways.

This pattern seems to have played out repeatedly throughout human history. Individually, we might take our own potential for wholeness, our inner authority, our capacity to be in the driving seat of our own lives— basically all the good integrated Self stuff—and hand it over to whichever popular figure is on the pedestal at that moment in time. Spiritual gurus, political leaders, celebrities, that influencer with perfect abs. First we're just fans. Then, we start admiring them a bit too much, believing they might have some special access to truth we lack. Before we know it? We're hanging on their every word, defending their obvious mistakes, rear-ranging our whole lives around their tweets, teachings or political promises.

Next thing we know? We've made them into gods. Not metaphorically —we literally worship them, convinced they've got the completeness and wisdom we can't find in ourselves. They become the ones who really know what's going on, who have all the answers, who'll save us from ourselves.

Meanwhile, we're still projecting our unintegrated shadow—all our darkness, fears, and rejected aspects of ourselves—onto whichever group is most convenient. We might demonize them: the immigrants "stealing our jobs," the other political party "destroying our country," the different religious group "threatening our values," or even just or even just that neighbor whose yard isn't perfect. They become responsible for everything wrong in our world, the embodiment of evil itself, the ones who must be stopped at all costs.

And when this individual pattern plays out collectively across entire societies and cultures? We get religions, political movements, and ideological systems built entirely on these projections. Whole populations can project their collective Self onto religious figures or political leaders, while simultaneously dumping their collective shadow onto other nations, ethnic groups, or anyone who thinks differently.

This double projection—our gods versus their demons—might help explain why we keep falling for charismatic leaders who seem larger than life. These figures seem to know exactly how to position themselves to catch both projections. They present themselves as the savior while pointing to specific groups as the enemy. And when a whole population is projecting their Self onto a leader while projecting their shadow onto scapegoats, we've potentially created the conditions for manipulation on a massive scale.

Every holy war, every ethnic cleansing, every ideological purge—don't they seem to follow this same blueprint? Our divine leader against their evil. Our righteousness against their corruption. We've handed over our wholeness and our shadow, leaving ourselves empty vessels just waiting for someone to tell us what to think.

The 20th century gave us horrific examples of this pattern. Hitler knew exactly how to work Germany's post-WWI wounded pride. He positioned himself as the receptacle for the population's Self-projections—their desperate hope for wholeness and restoration—while aiming their shadow projections at Jews, communists, and others. When people project their own inner authority onto a leader like this, they might be handing over their moral compass. It's like they stop thinking for themselves because they've outsourced their own wholeness.

And this pattern isn't just historical. I catch myself doing versions of it today—getting way too invested in some politician or celebrity, as if they're carrying something that belongs to me. We put these figures on impossible pedestals, then act shocked and betrayed when they turn out to be regular flawed humans who can't possibly live up to what we've projected onto them.

But there's another trap that's just as dangerous—and it swings in the opposite direction. Instead of projecting the Self's power outward, the ego can get intoxicated by it. Jung called this inflation, and it's what happens when we mistake a glimpse of the Self for personal godhood. History's graveyards are full of people who fell for this one. Napoleon started as a revolutionary general fighting for liberty, then got so high on his own supply that he literally crowned himself Emperor. Alexander the Great went from military genius to demanding people worship him as an actual god.

Mythology's been warning us about this forever too. King Midas and his golden touch—perfect example of how inflation makes us too stupid to see consequences. When mythological heroes get swallowed by monsters or turned to stone? That's negative inflation—the Self basically eating the ego alive. Complete identity meltdown. The ego gets so overwhelmed by the Self's power that the person loses touch with consensus reality. In extreme cases, we're talking severe psychological breaks—people who can't find their way back to ordinary consciousness.

We can spot this ancient pattern in our modern stories too. Tony Stark gets so confident in his genius that he thinks his tech can fix everything, making increasingly reckless calls that endanger everyone. The Joker in *The Dark Knight* gets so inflated with his own twisted brilliance that he thinks he's playing chess while everyone else is playing checkers—but his "genius" just leads to chaos and self-destruction.

These are our cautionary tales—when the ego grabs the Self's power without humility, it doesn't become godlike. It becomes the architect of its own annihilation. And the scariest part? We're all capable of walking that same path.

WITCHY WOMEN AND ALIEN PEARLS: A DREAM GUIDE TO INDIVIDUATION

We've covered a lot of ground with this individuation journey—the psychological stages, the shadow work, the whole dance of integrating opposites. But reading about it and actually experiencing it are two different animals. Sometimes the psyche has its own way of showing us what's really going on beneath the surface. I had a dream that did exactly that—condensed the entire individuation journey into one intense inner experience that finally made all the theory click into place.

During a bit of a soul searching period after a particularly messy breakup, I started examining how my childhood might've shaped my relationship patterns. Not the most comfortable exploration, but necessary. That's when I stumbled onto a pattern I'd been blind to: throughout my childhood, my mum's emotional availability swung between extremes. She loved me and my brothers with everything she had—that was never in question. But being a young parent juggling three energetic boys while life kept throwing curveballs? The pressure had to go somewhere. Some days she'd be wonderfully present—patient, nurturing, everything we needed. Other days, when it all became too much, her overwhelm would spill out in ways that scared us as kids—tears, frustration, sometimes anger that seemed to come from nowhere. Looking back now, I can see she was drowning and had no life raft. Just a young woman doing her absolute best with no roadmap and more on her plate than anyone should have to carry alone.

That unpredictability though—the constant shift between nurturing presence and emotional overwhelm—left its mark. I'd developed this growing suspicion—and it wasn't a comfortable one— that I was unconsciously drawn to women who carried that same emotional complexity. Women who could be passionate and warm one moment, then unpredictable and distant the next. Somehow I'd internalized that emotional rollercoaster as familiar, maybe even exciting, and kept seeking it out in my romantic life. Like I was trying to solve an old puzzle by recreating it over and over again. This pattern had been running my love life for years, completely under the radar. But it was just a suspicion, something I couldn't quite put my finger on—until one night a dream laid it all bare:

I found myself being led by a friend through an unfamiliar downtown city landscape towards a particular building, ordinary from the outside but pulsing with an uncanny energy I could feel in my bones.

"They're waiting for you," my friend said, gesturing toward a door that seemed to appear from nowhere.

As I stepped through the threshold, a room opened before me, the air itself charged with something ancient and unsettling. And there they were, a group of women with otherworldly, almost witchy qualities. The scene felt like the Oracle's waiting room in *The Matrix*, except instead of gifted children, there were these witchy women deeply absorbed in their craft. At least until they noticed me.

"He's here," one of them, the leader, seemed to announce telepathically, while scurrying toward me.

Immediately, the rest of them dropped everything and rushed over, greeting me like some long-lost family member returning from war. They quickly swarmed me with what at first felt like a welcomed warmth of love but then quickly turned into an overwhelming energy that was simultaneously alluring and suffocating.

I felt myself being consumed and suffocated by them, a mixture of desire, power, and something hungrier as if they were unaware that their power and good intention would harm me.

They started ramping up whatever power they were channeling, their circle tightening. By now, I felt myself being pulled under, dissolving into their circle, drowning in the whirlpool of their collective energy. Part of me wanted to surrender completely, to be consumed by this pull toward powerful feminine energy.

And then just as I was about to be completely engulfed—out of nowhere another powerful force, a translucent, alien being suddenly materialized in the room and jolted the women to a stop, causing them to scatter instantly, their power diminishing in the presence of this otherworldly entity. It stood about 5 feet tall, its skin a glowing, pearlescent white that seemed to emit its own soft light. No real facial features except for these large, almond-shaped eyes. Think classic grey alien, but somehow more... benevolent?

The being turned its attention to me, and I felt seen in a way I had never experienced before—as if it could perceive every layer of my existence simultaneously. Unlike the chaotic energy of the witchy women, the alien radiated calm, this tranquil but powerful wisdom that felt completely beyond ordinary understanding.

Curious and compelled by an inexplicable fascination with this new presence, I moved toward it, only to be stopped in my tracks by an assertive and commanding gesture. The alien in a sudden, sharp motion snapped its arm up—palm out, as I heard this crystal clear command in my mind: "STOP!" Then, with the tension easing, the alien slowly opened its mouth and appeared to regurgitate something from its belly that rose up into its throat, producing a small, radiant pearl from its mouth and placing it gently into my hands. As I received the pearl in my hands, an all-knowing white light of wisdom emanated from it and consumed me. I awoke from this revealing dream.

When I woke up, the dream's meaning was unmistakable. This wasn't just my subconscious sorting daily events—this was a powerful initiation, a message from the deepest part of myself that refused to be ignored any longer.

This was it—the pattern laid bare.

Those witchy women were the shadow feminine energies I'd been drawn to my whole life—magnetic, compelling, but ultimately consuming. They represented my unconscious attraction to women who embodied the same unpredictable intensity I had experienced with my mother. This pattern had manifested as a subtle savior complex where I'd unconsciously cast myself as the rescuer, finding identity and purpose in being the stable one for women in emotional turmoil.

With startling clarity, I saw that I had spent years seeking the maternal in the romantic, attempting to heal childhood wounds through adult relationships. I'd been unconsciously trying to recreate and somehow resolve those early experiences through my partners—seeking a kind of love that could never actually fulfill me.

That alien being—translucent, radiating this incredible calm—was what Jung would call the Self archetype. Unlike the chaotic, consuming energy of the witchy women (my unintegrated anima projection), the alien embodied the integrated center of the psyche that transcends and includes all aspects of our being. It arrived at precisely the critical moment when I was about to be consumed by my unconscious patterns.

That pearl it gave me? Jung would call it the "treasure hard to attain"— the distilled wisdom that emerges when you've really done the work of integration. This pearl represented the understanding that partner love must be different from parental love—a union of equals rather than a recreation of the parent-child bond.

What happened next went way beyond just "getting it" intellectually. As the pearl's light engulfed me, I experienced what can only be described as a moment of profound awakening—a dissolution of boundaries between knowing and being. This wasn't just receiving information; it was a complete reconfiguration of my consciousness. In that glowing moment, I was simultaneously the witchy women, the alien, the pearl, and the one witnessing it all. A visceral experience of wholeness that somehow held all these contradictory elements in perfect harmony.

The light radiating from that pearl seemed to rewrite neural pathways that had been carved since childhood. Attachment patterns, fear responses, defensive structures that had been running the show below my awareness for decades—suddenly they were visible. Not as enemies to fight, but as protective parts that could finally be seen, acknowledged, and woven into something larger. What had previously required years of intellectual analysis was transformed in an instant of direct experience.

This is what Jung meant by encountering the Self. Not some concept to figure out, but a living reality to experience directly. In that moment, I glimpsed what every mystical tradition has pointed toward: that beneath our fragmented, conflicted surface consciousness lies an already-whole core of being. This wasn't about becoming something new. It was recognizing what had always been there, underneath all the noise and struggle of my ego trying to manage life solo.

The transformative power of this experience extended far beyond the dream itself. Within weeks, I met the woman who would become my wife, but this wasn't mere coincidence or happy timing. That internal shift had created this completely different energy around me. I was no longer unconsciously seeking someone to fulfill unresolved maternal needs; I was finally free to recognize and connect with a true partner.

What surprised me most was the ease of this new relationship. After years of exhausting romantic struggles, I was experiencing something that flowed naturally. Not because it lacked depth or challenges, but because I was approaching from wholeness rather than emptiness.

Jung saw individuation as the central task of being human, and I get why now—it fundamentally transforms how you experience everything. The outer circumstances of my life hadn't magically changed overnight, but my relationship to those circumstances had undergone a radical shift. I was responding to challenges with this flexibility and creativity that just hadn't been there when I was caught in those unconscious patterns. Decisions that would have previously triggered anxiety and intense deliberation now seemed to arise naturally from a deeper wisdom.

In that alchemical language we talked about earlier, this dream was the culmination of the *Great Work*. The moment when the lead of unconscious projection was transformed into the gold of conscious relationship. The alien's pearl was my philosopher's stone, the key that made this transformation possible. Like those alchemists who understood they were transforming consciousness, not metals, I experienced how one moment of integration can reshape everything.

This dream basically gave me the whole individuation journey in one wild download. First came the shadow work—finally seeing my addiction to emotional intensity disguised as love. Then the anima integration—suddenly recognizing how I'd been trying to date my way to maternal healing. Meeting that alien? That was my Self encounter—my higher consciousness showing up in otherworldly form. The pearl of wisdom he gave me literally rewired my whole system. And the real-world transformation? Meeting my wife once I'd finally stopped seeking a therapist-mother-lover combo and could actually recognize a real partner.

But maybe most importantly, this showed me that individuation isn't just some psychological theory or self-improvement project. It's a sacred journey toward becoming who we already are beneath the layers of adaptation, protection, and unconscious programming. The Self isn't something we build through effort. It's what's left when we clear away everything that isn't authentically us.

Since that dream, I've continued to encounter challenges and growth opportunities—individuation is never "complete" in the sense of reaching a final, static endpoint. But something fundamental shifted that day, and it's never gone back. Like Neo in *The Matrix* who could never again unsee the code behind apparent reality, I could never return to the unconscious patterns that had previously defined my relationships. That pearl of wisdom wasn't just information I might forget someday. It was consciousness itself being transformed.

This is the real gift of the individuation journey—not becoming perfect (still waiting on that miracle), but fundamentally changing how we experience being alive. We go from scattered pieces reacting to life to something more whole that can actually respond. From wearing borrowed personalities to finding what's authentically ours. My specific dream was mine, but the pattern? That's universal. It's how we become fully human—not by adding more, but by integrating what's already there into something that finally feels alive and real.

SELF-INTEGRATION AND THE WORLD

The Self isn't just personally healing; it ripples outward into how we relate to others, how we respond to challenges, and ultimately, how we contribute to the world. A person connected to their Self brings something essential to every relationship and situation—a quality of presence, authenticity, and wisdom that sparks growth in everyone they encounter.

Jung had this idea—and it makes sense to me—that a society made up of individuated people would naturally be less oppressive and create more space for everyone to fulfill their potential. When more of us do this inner work of integrating our shadows and connecting with our deeper wisdom, we create more space for others to do the same.

The key thing about this Self-integration journey is that it doesn't wrap up with a single insight or dream, no matter how powerful. It's an ongoing process of maintaining authentic Self-connection in a world that sometimes actively resists it. Integration means taking all those fragmented parts we've discovered—shadow material, anima/animus energies, archetypal encounters—and weaving them into our conscious daily life. It's one thing to meet your shadow in a dream; it's another to recognize it when it shows up at the office or in your marriage.

When we begin living from our true Self, we'll likely run into resistance—not just from our own doubts, but from relationships, systems, maybe even entire social structures that feel a little threatened by our authenticity.

But with each cycle of awareness, each dream that reveals a hidden pattern, each synchronicity that confirms we're aligned with something larger than our ego's plans, we deepen our connection to this wise inner core. We become more authentically who we were always meant to be. Not perfect, but whole. Not flawless, but genuine. Not finished, but always becoming.

As we wrap up this exploration of Jung's model, remember that these aren't just interesting theories. They're maps for our own inner journeys. Whether you recognize these patterns in your dreams, your relationships, or your life challenges, the invitation is the same: to know yourself deeply, to integrate all parts of who you are, and to live from the authentic center that emerges when you embark on this Hero's Journey of self-discovery.

Know thyself—not just as a philosophical ideal, but as a lived practice. Because when we truly know ourselves, we discover this beautiful contradiction: we're both smaller and larger than we ever imagined. Unique individuals and expressions of something universal. Limited beings with access to limitless wisdom. This mysterious duality is the gift of the Self, the treasure at the center of the labyrinth, and it's available to anyone courageous enough to undertake the journey.

CONCLUSION: THE NEVER-ENDING JOURNEY OF GROWTH AND TRANSFORMATION

As we come to the end of this exploration into the science behind the hero's innate desire to grow, let's remember that the journey of personal evolution is an ongoing process—one that requires a delicate balance between light and darkness, stability and change, the ego and the soul.

We've dipped into psychology, biology, and sociology, looking for insights into what drives our relentless pursuit of growth. From Maslow's Hierarchy of Needs to the Barrett Model of Consciousness, we've seen how our basic and growth needs shape our motivations, behaviors, and aspirations.

And I hope you've seen, as I have, just how crucial shadow work is for real self-actualization and the importance of establishing a strong foundation by addressing our deepest fears and traumas. Through personal anecdotes—from my boxing misadventures to that cave experience with Joey—and cinematic examples, we've witnessed the transformative power of aligning with our authentic selves and contributing to something greater than ourselves.

As we continue on our own Hero's Journeys, let's remember that growth isn't a destination but a never-ending adventure. By embracing both the light and the darkness within us, by tending to our roots while reaching for the stars, we can cultivate the internal stability and external equilibrium necessary to thrive in an ever-changing world.

So let's keep moving on this path—sometimes stumbling, sometimes sprinting—with whatever courage, curiosity, and compassion we can muster. Every step, no matter how small, brings us closer to our potential and to making a real difference for others. For it's in the pursuit of growth and self-discovery that we find the true essence of what it means to be a modern hero.

In the next section, we'll explore how these Western psychological insights connect with Eastern contemplative traditions that have been guiding people toward Self-realization for thousands of years. We'll look at specific meditation practices, non-dual awareness techniques, and embodiment disciplines to complement the theoretical framework we've been exploring.

It's fascinating to me that there are so many parallels between modern psychology and ancient spiritual teachings. The path to wholeness, it seems, has been understood across cultures—just described in different languages and frameworks. The Buddhist concepts of no-self and mindfulness, the Taoist principles of wu-wei and harmony, and Hindu yoga practices all offer complementary approaches to the individuation process Jung described.

When we bring together these diverse wisdom traditions with our modern psychological understanding, we can develop a more complete roadmap for this Hero's Journey of self-transformation. One that honors both the universal patterns we all share and the unique path each of us must walk.

———

CHAPTER 4 SUMMARY

Chapter 4 was a long one, eh? And bloody hell, did that mirror hurt to look into. We explored the ego (trying to protect you while occasionally sabotaging your life), the shadow (your psychological junk drawer), and that wild dream where an alien gave me a pearl of wisdom. Turns out individuation isn't about becoming perfect—it's about becoming whole, which is messier but way more interesting.

KEY LEARNINGS:

- Your ego isn't evil—just poorly trained and scared shitless
- Whatever drives you crazy about others? Yeah, that's your shadow waving hello
- Dreams aren't random Netflix for your brain—they're actually trying to help
- The Self is bigger than your ego's wildest power fantasies

KEY TAKEAWAYS:

- Integration beats repression—unless you enjoy unexpected explosions
- That pool party punch? Perfect example of untrained ego meets shadow
- Your triggers are your teachers (annoying but true)
- Wholeness includes your weird bits—especially your weird bits

Reflective Question: Who's that person who makes your blood boil, and what disowned part of you might they be wearing like a costume?

"Until you make the unconscious conscious, it will
direct your life and you will call it fate."

- Carl Jung

Chapter Five

EASTERN SPIRITUALISM: ANCIENT WISDOM FOR MODERN GROWTH

So far on this journey together, we've explored growth through some pretty diverse lenses—we've geeked out on scientific theories, dissected psychological frameworks, and even wandered through the mythological wilderness. And you know what keeps showing up, regardless of which map we're following? This persistent idea that growth requires balance—finding that sweet spot between inner stability and how we engage with the world around us.

Honestly? I'm no chakra master or meditation guru. I've stumbled through enough weekend warrior meditation intensives to know my limitations. But I've found that these ancient energy systems offer some surprisingly practical wisdom that lines up beautifully with everything we've been exploring so far. So let's dive into the chakra system together—not as some exotic spiritual curiosity, but as a map that might just help us navigate our own Hero's Journey with a bit more clarity.

The chakra system maps seven energy centers from the base of the spine to the crown of the head, each representing both a physical location and a stage of development. As you'll see in Figure 5.1, what ancient yogis described thousands of years ago mirrors exactly what Maslow, Barrett, and Jung would later map—same journey, different language.

Figure 5.1: The Seven Chakras and Their Meaning. Ancient wisdom mapped onto the body—from root survival needs to crown transcendence. Notice how it's the same developmental journey as Maslow, Jung, and the Hero's Journey, just described thousands of years earlier. Turns out the yogis had this figured out while we were still inventing psychology.

THE ROOT CHAKRA: THE FOUNDATION OF STABILITY AND SECURITY

Okay, let's talk about the root chakra—or *Muladhara* if you want to impress people at yoga class. Think of it as the foundation of the whole chakra system—it's all about feeling grounded, stable, and secure in the world. You know that feeling when you're financially stressed and can't think about anything else? That's your root chakra basically screaming for attention. In Hindu and Buddhist traditions, this chakra is connected to the element of earth and is believed to govern our sense of smell, as well as the health of our bones, teeth, and large intestine.

When the root chakra is balanced, we may experience feelings of groundedness, stability, and security, along with a strong sense of belonging and connection to the physical world. On the other hand, an imbalanced root chakra is said to lead to that awful floating sensation of disconnection, the jitters of instability, and the gnawing edge of anxiety. Practices such as meditation, yoga, and spending time in nature are believed to help restore balance to this crucial energy center.

It's kind of funny to me how these diverse frameworks—emerging from wildly different cultures, disciplines, and millennia—all converge on the same fundamental truth: the importance of cultivating a strong foundation to help create genuine growth and thriving. The root chakra's association with safety and security is so eerily similar to the basic needs we learned about in Maslow's hierarchy of needs. Both of these frameworks emphasize the importance of meeting basic physiological and safety needs before progressing to more complex levels of personal growth and development.

But it doesn't stop there. Look at how the root chakra mirrors the "Ordinary World" and "Crossing the Threshold" stages of the Hero's Journey, where the hero must first establish who they are before venturing into the unknown. Or how it reflects the Tree of Life metaphor, where roots must grow deep and strong before branches can reach skyward. Even Barrett's levels of consciousness start with that crucial "survival" level that forms the foundation for all higher development. And Jung's individuation process begins with creating that stable ego-identity before we can integrate the deeper aspects of our psyche.

I mean, seriously—how many ways do we need to hear "get your basics sorted first" before we actually do it? And yet, it took me exploring the ancient chakra system to finally have the penny drop about these connections. Yep, I know—how very mindfulness-app-subscriber of me to find clarity through energy centers when the same message has been staring me in the face through every other framework we've explored. Better late than never, I suppose.

And if you think the parallels with the root chakra are striking, just wait until we explore the rest of the chakra system. As we move upward from survival needs toward creativity, personal power, love, expression, insight, and ultimately, connection to something greater than ourselves— you'll see that same developmental journey reflected in every framework we've explored. It's almost as if these ancient wisdom keepers were mapping the same territory our modern psychologists, mythologists, and researchers are just now rediscovering with different tools and language.

THE SACRAL CHAKRA: CREATIVITY, SEXUALITY, AND EMOTIONAL EXPRESSION

The sacral chakra, traditionally understood to be nestled in your lower abdomen, is said to carry the vibrant energy of orange and supposedly connects with the flowing element of water. I've always found it fascinating how this energy center seems to house so much of what makes life rich and worth living—our emotional landscape, intuitive nudges, capacity for pleasure, and creative expression. It's also where our sexual and reproductive energies take root.

This area aligns with what Eastern martial artists have cultivated for centuries as the "hara" (in Japanese traditions) or "dantian" (in Chinese practices). If you've ever watched Aikido or Tai Chi masters demonstrate their seemingly effortless power, you're witnessing the cultivation of this exact energy center. They don't generate force from tense muscles but from this centered, flowing energy in the lower abdomen—the same region as our sacral chakra.

The Taoist concept of *wu wei*—effortless action or "going with the flow"—perfectly embodies what a balanced sacral chakra supposedly feels like. It's that state where creativity and action arise naturally, without forcing or straining.

When we look at the frameworks we've explored earlier in this book, the sacral chakra's domain remarkably mirrors Barrett's second level of consciousness focused on relationships and belonging, as well as Maslow's level of love and belonging needs. It represents that crucial stage in our Hero's Journey where we begin to form connections beyond mere survival, expressing ourselves authentically and experiencing the pleasure of creative engagement with life.

When this chakra finds its balance, you might notice yourself feeling more confident in your creative endeavors and self-expression. There's a natural ease in connecting with your sexuality and sensuality—not in some performative way, but in that authentic feeling of being comfortable in your own skin. But when the sacral chakra becomes imbalanced? That's when we might experience those frustrating blockages in creativity, that disconnection from our emotional truth, or those struggles with expressing ourselves authentically.

In our journey of personal growth, I've come to believe the sacral chakra acts as a vital energy hub that we need to engage with if we want to feel fully alive and connected to our own sense of enjoyment. Think about it—how often do we push aside pleasure and creative expression in favor of productivity and obligation? Yet without this flowing, orange energy, life can quickly become a colorless routine.

Jung's framework offers us another lens to understand this area. He saw emotions, sexuality, and creativity as significant aspects of our authentic self that need exploring and integrating during our individuation process. This perfectly parallels our discussion of shadow work earlier —the sacral chakra often holds those disowned parts of ourselves related to pleasure, emotion, and creative expression that we've been conditioned to suppress or ignore. Our emotions aren't just fleeting sensations to be managed or suppressed—they serve as essential bridges between our conscious and unconscious mind. When we take the time to understand and integrate our emotional landscape, we make crucial progress on our individuation journey.

Similarly, our sexuality and creative impulses are intimately connected to the unconscious realms of our psyche. These aren't peripheral aspects of who we are—they can become powerful wellsprings for self-expression and personal growth when we honor and channel them consciously.

THE SOLAR PLEXUS CHAKRA: PERSONAL POWER, SELF-ESTEEM, AND DETERMINATION

Believed to sit in your upper abdomen, just above the navel, the *Manipura* or solar plexus chakra is thought to radiate with bright yellow energy. I think of this center as our internal sun—the source of our personal power, self-esteem, and determination. It's that spot you might feel ignite when you stand your ground or make a difficult decision.

Remember that scene in *The Karate Kid* when Daniel finally executes the crane kick after doubting himself for so long? That moment captures pure solar plexus energy—claiming your power and trusting your capabilities despite the odds.

When in balance, you'll recognize the feeling—a natural confidence flows through you, a sense of being in control of your own life and choices. Not controlling in a rigid way, but that empowered feeling of knowing you can navigate challenges on your own terms.

This chakra's attributes align with the frameworks we've been exploring. The qualities of a balanced Manipura mirror what Maslow described in the esteem and self-actualization levels of his hierarchy. In our Hero's Journey framework, this energy manifests as the "Tests, Allies, and Enemies" stage, where the hero begins to actively engage with challenges rather than simply reacting to them.

True personal power isn't about controlling others—it's about developing an internal locus of control where we respond to life's challenges from a centered place. I've found that this balance creates the foundation from which we can develop the heart-centered qualities found in the next chakra.

THE HEART CHAKRA: LOVE, COMPASSION, AND CONNECTION

Glowing with a vibrant green energy in the center of your chest, the *Anahata* or heart chakra is believed to serve as the bridge between our lower and higher energy centers. I've come to see this chakra as the great connector—the source of our capacity for love, compassion, and meaningful connection with others and the world around us.

Think about those moments when you've felt your heart truly open—

perhaps watching a sunrise over the ocean, holding a loved one close, or experiencing a random act of kindness from a stranger. That warm expansion in your chest? That's your heart chakra in full bloom.

When this chakra finds its balance, the feeling is unmistakable—a natural flow of giving and receiving love, genuine compassion for yourself and others, and a deep sense of connection that transcends surface-level interactions. When blocked or imbalanced, we might experience feelings of isolation, difficulty trusting others, or walls around our heart that keep genuine connection at bay.

This chakra represents the second and third evolutionary stages we explored earlier in our journey. Remember how we discussed that all of existence evolves through establishing viability, bonding, and cooperation? The heart chakra represents that crucial transition from Stage 2 (bonding) to Stage 3 (cooperation). Just as atoms that form chemical bonds create more stable molecules, and cells that communicate effectively form healthier organisms, humans who open their hearts to authentic connection create more resilient communities and relationships.

In the Hero's Journey framework, the heart chakra reflects that pivotal moment when the hero, having discovered their own strength, learns that true power comes through connection and alliance with others. It's no coincidence that the most compelling hero stories show protagonists who succeed not through isolation but through the bonds they form along the way.

I've grappled with this aspect of my journey more than I care to admit. My natural British reservedness combined with some hard lessons about trust has led me to maintain a very small, tight circle of connections. I can dive deep with those few I let in, but widening that circle? That's been my Everest.

A turning point came when a mentor gently observed, "You don't have to go it alone anymore." Those words hit me like a revelation. I realized how my tendency to handle everything myself—never asking for help— wasn't just independence but possibly a manifestation of the darker side of the classic hero archetype—that ego-driven model where personal glory and recognition become the primary motivation, where the need for attention and admiration keeps us isolated at the center of our own narrative. It was exactly the opposite of the modern hero path I've been advocating throughout this book.

I'm still working on this balance—wondering sometimes if my small circle is enough, other times feeling the pull toward broader connection. But I've come to see that the heart chakra isn't about the quantity of connections but their quality and authenticity. It's about the courage to remain open despite past wounds.

And perhaps this is where our personal journey with the heart chakra connects most deeply with the universal pattern. This essential principle of connection and cooperation extends beyond our personal relationships to our very understanding of evolution and growth at every level of existence. From atoms to galaxies, from individuals to societies—connection isn't just a nice-to-have, but a fundamental requirement for flourishing and advancement to the next level of development.

THE THROAT CHAKRA: COMMUNICATION, SELF-EXPRESSION, AND AUTHENTICITY

The *Vishuddha* or throat chakra is said to pulse with brilliant blue energy at the base of your throat, governing our capacity for authentic expression, communication, and speaking our truth. If the heart chakra is about connecting with others, the throat chakra is about how we share ourselves authentically with the world—not just through words, but through every form of creative expression that emerges from our depths.

The throat chakra perfectly shows what we've been exploring throughout this book about the tension between authenticity and social adaptation. Remember our discussion of Jung's persona—that necessary mask we wear to navigate social situations? The throat chakra is where we negotiate the delicate balance between honoring our authentic voice and communicating in ways that create connection rather than division.

When the throat chakra is balanced, there's this beautiful flow between your inner truth and outer expression. You say what you mean, mean what you say, and somehow manage to do it in a way that honors both your authenticity and your relationships. People with balanced throat chakras often become natural teachers, artists, or communicators—not because they're louder than others, but because their words carry weight and authenticity that resonates deeply.

But when it's blocked or imbalanced? The patterns vary widely. Some people swallow their truth entirely, becoming chronic people-pleasers who never quite say what they mean. Others swing to the opposite extreme—speaking without consideration for timing, context, or the emotional capacity of their audience. And then there are those who toggle between these extremes, sometimes holding perfect space for others while other times delivering their truth with such raw intensity that it overwhelms the very connection they're trying to create.

I have to confess something here: for someone who's written a book about authenticity, I've spent an embarrassing amount of my life struggling with this particular energy center. You'd think after all that shadow work and individuation talk, I'd have mastered the art of speaking my truth. But the throat chakra? It's one of my trickiest teachers.

Here's my particular pattern: I'd actually consider myself quite good at holding space for others. I try to listen deeply, give conversations room to breathe, and create the kind of container where people feel heard. But often when it's my turn to speak—especially in intense situations—what emerges to the surface is often too direct, too emotionally unfiltered for the context I'm operating in.

It's like I toggle between two extremes: patient, spacious listener and then—when something really matters to me—I speak with this raw emotional intensity that can catch people off guard. Not loud or dominating, but perhaps too real, too unvarnished for environments that expect emotional regulation and diplomatic language. What comes out often lacks the emotional regulation that the situation requires.

But here's what I've learned through examining this pattern: the key question isn't whether my response was "too intense"—it's what was driving that intensity in the first place. When my deeper values are genuinely threatened, that raw response might actually be justified, even necessary. But when it's my ego needs being triggered—my need to be right, to be respected, to maintain my image—then it's likely a reactive response that won't serve anyone well.

The real throat chakra work lies in developing the discernment to recognize the difference in the moment. And even when my values ARE being legitimately challenged, that initial intensity should serve as a signal to step back and evaluate: "Is this situation fundamentally incompatible with who I am?"

This connects back to those evolutionary stages we explored earlier—how we need to bond with compatible others to continue growing, but that bonding requires being on the same wavelength. Sometimes the wisest response isn't to keep fighting for your values in a particular context, but to recognize the mismatch and find your compatible tribe. Just like atoms that can't bond with certain other atoms, sometimes authentic communication requires finding the right environment where your truth can actually be received.

My challenge isn't about learning to speak up—it's about learning to modulate the emotional intensity of my truth-telling so it can actually land with others, while also developing the wisdom to recognize when I'm simply in the wrong environment for authentic communication to serve evolution rather than just create friction.

True throat chakra balance means becoming a clear channel for truth that serves both self and others. Not suppressing the emotional authenticity that makes communication real, but learning to express it in ways that invite connection rather than triggering defensiveness, and having the wisdom to recognize when you're simply not in the right container for that level of authenticity.

The gift of a balanced throat chakra is becoming someone who can speak difficult truths with both courage and skill—honoring the emotional reality of what needs to be said while considering how it can best be received. It's the difference between emotional authenticity and emotional intelligence, between speaking your truth and speaking your truth wisely.

As we move into the higher chakras, I've noticed something interesting about how these energy centers seem to build on each other. At least in my experience, the throat chakra works best when I've got some stability in those foundational areas—feeling secure enough to be vulnerable (root), emotionally flowing (sacral), confident in my own power (solar plexus), and coming from an open heart. When any of those are wobbly, my communication tends to get wobbly too. It's less mystical theory and more like practical psychology playing out in real time—the same developmental progression we've seen mapped in Maslow's hierarchy, Barrett's levels of consciousness, and Jung's individuation process.

THE THIRD EYE CHAKRA: INTUITION, WISDOM, AND HIGHER CONSCIOUSNESS

The *Ajna* or third eye chakra radiates with deep indigo energy from the space between your eyebrows, governing our capacity for intuition, insight, and what I can only describe as "inner knowing." If the throat chakra is about expressing our truth, the third eye is about perceiving truth—not just the surface-level information our regular senses provide, but those deeper patterns and connections that exist beneath ordinary awareness.

I'll be honest—writing about the third eye chakra feels like stepping into territory where I risk sounding like I've gone full crystal-clutching mystic. But stay with me here, because what we're really talking about is something far more practical and grounded than you might expect. We're exploring that mysterious capacity we all have for sensing what's not immediately obvious—those moments when you just "know" something without being able to explain how.

When this chakra is balanced, there's this beautiful integration between rational thinking and intuitive knowing. You can analyze a situation logically while simultaneously picking up on subtler dynamics that pure logic might miss. It's like having access to a broader spectrum of information—not just what's being said, but what's being communicated through energy, presence, and those indefinable qualities we often dismiss as "just feelings."

In our Hero's Journey framework, the third eye represents that stage where the hero begins to receive "supernatural aid"—guidance that comes from sources beyond ordinary perception. Think of Obi-Wan's voice guiding Luke to "use the Force" or the Oracle's cryptic wisdom in *The Matrix*. This chakra captures that capacity to perceive deeper patterns and receive guidance that transcends logical analysis.

But when the third eye is imbalanced? That's when we either become disconnected from our intuitive faculties entirely—relying solely on rational analysis and missing crucial guidance—or we swing to a potentially more dangerous extreme: becoming so identified with our spiritual insights that we start wielding them like weapons of superiority rather than tools of service.

And here's where I need to get brutally honest about my own journey with this energy center, because it connects directly to one of the most humbling lessons I've learned about the integration process we've been exploring throughout this book.

After experiencing some particularly intense spiritual insights—the kind of downloads and revelations that genuinely alter your understanding of reality—I found myself in a precarious psychological position. My ego, that clever shape-shifter we've discussed extensively, had found a new costume to wear: the enlightened teacher. Instead of using these insights to deepen my own integration and service, I started unconsciously positioning myself as someone who had figured it all out, someone uniquely qualified to guide others toward their own awakening.

It was sneaky because it felt so righteous. I wasn't consciously trying to be arrogant or superior—I genuinely wanted to help people. But what was actually happening was that I'd become intoxicated by my own insights, using them as a new form of ego inflation rather than allowing them to humble me into deeper service.

This played out in exactly the way you might expect: I started showing up in conversations as the one with answers rather than questions. When friends shared their struggles, instead of creating space for their own discovery, I'd jump in with spiritual interpretations and guidance that they hadn't asked for. I was operating from my head—analyzing their experience through the lens of my newfound wisdom—rather than meeting them heart to heart in their actual reality.

The reckoning came during a men's council I attend regularly—one of those sacred containers where authentic feedback is not just welcomed but essential for everyone's growth. We were engaged in what we call "fire council," a practice where we literally pass a talking stick around a circle while sitting around a fire, each person speaking from their heart while others listen without interrupting or offering advice. It's designed to create space for truth-telling that might be too tender or challenging for ordinary conversation.

For several days leading up to this gathering, I'd been in full "spiritual teacher" mode, offering unsolicited wisdom to anyone who'd listen. I was riding high on recent insights and completely unconscious of how my energy was affecting others. During the fire council, when it was my turn to receive feedback from the group, one of the men looked directly at me and delivered what felt like a lightning bolt: "Lee, you're riddled with insights."

The way he said it—not with cruelty, but with that unflinching honesty that true brotherhood requires—cut straight through my spiritual persona to the uncomfortable truth beneath. I wasn't embodying wisdom; I was performing it. I wasn't serving others; I was serving my ego's need to feel special, important, elevated above the ordinary struggles of human existence.

This feedback connected directly to that Rothko painting experience I shared earlier—remember the two fields of red, one representing mental understanding and the other embodied heart wisdom? I'd become completely caught up in the upper field, intellectualizing and analyzing spiritual insights rather than allowing them to drop into my heart and transform how I actually showed up in the world.

The fire council moment was a perfect example of what Jung called "inflation"—that psychological state where we become identified with archetypal energies rather than being a conscious channel for them. I'd encountered genuine wisdom through my third eye chakra, but instead of remaining humble before these insights, my ego had claimed ownership of them.

This is one of the most dangerous pitfalls of third eye chakra development, and it's particularly relevant to anyone on the path of conscious growth. The very insights that are meant to serve our individuation can become new forms of ego identification if we're not careful. Instead of making us more humble and compassionate, they can make us feel special and separate.

This connects to what we see in Maslow's hierarchy when people prematurely attempt self-actualization without properly integrating the lower levels. The third eye chakra's insights are meant to serve our growth and connection, but when we're still operating from unmet esteem needs or unhealed wounds, these spiritual experiences can become just another way to feed the ego rather than transcend it.

What makes this especially tricky is that the line between being a guide and being a guru is often razor-thin, and it's a balance I continue to navigate even as I write this book. My intention is always to serve as a fellow traveler or guide sharing what I've learned rather than positioning myself as someone who has all the answers. But given my patterns around recognition and the savior complex we've explored throughout this journey, I have to maintain constant vigilance against slipping into that guru energy.

The beauty of having an authentic community—whether it's a men's council, a women's circle, or any group committed to mutual growth—is that they serve as mirrors for these blind spots. That fire council feedback didn't destroy me; it recalibrated me. It reminded me that true wisdom expresses itself through humility and presence, not through clever insights and spiritual performances.

The third eye chakra, when properly integrated, offers us access to inner knowing and guidance. But this gift comes with a responsibility: to remain humble before the mystery, to use insights in service of connection rather than separation, and to remember that wisdom is meant to be lived, not just accumulated or displayed.

This connects beautifully with Jung's understanding of the individuation process. Remember, the goal isn't to become someone special or enlightened, but to become fully human—integrated, authentic, and capable of serving something larger than ourselves. The third eye chakra supports this process by offering access to guidance and understanding that transcends our personal perspective, but only when we approach it with authentic respect and humility.

The third eye's capacity for insight and intuition is most valuable when it's grounded in security (root), flowing with creativity (sacral), empowered by authentic strength (solar plexus), guided by an open heart (heart), and expressed with conscious communication (throat).

When all these elements work together, the third eye becomes not a source of spiritual superiority but a tool for deeper service—helping us perceive what's needed in each moment and respond with wisdom rather than simply reacting from old patterns. It's the difference between spiritual insight and spiritual intelligence, between receiving guidance and being guided by guidance.

The question the third eye poses isn't "How enlightened am I?" but rather "How can I serve?" And that shift in orientation makes all the difference between wisdom that inflates the ego and wisdom that serves the soul's evolution.

THE CROWN CHAKRA: WHEN THE MAP DISSOLVES

So here we are at the crown chakra—that shimmering violet energy at the top of the head that's said to represent our connection to the divine, to unity consciousness, to whatever you want to call that sense of being part of something infinitely larger than yourself.

And honestly? I almost didn't write this section at all.

Not because I don't think the crown chakra matters, but because every time I try to write about it, I end up sounding like I'm channeling some new-age greeting card. "Connect with the infinite! Dissolve into universal love!" That kind of thing. Which is exactly the opposite of what this energy center actually feels like when you encounter it in real life.

The truth is, crown chakra experiences can happen in the most unexpected moments—while making coffee on a Tuesday morning, sitting in a hospital waiting room, or standing in line at the grocery store. But for me, the most transformative awakenings came in a place and way I never could have predicted.

I was in the Mayan Riviera, staying in a simple beach bungalow after coming through some significant personal challenges. I'd spent the day in a cacao ceremony—a traditional healing practice that's become popular in the region. By evening, I was back in my room, winding down as the sun set over the Caribbean, about to take a shower before bed. I had my headphones on, Eric Prydz's "Opus" playing—a ten-minute electronic house track that builds and builds.

Now, here's something you need to understand about me, and it's embarrassing to admit: I hate dancing. Always have. My ego is way too invested in trying to be "cool" to let my body move freely in front of anyone, especially myself. Dancing feels vulnerable, exposed, ridiculous.

I'm usually the guy who stands at the edge of wedding receptions nursing a beer while everyone else loses themselves on the dance floor.

As I caught my reflection in the mirror, something shifted. I found myself really looking at myself—maybe for the first time ever. Not checking my appearance or fixing my hair, but actually seeing myself with something approaching compassion. We spend so much time looking at ourselves through other people's eyes that we forget how to see ourselves through our own. In that mirror, I was finally meeting myself.

Suddenly, something dissolved within me. What I now recognize as my ego, that protective shell that keeps me performing "cool" all the time. There's this part of us that exists beneath all our adaptations and defenses, and I felt like I was touching that self for the first time.

The next thing I knew, my cells felt like they were vibrating intensely, as if my body was being called to move from some source deeper than conscious decision. And then I was dancing. Really dancing. For the full ten minutes of that song, completely alone, completely unselfconscious, tears of joy streaming down my face.

It wasn't graceful or beautiful or Instagram-worthy. It was raw and honest and free. The most liberated I'd ever felt in my own skin. Everything I'd been protecting myself from—looking foolish, being seen, taking up space with my joy—suddenly felt irrelevant compared to this overwhelming gratitude for being alive.

What moved me most wasn't the dancing itself, but what it represented —a willingness to be foolish in service of aliveness. There's a difference between happiness and joy. Happiness depends on circumstances; joy is our natural response to being fully present to life. In that mirror, dancing to electronic music in a beach hut thousands of miles from home, I touched that joy for the first time.

Cliché? Absolutely. Powerful? Beyond words. Something about that place—with its cenotes, ancient Mayan ruins, and the lingering energetic resonance from the meteor impact that ended the dinosaur era—seemed to create a connection I'd never experienced before. It was pure crown chakra activation: ego dissolution followed by spontaneous expression of joy and gratitude for existence itself.

The crown chakra experience I had three weeks before my first son was born was different but equally unexpected. For an entire week, I was in this constant flow of unexplainable emotion and tears of gratitude. Not anxiety about becoming a father—pure, overwhelming love for life itself. It felt like my higher self was preparing me, getting me ready to be present and supportive for my wife during the birth rather than being caught up in my own fears and excitement.

Our souls have their own timing, their own curriculum for our becoming. That week of inexplicable love felt like my soul's way of preparing me for the most important transformation of my life. Then, just as mysteriously as it had arrived, this heightened state settled back into normal consciousness the week before my son was actually born. But I was different—more prepared, more grounded, more available for what was coming.

These experiences mirror what we've explored throughout this journey. Maslow's self-actualization—that peak of his hierarchy where you've supposedly reached your full potential? Those moments of spontaneous dancing and overwhelming love feel exactly like what he was pointing toward. Not some constant state of bliss, but these natural arising moments of creativity, self-acceptance, and deep purpose that seem to emerge when we stop performing and start being.

Barrett's seventh level of consciousness—that place of service and unity with something larger than yourself? Both experiences shared this quality of ego dissolution that revealed not emptiness, but connection. The boundaries between self and everything else became suddenly negotiable.

The crown chakra has zero interest in our spiritual achievements or how evolved we think we are. It shows up in moments of authentic vulnerability, when we're brave enough to let our defenses down and meet life as it actually is rather than as we think it should be.

This completes the circle we've been traveling throughout this entire journey. We started with the root chakra's need for safety and survival, moved through creativity and power and love and expression and wisdom, only to discover that what we were seeking was never actually separate from where we began.

I'm writing these words while my son plays with his toys and throws them on the ground, delighting in watching them fall and immediately wanting them back so he can do it all over again. Watching him reminds me that joy doesn't require justification or achievement. It's our natural state when we're not busy protecting ourselves from life.

So there you have it—ancient Eastern wisdom confirming everything our Western psychologists spent centuries figuring out. Bit embarrassing for us Westerners, really. The chakras just walked us through the exact same developmental journey as Maslow's hierarchy, Jung's individuation, and Campbell's Hero's Journey. Different language, same territory. Makes you wonder what else these ancient traditions figured out while we were busy inventing psychology. But let's see what this Eastern detour actually taught us about the journey we've been on.

––––––

CHAPTER 5 SUMMARY

Chapter 5 brought Eastern wisdom to our Western psychology party—and guess what? They've been saying the same things for thousands of years, just with better incense. The chakra system maps perfectly onto our psychological development, from root survival needs to crown experiences (yes, including my mortifying dance session in Mexico). Turns out enlightenment might involve looking ridiculous.

KEY LEARNINGS:

- Chakras aren't woo-woo—they're describing the same journey as Maslow and Jung
- Ancient wisdom had this figured out while we were still inventing the wheel
- Each energy center = specific life challenge you can't bypass
- East and West are dance partners, not competitors

KEY TAKEAWAYS:

- Balance all chakras—spiritual bypassing via crown chakra doesn't work

- Your body knows things your mind hasn't figured out yet
- Sometimes transcendence looks like a middle-aged man dancing alone and crying
- Integration requires both grounding and flight

Reflective Question:

Which chakra has you stuck—and what would your life look like if that energy started flowing?

"When I let go of what I am, I become what I might be."

– Lao Tsu

PART ONE CONCLUSION

The Integration of Being

So here we are at the end of Part 1, having journeyed from the hero's call to adventure through the depths of the psyche, from ancient chakras to modern consciousness research. And if you're feeling a bit like I did after that spontaneous dance session in Mexico—simultaneously enlightened and slightly ridiculous—then we're probably on the right track.

What I find beautiful about bringing Eastern wisdom into conversation with Western psychology is how they complement rather than compete with each other. Jung's shadow work prepares us for the deeper surrender that some Eastern traditions call enlightenment. Maslow's hierarchy gives us a practical framework for the developmental stages that yogis have mapped for millennia. The Hero's Journey provides a narrative structure for the ego death and rebirth that mystics across cultures have experienced.

You don't need to choose between being psychologically healthy and spiritually awake—they're the same process described in different languages. The goal isn't to transcend your humanity but to embrace it so fully that you discover the divine hiding in plain sight within your ordinary, messy, beautiful human experience.

As I've reflected on these diverse frameworks, I'm struck by a humbling truth: we've been mapping the same territory all along. Think about it: we start with survival and safety (root chakra/Maslow's basic needs/hero's ordinary world), move through creativity and relationships (sacral/love and belonging/finding allies), claim our personal power (solar plexus/esteem needs/tests and trials), open our hearts to connection (heart chakra/self-actualization beginning/supernatural aid), learn to express our truth (throat/full self-actualization/approaching the ordeal), develop wisdom and insight (third eye/transcendence/receiving the elixir), and finally experience moments of unity with something larger than ourselves (crown/service to others/return with the gift).

It's the same spiral, whether described by ancient yogis in Sanskrit, modern psychologists with clinical terminology, or mythologists studying stories. The names change, but the territory remains constant: we grow from fragmentation toward wholeness, from isolation toward connection, from survival toward service.

This spiral IS the modern Hero's Journey—not battling external monsters but navigating internal territories, not conquering kingdoms but transforming consciousness, not achieving glory but achieving integration.

What modern psychology is "discovering," ancient wisdom keepers—whether through chakras, the Tree of Life, the Medicine Wheel, or Egyptian soul mapping—had already understood millennia ago. Perhaps consciousness itself, when refined through practice and attention, becomes its own instrument of discovery.

This recognition brings us full circle to where we began—with that fundamental question: What transforms an ordinary person into a hero? Now I think we can see that the question itself contains a beautiful misconception.

There are no ordinary people. There are only heroes who haven't yet recognized their journey. So what does this mean for how we actually do the work?

Throughout these chapters, we've looked at transformation through multiple lenses, yet underneath all the different ways of describing it is one simple truth: wholeness requires integrating all aspects of our being.

The mind seeks to understand and make meaning—it's likely what brought you to this book. But alone, as I learned during that fire council feedback about being "riddled with insights," it becomes a trap. The body holds our history and knows truths the mind hasn't grasped—those boxing matches in the Outback taught me that. The soul yearns for expression beyond the ego's concerns—it's what recognizes synchronicities and feels called to something greater.

I've learned the hard way that these frameworks are maps, not merit badges. The moment we use spiritual experiences or psychological insights as weapons of superiority, we've missed the point entirely. My "riddled with insights" moment was the universe reminding me that wisdom without humility is just a fancy ego trip.

What makes the modern Hero's Journey unique isn't the battles we fight but the battlefield itself. We're not facing dragons in caves but shadows in our psyche. We're not seeking magical elixirs but integration and wholeness. We're not conquering kingdoms but transforming consciousness—first our own, then contributing to the collective transformation our world desperately needs.

As we prepare to enter the next stage, reflect on which aspects of this journey have called to you most strongly—and which ones you wanted to skip past. Our resistances often point toward where our next growth lies waiting.

Maybe you resonated with the Hero's Journey but felt skeptical about chakra energy. Maybe Jung's shadow work triggered your protective mechanisms, or the mystical experiences stretched your belief system. Whatever your response, I'd say trust it. Take what serves your growth and leave the rest for another cycle of your spiral journey.

Part 2 is where things get a little wild! It shifts from understanding the modern hero's inner landscape to exploring the expanded territories of consciousness itself. What happens when the modern hero starts noticing synchronicities everywhere? When ancient practices suddenly make sense? When you find yourself in a sweat lodge wondering how you got there? How do we connect with collective consciousness through ritual and community? We've mapped the psychological territory; now we'll explore the frontiers beyond ordinary perception. Fair warning: the modern hero's path gets stranger before it gets clearer—but that's exactly why it matters in these times when the old maps aren't working anymore.

So take a breath. Maybe even dance a little—ridiculous and unselfconscious—to whatever music makes your cells vibrate with the simple joy of being alive. Because that's where all the real wisdom lives: not in the frameworks we can explain, but in the moments when we're brave enough to let ourselves be moved by the mystery of it all.

The journey begins the moment you say yes to your own becoming. Everything else—the challenges, the allies, the transformations—comes from that first courageous step into the unknown.

Welcome to your adventure. Part 2 awaits, with practical tools and specific practices to support your heroic emergence. But remember: the journey has already begun. It began the moment you picked up this book, drawn by something in you that knows it's time.

The only way out is through. The only way up is down first. The only way to become who you're meant to be is to release who you're not.

Let's continue this journey together.

———

PART 1 SUMMARY: YOUR HERO'S JOURNEY ROADMAP

Right, let's get practical about what we've covered. Part 1 has given you five different maps for the same journey—here's your quick reference guide for when you need it:

THE JOURNEY SO FAR:

- **Chapter 1:** The Hero's Journey pattern—from boxing tent beatdowns to recognizing we're all on this ancient path
- **Chapter 2:** Universal growth patterns—that cosmic itch is evolution itself (viability → bonding → cooperation)
- **Chapter 3: Maslow's hierarchy meets shadow work**—why having everything can leave you empty (basic needs → growth needs, Barrett's 7 levels of consciousness, the Tree of Life as metaphor)
- **Chapter 4: Jung's complete psyche map**—ego, persona, shadow, personal unconscious, collective unconscious, anima/animus, complexes, archetypes, individuation, and the Self

- **Chapter 5: Eastern wisdom via chakras**—7 energy centers mapping the same journey Western psychology "discovered" (root to crown, each chakra corresponding to psychological development stages)

YOUR QUICK-REFERENCE TOOLKIT:

- Feeling stuck? Check which stage you're in (surviving, conforming, differentiating, etc.)
- Triggered by someone? That's your shadow material wearing their face
- Can't access creativity? Probably neglecting basic needs or lower chakras
- Ego acting up? It needs training, not destruction
- Spiritual bypassing? Go back and do the shadow work
- Projecting on partners? That's anima/animus material asking for integration
- "Riddled with insights"? You're in your head, not your heart

RED FLAGS YOU'RE AVOIDING THE WORK:

- Reading more books instead of applying what you know
- Focusing only on "love and light"
- Triggered by everyone around you
- Stuck in your head (hi, "riddled with insights" me)
- Waiting to feel "ready" before starting

GREEN FLAGS YOU'RE ON TRACK:

- Comfortable with paradox and "both/and" thinking
- Less triggered, more curious about reactions
- Shadow work feels necessary, not optional
- Integration over perfection
- Helping others without savior complex

YOUR PART 1 HOMEWORK:

1. Identify which framework resonates most (that's your entry point)
2. Notice your biggest resistance (that's your growth edge)
3. Pick ONE shadow aspect to work with
4. Find your support system (no solo heroes)
5. Start before you're ready

BOTTOM LINE:

Every framework we've explored is saying the same thing: grow roots before branches, face your shadow before seeking light, integrate your weird bits, and remember—the journey spirals. You'll revisit these themes at deeper levels. That's not failure; that's the design.

PART 2 PREVIEW:

We're going from understanding to experiencing, from maps to territory, from "that's interesting" to "holy shit, this is real."

Ready? Good. Neither was I.

BEYOND THE VEIL

Journeys into Expanded Consciousness

WHEN REALITY GETS A BIT WEIRD

As I lay in bed, frozen by some unseen force, my mind raced trying to make sense of what was happening. The angelic music that had somehow lulled me into a trance-like state now gave way to an overwhelming sense of fear as my teeth chattered uncontrollably, vibrating at an impossible speed. It felt as though my very being was being lifted from this earthly plane, pulled somewhere else by a force I couldn't name or understand.

But I'm getting ahead of myself. Let me back up.

I never expected to find myself living in Sedona, Arizona, in my late 20s, but life has a way of putting you exactly where you need to be—even when you're convinced it's the last place you want to be. If you've never been, imagine Mars decided to take mushrooms: these surreal red rock formations that look completely otherworldly. As I drove through the town for the first time, out of nowhere I suddenly became overwhelmed with emotion. Should've been my first clue that Sedona was going to get weird. I never intended to make Sedona my home and was always looking for ways out. My partner at the time, though? She was perfectly happy there, so I stayed. You know those relationships where you're physically present but mentally browsing real estate listings in other cities? Yeah, that was me.

Sedona is famous for its vortexes—supposedly swirling centers of energy that transform your life, heal your soul, or at least separate tourists from their money. Initially I was about as convinced as you'd expect a skeptical Brit to be. Vortexes? You're taking the piss, mate!

But three months in, the weirdness escalated. Nothing dramatic at first. Just... off. The kind of thing you'd dismiss once or twice. But it kept happening. I would often wake up to the distant sound of children playing outside, naturally assuming they were from the school across the street. Except when I'd check my phone, it was between 5 and 7 am, long before the school day began. Odd. I must just be dreaming.

One particularly unsettling incident happened early one morning. As I lay in bed, bathed in the warm morning sun filtering through the curtains, I was suddenly awakened by the sensation of something moving around my bed. Fully conscious and aware of my surroundings, I listened as the presence of children playfully moved around my bed, their laughter filling the room. It felt as if they were running from the foot of the bed to the sides, their energy and excitement right there in the room. I could hear their feet—actual feet—padding on the floor. The mattress even shifted slightly, like when a cat jumps on your bed. Except I didn't have a cat. Or children.

As the children's laughter faded away, I lay there in the quiet of my bedroom, proper freaked out, my mind racing through increasingly desperate explanations. What the hell had just happened?

Then came the night with the music. As I drifted off to sleep, I was abruptly awakened by the most beautiful and heavenly music I had ever heard. It was as if an angelic choir was singing, accompanied by the sound of harps and piano. I wondered if I was somehow creating this music in my dreams. The feelings it evoked were indescribable—a sense of unity and peace that dissolved everything else.

As the music enveloped me, I found myself in a trance-like state, lost in its beauty and the emotions it stirred within me. It felt like being inside a cathedral made of sound—sacred, ancient, overwhelming.

Suddenly, I was jolted awake by an intense feeling of fear. My heart raced as I realized something was terribly wrong. My teeth began to chatter uncontrollably, vibrating at a frequency unlike anything I had ever experienced. It felt as if my entire skull was shaking, the vibrations getting stronger with each passing moment.

I was trapped in my own body, unable to move as the vibrations consumed me. It was as if I was being lifted off the ground, pulled into an unknown realm by the force of the vibrations. My mind raced faster than before, trying to make sense of what was happening. Was this a dream? A nightmare? Was this a seizure? A stroke?

Despite the fear that gripped me, I couldn't resist the temptation to see how long I could allow the vibrations to continue. Part of me wanted to know what lay on the other side of this experience. But as the vibrations intensified, raw terror won out. And I somehow managed to shake myself out of the situation.

As the vibrations subsided, I lay in bed, my heart pounding in my chest. Whatever had just happened, it wasn't normal. And it certainly wasn't over.

The strange incidents I experienced in Sedona were unsettling, to say the least. I couldn't help but wonder if there was a deeper meaning behind them and if the town's vortexes and spiritual energy were somehow connected. Initially, I tried to write these events off to sleep paralysis— that phenomenon where your body is temporarily paralyzed while your mind remains awake. Nice, tidy, scientific explanation.

But as I dug deeper into what might be happening, a new possibility emerged. What if the sleep paralysis explanation was right, but incomplete? What if these paralysis states weren't just glitches in our sleep cycle, but actual doorways—means to access realms of consciousness beyond our normal understanding? And what if Sedona's famous vortexes somehow amplified or triggered these experiences? Maybe our ancestors knew something when they treated these liminal states as sacred rather than medical.

Little did I know that this bizarre experience would set me on a path of investigating the nature of consciousness and its mysterious manifestations itself. Fueled by equal parts curiosity and the desperate need to understand what the hell was happening to me, I embarked on a quest to unravel the enigmatic nature of the weird, eerie, and almost supernatural events that had unfol—sorry, let me try that again without sounding like a

BBC documentary about Victorian séances—I needed to figure out what in the actual hell was happening to me!

This search led me down a rabbit hole of esoteric knowledge, ancient wisdom, and cutting-edge scientific research. From the earliest traditions of Indigenous cultures to the frontiers of quantum physics, I pursued answers to the fundamental questions sparked by my Sedona experience. And yes, I realize how mental that sounds—one minute you're a skeptical Brit, the next you're reading about shamanic journeying and quantum entanglement. But desperate times, desperate measures, right?

As my stay in Sedona continued, more weird stuff started happening. Synchronicities everywhere—and I know how cliché this sounds, but yes, I became one of those people seeing 11:11 constantly and thinking the universe was trying to tell me something. I'd think about someone I hadn't seen in years, and they'd call that afternoon. I'd have a dream about a specific symbol, then see it three times the next day. Lucid dreams became a nightly thing. And sometimes I'd just know things—like answers would arrive fully formed in my head without any logical process behind them.

It was like those first experiences had thinned the veil of the physical world and given me a glimpse into another world. And being in Sedona—with its vortexes and whatever else was going on there—just seemed to amplify everything.

Through all this madness, one thing became clear: consciousness is way stranger than we give it credit for. Humans have always known this—from shamanic journeying to remote viewing, we've been poking at the edges of awareness since forever.

So in this chapter, we're going to look at how people throughout history have tried to understand these experiences. We'll dig into mythology, folklore, and yes, even those alien encounters people keep reporting. Because once you've had invisible children playing in your bedroom at dawn, your definition of "impossible" gets a bit more flexible.

Are these experiences just our brains misfiring? Psychological projections? Glimpses into other dimensions? Honestly, I still don't know. But the questions themselves changed how I see everything.

Buckle up. It's about to get weird. But if you've made it through shadow work and chakras, you can handle weird.

UNKNOWN FORCES & PHYSICAL MANIFESTATIONS OF OUR HIGHER SELVES

After Sedona 'twisted my melon' with invisible children and angelic choirs, I needed answers. And it turns out, once you start tugging on that thread, you end up in some seriously weird territory.

By now we're well aware of how humans have always felt this pull toward something more, aren't we? I think we've also established how different cultures dress it up in different costumes—some refer to it as a "calling," others say it's your "higher purpose," and your yoga teacher probably has seventeen Sanskrit words for it. But strip away all the fancy language and what you've got is this universal itch we're all trying to scratch.

Religious and spiritual traditions have always talked about it as a 'calling' or 'mission' from a higher power. Different cultures have their own names for this force—God, Brahman, the Great Spirit—but they're all pointing at the same thing.

Now, mythology, folklore, and even the concept of aliens—they've played a massive role in human culture and spiritual traditions. Think about it: from ancient mythology to modern science fiction, these themes keep capturing our imagination. Ancient mythology depicted gods and goddesses as otherworldly beings with superhuman powers. Folklore passes down traditional stories about mysterious encounters through generations. And the concept of aliens? It's driving scientific advancement in our search to understand life in the universe.

But the thing I find most fascinating is that these themes haven't just shaped our stories. They've actually changed how we see the world. Ancient myths and folklore helped people make sense of natural phenomena, gave them meaning and purpose. Similarly, the search for extraterrestrial life has expanded our understanding of the universe and where we fit in it.

These themes have captured imaginations worldwide and significantly impacted society. But why do they still have such a strong hold on us? Maybe they're a way for us to explore and understand our own humanity, to confront our mortality, or—and here's where it gets interesting—to represent our higher selves. These themes often depict beings more advanced than humans, and it's possible they're projections of our own aspirations and potential. They might be showing us what we could become, pushing us toward higher understanding and enlightenment.

Look at mythology, folklore, and religion—they're packed with stories about beings believed to be physical manifestations of our higher selves. These higher selves often show up as gods or goddesses descending from heaven or celestial realms to interact with humans and help us evolve. Take ancient Greek mythology—Zeus descending from heaven on golden rain (bit dramatic, but effective). Or Hindu mythology, where Indra, king of the gods, comes down from his celestial home with lightning bolts. Now, these stories aren't necessarily meant to be taken literally—that's not the point. They represent the idea that we're all connected to a higher power that's guiding our journey through life.

Folklore's got its own examples too. Take the Native American legend of "The Great Spider Grandmother"—an old woman who comes from another world, born out of lightning strikes. She teaches children how to weave baskets and serves as a spiritual guide. Notice a pattern here?

Carl Jung—you remember him from our shadow work chapters—once said "we can't make it alone," suggesting we need guidance from higher powers to grow and evolve. This idea shows up everywhere in stories depicting higher beings as guides and helpers on our journey. These higher powers represent our desire to connect with something greater than ourselves, our search for meaning and understanding. Through their enduring appeal, these stories continue inspiring and guiding us, helping us grow and evolve.

And honestly? This theory that mythological and folkloric beings are physical forms of our higher selves becomes pretty convincing when you consider what we've learned about the subconscious and the importance of personal growth. It aligns perfectly with Jung's concept of archetypes and the shadow—remember the anima and animus we explored? These archetypes often guide us toward self-exploration and facilitate development on all levels. By interacting with them, we can gain a deeper understanding of ourselves and our place in the world, potentially accessing our higher selves.

But then I started wondering—and stay with me here because this is where it gets a bit wild—what if these archetypal energies don't just live in our heads? What if, under certain conditions, they could somehow... leak out? Or show up in ways we can actually perceive?

I know, I know. I'm suggesting that psychological concepts might show up in the 'real' world. But remember, I'd just had invisible children playing in my bedroom and angelic music that left me vibrating like a tuning fork. So I was pretty open to possibilities that would've made rational-me laugh out loud.

Trust me, if you'd told me five years ago I'd be seriously considering whether fairies might be Jung's anima archetype having a laugh, I'd have checked what was in your tea.

Here's what was nagging me: people have reported encountering beings that seem suspiciously like personified archetypes for literally thousands of years. And I'm not talking about one or two 'crazies'—I'm talking about consistent reports across cultures and centuries. What if, when our psyche really needs to get our attention and dreams and synchronicities aren't cutting it, these archetypal forces find other ways to break through?

So if these mythological beings represent universal patterns in our psyche, how might specific patterns like the anima and animus appear? One possibility is through those mysterious beings we find in old stories—sirens, nymphs, fairies, elves. They're often portrayed as almost human, deeply connected to us, while living in their own separate world. Fairies especially have been important in how folk stories have changed over centuries, becoming popular through local legends and characters like Tinkerbell. They're frequently shown as helping humans while existing in their own magical space.

THE ORIGINS OF FAERIES IN THE DIFFERENT STATES OF CONSCIOUSNESS

Things get interesting when we step back in time, approximately 40,000 B.C.E to be exact. Cave paintings from this period might just give us a good idea of the universe and humanity's place within it. These paintings often feature humans alongside half-human, half-animal creatures with geometric imagery and landscapes. And before you think "oh, they just had vivid imaginations," consider this: anthropologist David Lewis-Williams believes these ancient artists were painting what they saw during altered states of consciousness.

Picture this: shaman-priests getting absolutely off their faces on whatever psychotropics they could find, tripping balls and then painting their visions on cave walls. Those beings that looked like fairies or demons? Maybe not just artistic license. Symbols in these cave paintings suggest that psychotropic substances, such as mushrooms, may well have been on the menu to induce visionary states. In recent years, this argument has gained more support due to the use of natural and plant-based medicine in therapy.

Lewis-Williams found that various cultures consistently experienced similar entities in altered states. His conclusion? The faeries from historical periods might be related to those depicted in prehistoric caves, suggesting humans have been interacting with alternative realities for a bloody long time.

And get this—folklorists have been collecting these stories for centuries and found that massive numbers of rural populations still believe in faeries. These aren't just quaint bedtime stories. People report actual interactions with entities in alternate realities full of strange humanoids, with recurring symbols and motifs suggesting a world with its own rules.

Sure, fairy folklore evolved into Disney movies and moral tales. But at their core, these stories describe how humans across cultures have reported similar experiences during altered states—whether through meditation, extreme stress, illness, or ritual practices. What's fascinating isn't necessarily what people see, but the consistency of these reports across time and culture.

Now, I'm not suggesting you go full Van Gogh—knocking back absinthe and chasing green fairies through the night. Because if you do, you might just lose an ear. That's definitely not the point here. What interests me is what these consistent patterns might tell us about consciousness itself—about those liminal spaces where our normal perceptual filters might work differently.

CLAIRVOYANCE AND THE MEMORY OF NATURE

During the early 1900s, folklorist WY Evans-Wentz went around Celtic communities and discovered something fascinating—loads of people claimed they could perceive information beyond their five senses through "clairvoyance." They called it "seer-ship" or "second-sight," and through it, they reckoned they could communicate with faeries and access alternate realities filled with nature spirits and mystical visions.

But here's the interesting part—Evans-Wentz noticed these abilities were declining because of technology and modernization. Enter the Theosophical Society in 1875, trying to bring these supernatural beliefs into mainstream culture. Their main tool? Clairvoyance.

Austrian Theosophist Rudolf Steiner took it further. He believed clairvoyants had to transform their passive thoughts into something more dynamic to access what he called the 'Supersensible World'—a realm supposedly inhabited by elemental beings who looked after landscapes, plants, and vegetation growth.

Okay, I need to pause here because I can hear how this sounds. "Supersensible World"? I know this sounds like Doc Brown explaining the flux capacitor while Marty stares at him like he's crazy. "You need 1.21 gigawatts to access the Supersensible World, Marty!" But remember, Doc looked like a complete crackpot right up until that DeLorean hit 88 miles per hour. Sometimes the maddest-sounding ideas are just waiting for the right conditions to prove themselves real. So here we are.

Now, Steiner thought these elemental beings—mythical creatures associated with earth, air, fire, and water—could use clairvoyance to cross between worlds. He reckoned humans had this ancient clairvoyant ability too, but we'd lost it through "spiritual decline" (cheery thought). According to him, we could get it back through spiritual practices like meditation or prayer.

Obviously, mainstream science thinks this is all bollocks. But here's what interests me: the consistency of these reports across cultures and time periods. Either humans are remarkably consistent in their delusions, or there's something here worth exploring.

Now, these elemental beings aren't just random fairy tale creatures.

They're mythical entities associated with the elements of nature—earth, air, fire, and water. Think gnomes for earth, sylphs for air, salamanders for fire, undines for water. They're often shown as having the ability to control and manipulate natural forces, connected to the physical world in ways that let them shape the environment. In many traditions, they're seen as powerful and wise beings who can bring blessings or curses upon those who encounter them.

Steiner believed these beings possessed an innate ability to see and understand the spiritual world, using this ability to communicate with humans and other beings on a higher plane of existence. But here's where it gets interesting—he argued that we humans have this same ancient clairvoyant ability. We've just lost it, largely forgotten it in modern times. According to him, this loss was the result of a general spiritual decline in the world. (Bit depressing, that.)

The good news? Steiner believed we could get this ability back through spiritual practices and disciplines. Some people believe the Supersensible world can be accessed through meditation, prayer, or special gifts.

Obviously, mainstream science thinks this is all bollocks. The existence of the Supersensible world and these abilities aren't generally accepted as scientific fact—they're considered matters of belief and interpretation. But here's what interests me: the consistency of these reports across cultures and time periods. Either humans are remarkably consistent in their delusions, or there's something here worth exploring.

And after my Sedona experiences, I'm leaning toward the "something worth exploring" camp. When you've felt your body vibrating at impossible frequencies while angelic music plays, suddenly elemental beings don't seem quite so far-fetched.

Then there's biologist Rupert Sheldrake, who really threw the cat among the pigeons with his theory of 'morphogenic fields' or 'the memory of nature.' Now, as a biologist, Sheldrake isn't denying genetics or DNA— he's proposing something additional, something that would work alongside our regular biological inheritance.

His theory? That there are invisible, non-material fields that somehow influence how things take form and behave. According to Sheldrake, every species has its own information field containing patterns from all previous generations—not encoded in DNA, but existing in some kind of field that connects all members of a species across time and space.

Think about his famous crystallization example: supposedly, once a new chemical compound crystallizes for the first time anywhere in the world, it becomes easier to crystallize everywhere else—even in completely sealed labs with no physical connection. No DNA involved, no genetic transmission. Just some mysterious field effect.

He even extended this beyond biology—to proteins, crystals, atoms. In his view, once something happens enough times, it creates a kind of groove in reality that makes it easier to happen again. But here's an interesting twist—these grooves aren't permanent. Without continued use, patterns can fade from the field, like forgotten cultural practices or lost abilities. This might explain why some ancient knowledge seems genuinely lost, not just hidden. It also might explain why myths and mystical experiences show similar patterns across cultures that never had contact. Not through shared DNA, but through some kind of connection we don't understand.

Now, I need to be clear here—this is NOT the same as the epigenetic inheritance we talked about in Part 1. That's proven science where trauma and experiences create actual, measurable changes in how genes are expressed. Sheldrake's talking about something completely different and, frankly, way more controversial.

But here's why I'm even bringing it up: epigenetics already shattered our old ideas about inheritance. We used to think DNA was destiny, that genes were fixed. Then we discovered experiences could switch genes on and off, that your grandmother's famine could literally affect your metabolism. If inheritance turned out to be that much weirder than we thought, who's to say it stops there?

I'm not saying morphic fields are real. Most scientists think Sheldrake's completely off his rocker. But after Sedona, after experiences that didn't fit any scientific model I knew, I've become more curious about the edges of what we think is possible.

The wild thing is, Sheldrake isn't the only one suggesting information might travel through non-physical channels. Jung had his collective unconscious—that vast repository containing all religious, spiritual, and mythological experiences of humanity. Remember from Chapter 4 when we explored how Jung believed these manifest in dreams as archetypes? Different framework, same basic idea: that we're connected through some layer deeper than physical inheritance.

And from Eastern spirituality, we get the Akashic Records—supposedly containing the entire history of the universe, accessible through prayer or meditation. It's like the ultimate cosmic hard drive, if you believe in that sort of thing. Again, same concept: information existing in some field beyond the physical.

What fascinates me is how these different traditions—scientific rebels like Sheldrake, psychologists like Jung, ancient Eastern mystics—all point toward the same possibility. That consciousness and information might travel through channels we can't see or measure. That myths, folklore, and yes, even alien encounters showing up with similar patterns across disconnected cultures might not be coincidence but some kind of connection we don't understand.

The point isn't to convince you that morphic fields exist. It's to recognize that every time science advances, we discover reality is stranger than we imagined. Radio waves were "impossible" until they weren't. Quantum entanglement was "spooky action at a distance" until it became accepted physics. Maybe consciousness and information travel in ways we simply haven't figured out how to measure yet.

For those of us navigating experiences that don't fit current models—whether that's synchronicities, mystical states, or whatever the hell happened to me in Sedona—maybe the lesson is to hold our maps lightly. Science is still catching up to consciousness. In the meantime, we can be curious rather than dismissive, open rather than certain.

Mental? Absolutely. But after everything we've explored in this book, is it any more mental than the proven fact that your ancestors' trauma lives in your cells? Or that your unconscious is populated by universal archetypes? Or that energy centers mapped by ancient yogis correspond to psychological development stages mapped by modern psychologists?

CELLULAR CONSCIOUSNESS: THE INTELLIGENCE WITHIN

Bear with me here, because we're about to take another step into the weird —though honestly, it's nothing compared to what's coming later in this chapter. If you thought morphic fields were out there, wait until we get to the bit about interdimensional beings possibly trying to nurse hybrid babies. (I'm joking. Sort of. Actually, disturbingly, that's not even that far off. But I'm getting ahead of myself.)

While Sheldrake's theory of morphogenic fields offers a fascinating perspective on how information travels through nature, I found myself wondering about something even closer to home: What about the consciousness within our own bodies, at the cellular level?

This question hit me during another one of those 3 AM existential crisis moments. If these morphic fields connect entire species across time and space, carrying accumulated wisdom through generations, then what about the trillions of cells in my own body? Might they have their own field, their own form of intelligence and awareness?

Now, I know this sounds a bit out there. But trust me, cellular consciousness is practically mainstream science compared to where we're headed.

Think about it. Our bodies do countless things without our conscious input—healing cuts, fighting off infections, keeping everything running smoothly. Our immune systems recognize threats we can't even perceive. If we had to consciously manage all that, we'd be dead in minutes. These processes aren't just happening to us; they're happening as us, yet completely independent of our conscious control. It's like discovering you've been sharing your flat with a brilliant roommate who's been quietly maintaining everything while you were oblivious!

Lucky for me, I'd just started dating someone studying molecular and cell biology (now my wife), which gave her a unique perspective on my metaphysical musings. As we got to know each other on a more meaningful level, our conversations naturally drifted into cellular consciousness (because apparently that's my idea of romance). Where I saw mysterious cellular intelligence, she could explain the precise biochemical pathways —yet rather than dismissing my more expansive interpretations, she helped me find the fascinating middle ground where science and spirituality meet.

"Your cells aren't just following instructions," she once said after one of my philosophical rambles. "They're making complex decisions constantly based on their environment." Coming from someone who spent their days peering at cells through microscopes, that carried weight.

This raises some proper head-scratchers: If our cells have this wisdom, why do we feel so disconnected from it? Maybe our ego acts like a filter, limiting our direct experience of cellular intelligence. Perhaps our cells, in their wisdom, work quietly in the background while we stumble around thinking we're in charge.

I've wondered if there might be ways to engage with this cellular intelligence. Could dreams, meditation, or other altered states allow us to tap into the perspective of our cells? It reminds me of trying to learn a foreign language—cellular consciousness likely doesn't speak in words but in sensations, energies, and vibrations that our thinking mind struggles to translate.

Indigenous traditions often view plant medicines as tools for accessing deeper intelligence—both within and beyond ourselves. Spiritually, it's connecting with higher consciousness. Scientifically, maybe it's accessing normally filtered cellular awareness. Your cells contain your complete genetic history and operate independently of your conscious mind. In altered states, perhaps you're bypassing the filters that normally separate your awareness from this cellular wisdom.

This connects to something we explored with the crown chakra—that dissolution of boundaries between self and everything else. What if that dancing session in Mexico wasn't just me connecting to some abstract "universal consciousness" but actually tuning into the intelligence of my own cells for the first time?

This perspective also extends Sheldrake's concept beautifully. If information can be transmitted across an entire species through morphogenic fields, might there also be a field operating within our own bodies, connecting all our cells in a web of shared intelligence? And if so, might this internal field be connected to the larger fields that extend throughout nature and the cosmos?

From this perspective, our bodies become microcosms of the universe

—each cell a star in our internal galaxy, participating in a cosmic dance. The boundaries between inner and outer start dissolving. If our cells really do have consciousness, then health isn't just about not being sick—it's about having a decent relationship with the trillions of tiny collaborators keeping us alive. Makes you think twice about that third pint, doesn't it?

And speaking of vast consciousness, this brings us back to Jung's collective unconscious and those Akashic Records the Eastern traditions bang on about. Imagine having access to the entire history of the universe through meditation—like the ultimate cosmic Google.

Mind-boggling, innit?

So we've got morphic fields possibly connecting entire species, cellular consciousness doing its thing inside us, and Jung's collective unconscious storing all of human experience. But here's where it gets even weirder—what if all these invisible connections and stored memories sometimes... manifest? What if they show up in ways we can actually perceive? Which brings me to something that's going to sound completely barmy...

FAERIES AND ALIENS: SAME PHENOMENON, DIFFERENT COSTUME?

Get ready for this one, because I'm about to tell you that the scientist who helped Steven Spielberg create *Close Encounters of the Third Kind* thinks aliens might just be faeries with spacecraft. No, really.

Jacques Vallée—the French astronomer and computer scientist who inspired that film's French scientist character—dropped this bombshell in 1969, and honestly, it's been messing with people's heads ever since, including mine! Spielberg was so intrigued by Vallée's ideas that he hired him as a technical consultant. And what were those ideas? That maybe, just maybe, all those alien encounters people keep reporting are the same phenomenon that our ancestors called faerie abductions. Just with updated 'special effects'.

I know. I KNOW. Stay with me here.

Vallée isn't some random conspiracy theorist. This is a proper scientist who worked on ARPANET (basically the internet's granddad) and has a computer science degree from Northwestern. When someone with those credentials says "I think we've been looking at this all wrong," it's worth at least hearing them out.

In his book *Passport to Magonia* (brilliant title, eh?), Vallée lays out the case in detail. Themes of folklore surrounding human abductions by faeries. There are numerous references to humans being taken away by fairies for various purposes, such as childcare, servitude to aid faerie children, and providing sexual intercourse or punishment because the faeries simply desire it. There is also a similar theme between those consistently found in the strange phenomenon of alien abductions, which have increased significantly since the 1950s.

He wasn't saying aliens are literally faeries or vice versa. He was suggesting they might be versions of the same phenomenon, adapted to whatever cultural framework the witnesses can handle. Medieval peasants saw faeries. We see aliens. Same experience, different interpretation.

Think about the similarities. Folkloric faerie abductions from centuries ago: humans taken for childcare, servitude, sex, or just because faeries fancied it. Modern alien abductions starting in the 1950s: humans taken for experiments, breeding programs, or mysterious purposes. The themes are eerily similar. Different costumes, same script?

In the 17th century, minister Robert Kirk described faeries as beings "like humans but without bodies," who could swim through air, appear and disappear at will, and carry mortals to underground spherical homes in ethereal vehicles. Now, I want you to really think about that description. Replace "faeries" with "aliens" and "underground spherical homes" with "UFOs," and you've basically got a modern alien encounter report. Same story, updated special effects. Kirk also believed that faeries were a hybrid of angels and humans, a belief that aligns with more recent alien abduction reports.

The similarities get even stranger when you dig deeper. Researchers John Mack (psychiatrist at Harvard, not exactly a quack) and David Jacobs spent years interviewing alien abductees. The stories are remarkably consistent: transport to spaceships, hybrid alien-human nurseries, traumatic experiences leading to PTSD. Just like historical faerie encounters, but with chrome and blinking lights instead of mushroom circles and moonlight.

What really makes you think, though, is how both types of encounters share the same bloody script. People report missing time—hours gone with no memory of what happened. They're taken to otherworldly locations that defy normal physics. There's often this deeply uncomfortable sexual or breeding component (yeah, I know, it's proper weird). They come back with mysterious marks or implants they can't explain. The details stay fuzzy unless they undergo hypnosis. But perhaps the most unsettling similarity? The aftermath. Whether the abductors were faeries or aliens, survivors don't just walk away with interesting stories— they're left with the kind of deep psychological scars that get diagnosed as PTSD.

The rational part of my brain is screaming as I write this. 'You're a reasonable person!' it says. 'You've read Jung! You understand psychological projection! Don't go down this rabbit hole!' But hang on—isn't the whole point that integration means holding opposites? Light AND shadow, rational AND mystical? What if the real growth happens when we, modern heroes, stop trying to force every experience into neat boxes labeled 'real' or 'imaginary' and instead ask what these encounters—whatever they are—are trying to teach us?

The idea of being whisked away to nurse alien-faerie hybrid babies is simultaneously terrifying and absurd. What is this, *Mary Poppins* meets *The X-Files*? Actually, scratch that—it's basically *Labyrinth*. You know, that bonkers David Bowie film where goblins steal babies and nothing makes sense but somehow it all feels weirdly meaningful? That's essentially what we're talking about here—otherworldly beings taking humans (often children) to their realm for mysterious purposes, playing by rules we don't understand.

Come to think of it, *Labyrinth* might be the most accurate documentary about faerie encounters ever made. Bowie's Goblin King with his reality-bending powers, stealing human babies, existing in a realm where time works differently... Jim Henson might have been onto something.

Here's what really gets me: if these are the same phenomenon appearing in different cultural costumes, what does that say about the nature of reality? Are these experiences showing us that consciousness is far stranger than our materialist understanding allows? Or am I just desperately trying to make sense of my Sedona experience by grasping at interdimensional straws?

The most unsettling part isn't the possibility that faeries and aliens might be real. It's the possibility that our entire understanding of what's "real" might be kindergarten-level compared to what's actually going on. And once that door opens in your mind... well, good luck closing it.

————

CHAPTER 6 SUMMARY

Right, quick recap of what just happened in Chapter 6: I shared my bizarre experiences while living in Sedona—invisible children playing at dawn, angelic music that left my teeth chattering like a jackhammer, and the growing sense that Sedona's famous vortexes might have amplified it all. This sent me investigating whether these weren't just brain glitches but glimpses of consciousness operating beyond normal boundaries. We explored how humans have always sensed 'something more,' from 40,000-year-old cave paintings to modern alien encounters. Dug into cellular consciousness, morphic fields, and Jung's archetypes possibly manifesting in perceivable ways. Oh, and Jacques Vallée thinks aliens are just faeries with updated special effects.

KEY LEARNINGS:

- Cave paintings from 40,000 BCE might document actual visions from altered states
- Folklore across cultures consistently reports similar entities and experiences
- Cellular consciousness operates independently of our aware mind
- Faeries and aliens share suspiciously similar abduction scripts across centuries

KEY TAKEAWAYS:

- Sleep paralysis might be a doorway to other states, not just a medical glitch

- Your cells might be having experiences your conscious mind can't access
- Mythological beings could be archetypal forces manifesting in perceivable forms
- Same phenomenon, different cultural costume (faeries then, aliens now)

Reflective Question: What if those strange experiences you've dismissed weren't malfunctions but glimpses of consciousness operating beyond its normal boundaries?

WHAT ARE THESE THINGS PEOPLE KEEP SEEING?

R ight then. We've covered invisible children, angelic music, vibrating teeth, and the possibility that my cells might be smarter than I am. Now comes the bit where we try to make sense of it all. Look, if Vallée's suggestion that faeries and aliens might be the same phenomenon is right—if what terrified medieval peasants in the woods and what terrifies modern Americans in the desert are somehow connected—then what the hell are they?

David Luke—a British psychologist who's made a career out of studying the strange things people experience in altered states (and God bless him for it)—offers three possible interpretations:

1. They're hallucinations: our brains creating something from nothing when they can't process what's happening, shaped by our culture.
2. They're psychological projections: emerging from the depths of our own minds—both personal and collective.
3. They're interdimensional visitors: actual entities from another reality.

Let me walk you through each possibility, because after almost vibrating out of my body to angelic music, I'm not exactly in a position to rule anything out.

INTERPRETATION 1: HALLUCINATIONS SHAPED BY OUR CULTURE

From the good old rational Western perspective, all these encounters might just be our brains having a bit of a moment. Hallucinations are perceptions that occur in the absence of an external stimulus, and can involve any of the senses, including seeing, hearing, feeling, tasting, or smelling things that are not actually present.

Let's be honest—nobody's caught a fairy in a jar or got an alien to pose for a selfie. Instead, people who claim to have had such experiences often report only seeing or hearing things, which can be explained as hallucinations.

There are many reasons why hallucinations may occur, even without recreational drugs. Mental and physical illness, sleep deprivation, and certain medications can all cause hallucinations. Plus, extreme stress or trauma can lead to hallucinations, as the brain may attempt to cope with overwhelming stimuli by creating a more manageable reality.

Take Charles Bonnet syndrome, where people with vision loss experience vivid visual hallucinations. This suggests that the brain, needing to make sense of the lack of visual input it is receiving, creates its own images to fill in the gaps. Bit like when I'm trying to see in the dark and suddenly that coat on the chair looks like a lurking intruder.

In the case of fairies and aliens, the brain might attempt to make sense of certain experiences that it can't parse by creating an interpretation that matches cultural views and beliefs. When the brain can't process its surroundings, it might whip up an explanation that makes sense within cultural beliefs.

Still with me? Let me give you a concrete example.

Picture this: You're walking through the woods at dusk, and you see a strange glowing light moving between the trees. Your brain goes into overdrive trying to file this under something familiar. A plane? Helicopter? Maybe a drone? But as you watch, you realize it's not behaving like any of those things—it's moving in ways that violate everything you know about normal aircraft.

Now your brain gets proper desperate. It NEEDS an explanation, any explanation, even if it means reaching for something completely unrealistic. And this is where culture steps in to save the day (or completely mess with your head). Your panicking brain grabs whatever supernatural explanation is culturally mainstream at the moment.

Rural Ireland, 1823? "Definitely a will-o'-the-wisp fairy!" Victorian London, 1890? "Ghost of a murdered child!" America, 1952? "Flying saucer from Mars!" Today, 2025? "Interdimensional being from the multiverse!"

Same unexplainable light. Same confused and desperate brain. Completely different interpretations based on whatever mythology is popular in your culture.

There's also pareidolia—a completely different mechanism where the brain sees patterns that aren't actually there. Unlike the desperate cultural interpretation of genuinely weird phenomena, pareidolia is when perfectly normal things get misidentified. Someone obsessed with extraterrestrial life might see an ordinary meteor and think "alien spacecraft!" Someone into fairies might see a bird's movement and go "fairy!" In these cases, there's nothing mysterious to explain—just our pattern-seeking brains getting carried away.

Mass hysteria adds another layer. Get a group of people sharing the same beliefs and fears, and suddenly everyone's seeing the same things. The Salem witch trials weren't just about political persecution—people genuinely believed they were seeing witches and experiencing demonic possession. Shared cultural beliefs created shared hallucinations.

Consider ayahuasca ceremonies. People who take this psychoactive brew report remarkably similar visions of entities—but notably, the entities often match their cultural expectations. Westerners see aliens or machine elves. Indigenous users see jungle spirits and ancestors. Same brew, different cultural filing system.

So from this perspective, all these encounters—faeries, aliens, angels, whatever—might just be our brains doing their desperate best to make sense of confusing input, heavily filtered through whatever explanatory framework is culturally available. It's a powerful explanation for how a shared belief can create a shared hallucination. But it doesn't fully explain why these specific patterns and figures show up in the first place, which brings us to an even deeper possibility.

INTERPRETATION 2: PSYCHOLOGICAL PROJECTIONS OF OUR UNCONSCIOUS

More and more thinkers, from quantum physicists to philosophers, are challenging the idea that the brain creates consciousness. What if, instead, it acts as a receiver or a filter? In this model, consciousness is fundamental, and our brains tune into a specific frequency we call "normal reality." Altered states, then, aren't malfunctions; they're the result of the brain changing channels, allowing us to access aspects of consciousness we normally can't perceive.

This is where Luke's second interpretation comes in, suggesting these entities are projections from the psyche. But we can break this down even further.

First, the Personal.

I've been thinking about my Sedona experiences through this lens. Those children's voices at dawn—what if they were my repressed inner child finally getting my attention? The angelic music that turned terrifying —perhaps my psyche showing me both the beauty and the horror of awakening? The vibrations that felt like they'd pull me apart—maybe that was my ego literally shaking as it confronted forces beyond its control.

This interpretation explains why these experiences often feel so intensely personal and transformative. A random hallucination wouldn't change your life, but a dramatic intervention staged by your own unconscious? That's going to hit different.

I don't know about you, but there's something oddly reassuring about this, isn't there? That terrifying entity that showed up in your bedroom at 3 AM? Just a part of you desperately trying to get your attention. Still scary as hell in the moment, but at least it's not some external demon with its own agenda. It's more like your psyche staging a dramatic intervention because you wouldn't listen to the gentle nudges.

But this is where it gets bigger, moving beyond our personal baggage and into a realm we've discussed before: the collective unconscious.

If an altered state can open a door to our personal psychic material, what happens when it throws open the gates to that deeper, shared reservoir of human experience? What if these entities are the contents of the collective unconscious, breaking through?

Suddenly, the baffling consistency of these encounters across cultures and millennia makes perfect sense. The entities aren't random figments; they are archetypes taking the stage.

The Trickster, the Wise Old Guide, the Shadow, the Divine Child— these universal patterns that we've discussed are now showing up in costume. In one era, they dress as fairies. In another, as aliens or angels. The underlying form is the same archetypal energy, just filtered through a different cultural lens. This also connects to ideas like Rupert Sheldrake's morphic fields—the notion of shared, collective patterns of memory and information.

This neatly solves a major problem with the pure hallucination theory. Why would random brain misfires create such consistent, meaningful experiences? They probably wouldn't. But if we're tapping into the fundamental, archetypal structures of the human psyche, it's exactly what we'd expect.

This reframes the entire question. The entity isn't just my projection; it's our projection. It's a message not just from my unconscious, but from the unconscious.

So, does it matter if they're "real" in the external sense? If an encounter with a "Machine Elf" is actually an encounter with a universal archetype that triggers genuine psychological integration, it is functionally real. It's the human psyche itself—in all its collective, ancient wisdom—staging an intervention for the good of your soul.

INTERPRETATION 3: INTERDIMENSIONAL VISITORS

Right then. Before we even get started on this next one, let's address the elephant in the room. "But what about group sightings?" I hear you say.

How can a whole gaggle of people, from a family on a road trip to an entire village, see the exact same, inexplicable thing at the exact same time? Doesn't that blow a rather large hole in the nice, tidy 'it's all in your head' theories?

It's a bloody good question. And while, yes, you can wave some of it away with 'mass hysteria', there are other cases where that explanation feels stretched thinner than a cheap pair of tights. The Phoenix Lights, for example. Thousands of people. Dozens of miles apart.

It's this very problem—the sheer, stubborn reality of credible mass sightings—that forces our hand. It pushes us past metaphors and projections and makes us confront Luke's third and, to be fair, most proper bonkers interpretation: these beings are real, independent entities from a higher dimension that we can only perceive under special circumstances.

The theory goes like this: we experience the world in three spatial dimensions. Our brains are perfectly designed for 3D stuff, like trying to catch a dropped piece of toast before it hits the floor, butter-side down. But there was never an evolutionary need to perceive a fourth spatial dimension, so our brains simply aren't wired for it. We're effectively blind to it.

Right, to get our heads around this without them actually exploding, let's use the classic "Flatland" analogy.

Imagine a universe that's just a flat sheet of paper. The residents, the Flatlanders, are two-dimensional shapes. They have length and width, but no concept of "up." To them, we'd be proper gods, wouldn't we? We could see inside their locked houses. We could lift a Flatlander out of their "inescapable" prison. If we stuck one of our fingers through their paper universe, what would they see? A mysterious circle of flesh that appears from nowhere, changes shape, and then vanishes. A miracle.

Now, flip it. What if we're the Flatlanders?

If a four-dimensional being were to visit our 3D universe, it would seem to have god-like powers. It could appear and disappear at will. It could walk through solid walls. If it stuck its 4D "finger" into our reality, we'd see a bizarre, wobbly blob of what-have-you that materializes out of thin air. Sound a bit familiar? Thought it might.

Plato had another way of thinking about this with his Allegory of the Cave. He imagined prisoners who could only see shadows on a wall, believing them to be reality. What if our entire three-dimensional reality is just the damp wall of Plato's cave? And what if the fairies, aliens, and angels are simply the "shadows" cast on our wall by beings moving through a fourth dimension just outside our perception?

This also opens up another fascinating possibility about how these encounters happen. What if the visits aren't always random? It's hard to ignore that many of these strange events happen around sites of collective, focused intent—group prayers, sacred ceremonies, mass meditations, or group plant medicine journeys. What if, through that collective focus, we are essentially ringing a dinner bell for the fourth dimension? Or at least putting out a welcome mat? It suggests that maybe, just maybe, this isn't a one-way street. They can pop in unannounced, but perhaps, under the right conditions, we can also invite them over for a chat.

So in this final interpretation, the entities aren't just functionally real projections of our psyche. They are actually real. Our brain might still frantically flick through its archetypal filing system to label the experience 'angel' or 'alien,' but the thing itself exists independently of us, paying us a visit from next door, dimensionally speaking.

Look, maybe the real answer is that it doesn't matter which interpretation is "right." Maybe consciousness is weird enough to be all three—hallucination, projection, AND interdimensional weirdness—depending on the day. What I do know is that these experiences seem to love certain environments. There's a pattern to where the strange stuff happens, and it's not random.

VAST OPEN SPACES: NATURE'S PROJECTION SCREEN

Okay, so we've covered hallucinations, psychological projections, and the possibility that we're all Flatlanders being poked by fourth-dimensional fingers. But closing the loop on my Sedona experience with its vortexes and late-night vibrations, there's one final thing to touch on: why do these experiences seem to happen more in certain places?

Think about it. Moses didn't get his burning bush in downtown Jerusalem. Buddha didn't find enlightenment in a shopping center. And modern UFO sightings? They love a good stretch of empty desert highway. There's something about vast, open spaces that seems to invite the weird in.

After my Sedona experiences, I started noticing this pattern everywhere. These expansive, wild places—deserts, forests, oceans—they've always been seen as supernatural hotspots inspiring awe, wonder, and a sense of the divine. From ancient civilizations treating them as sacred to modern people having "spiritual awakenings" or alien encounters, there's a consistency here that's hard to ignore.

In Jungian psychology, these vast expanses serve as perfect projection screens for our unconscious material. When you're standing in the middle of nowhere, with no human constructions to anchor your everyday consciousness, something shifts. Your psyche suddenly has room to breathe—and sometimes, to manifest in ways that would be impossible in the confines of civilization.

It's like our consciousness needs space to properly unfold. Jung reckoned that these unknown regions become canvases where we can project our deepest unconscious material—desires, fears, archetypal energies that have no outlet in normal life.

This actually makes sense when you think about it. In a city, your consciousness is constantly bouncing off walls, both literal and metaphorical. But out in true vastness? That's where things can get really odd.

Or there's the universal Temptress of the Sea or the Siren on the Shore. That seductive archetype who appears in every maritime culture. Beautiful, enticing, singing songs that lure sailors to their doom. She represents everything alluring and terrifying about the unknown depths. Disney turned her into Ursula, which, when you give it some thought, is just a modern expression of the same ancient archetype—dangerous feminine power from the deep.

And Pan, the Greek god of wild places? He literally gave us the word "panic"—that primal terror people feel in wilderness that can make them run blindly until they collapse. The slightest unexpected sound in his domain could trigger overwhelming fear. But treat his sacred spaces with respect, and he'd bless you with nature's abundance.

Notice how these beings are always tied to specific environments? You don't get sea sirens in the desert or wild women of the suburbs. It's like each type of vast space has its own particular flavor of strange.

Here's something I thought a lot about: what happens to human consciousness when it's constantly confined? In cities, where everything is walls and boundaries and human-made structures, our consciousness literally has nowhere to go. It's constantly being reflected back at us.

The bombardment of stimuli, the lack of horizon, the absence of true darkness or silence—it creates what I can only describe as psychic constipation. Our consciousness, unable to project outward into vastness, turns inward in ways that might not be healthy.

Is it any wonder then, that anxiety and depression rates are often higher in cities? Or that people—and to be honest, I'm one of them—pay thousands of dollars for wellness retreats in nature just to feel "normal" again? (Guilty). We're beings designed for occasional encounters with the infinite, stuck in boxes stacked on boxes.

Who knows, this might just explain why I initially wanted to flee Sedona for a bigger city. Part of me knew that staying in that vast desert meant I couldn't hide from whatever was trying to emerge. Cities let us avoid ourselves. Deserts don't.

The irony? When I finally did escape Sedona for the "safety" of city life, I had the most difficult few months of my life. As if leaving that vast, strange space created some kind of psychic whiplash. Make of that what you will.

And so looking at my Sedona experiences through this lens, things start making a different kind of sense. Sedona sits in the middle of a red rock desert—massive vistas, ancient geological formations, the kind of silence you can actually hear. It's exactly the type of environment where consciousness might... stretch out a bit.

Those children's voices at dawn? In a city, my brain would have immediately filed that under "kids from next door" and moved on. But in that vast desert silence, with no easy explanation available, my consciousness had to grapple with it differently.

The angelic music and vibrations? Try having that experience in a studio flat with neighbors banging on the walls. The environment itself seemed to allow—maybe even invite—experiences that wouldn't have been possible elsewhere.

And let's not forget Sedona's reputation for "vortexes". Whether you believe in swirling energy centers or not, there's something about that landscape that has been affecting people for centuries. The Native Americans considered it sacred long before new-age shops started selling crystal pyramids.

And speaking of the Native Americans, Indigenous cultures have always understood something we've forgotten: not all space is the same. Some places are thin, where the veil between ordinary reality and... whatever else... is barely there at all. Like tissue paper instead of a brick wall. These cultures don't see the supernatural as separate from nature—they see certain natural places as inherently more connected to the mystery.

We modern folks have largely lost this understanding. We treat all space as real estate, as resources, as Instagram backdrops. But what if some spaces really are different? What if certain environments actually do create conditions for experiences that are impossible elsewhere?

This isn't just about belief or suggestion. There's something about the actual physical qualities of these spaces—the vastness, the silence, the absence of human electromagnetic interference, the geological formations —that might create conditions where consciousness behaves differently.

When you start looking, this pattern is everywhere: Aboriginal Australians going walkabout in the outback for spiritual visions, Native American vision quests in wilderness, Christian mystics retreating to desert caves, modern alien encounters on lonely highways. Hell, even Burning Man happens in a desert—coincidence? I think not. It's like humanity has always known: if you want to encounter the mysterious, the transformative, the weird—you go to the wild places. You find somewhere vast enough to hold whatever needs to emerge.

CONSCIOUSNESS NEEDS ROOM TO ROAM

What I'm starting to understand is that consciousness might be like water —it takes the shape of its container. In small, rigid containers (cities, buildings, structured lives), it stays small and rigid. But give it a vast space, and it expands to fill it, sometimes in ways that surprise us.

Those beings people encounter in wild places—whether we call them faeries, aliens, or psychological projections—they seem to emerge specifically where consciousness has room to show up as them. It's not that these places are "magical" in some supernatural sense. It's that they provide the conditions where the magic that's always potential can become actual.

And here's something Jung understood that we've largely forgotten: consciousness needs to project itself somewhere. When it can't project outward in healthy ways—through creative expression, spiritual practice, or encounters with vast nature—it turns inward and gets twisted. Those projections still happen, but now they're aimed at other people, or they become anxiety loops, or they show up as all sorts of psychological knots.

Think about it. In vast spaces, people naturally find themselves praying, meditating, creating art, or just sitting in profound contemplation. Nobody needs to tell them to do this—it happens spontaneously. The environment itself seems to invite these healthy forms of projection. Your consciousness, finally given room to breathe, naturally flows into prayer, creative expression, or deep introspection.

But in confined spaces? Those same energies that might have become a vision quest or a profound insight instead become road rage, Twitter arguments, or that fun thing where you lie awake at night replaying every embarrassing moment from the last decade. The energy has to go somewhere.

Have you ever had a profound or inexplicable experience in a vast open space? How did it change your perspective or sense of self?

I realize Sedona wasn't just showing me that consciousness is stranger than we think—it was preparing me for something even more profound. What happens when we stop experiencing consciousness as isolated individuals and start tapping into something collective? That's where we're headed next.

BEYOND THE VEIL: WHEN THE UNCONSCIOUS MAKES ITSELF KNOWN

Alright, hold on to your hats, because if you thought invisible children and interdimensional fingers were unbelievable, we're about to crank the weird dial up to eleven. And I mean proper off-the-charts, question-your-sanity, what-the-actual-hell-just-happened levels of strange.

Remember how I mentioned things went sideways when I left Sedona? Well, that was putting it mildly.

The moment I escaped that red rock vortex madness for the "safety" of city life, everything went catastrophically wrong. And I mean catastrophically. It was like leaving Sedona had triggered some kind of cosmic domino effect. The relationship I was in? Let's just say it spiraled into dark territory. Quite simply, the kind of experiences that turn your world upside down.

For months after, I stumbled around in this fog, traumatized and desperately trying to piece together who I was after everything had shattered. I was functioning on the outside—going through the motions—but inside? Complete wreckage. The irony wasn't lost on me: I'd run from Sedona's supernatural weirdness only to find myself in a very real, very human horror show that made vibrating teeth and angelic music seem quaint by comparison.

So when one of my mentors—seeing me barely holding it together—suggested I attend an intensive self-discovery retreat in the Appalachian mountains, I was simultaneously desperate and skeptical. Another bloody retreat? But what else was I going to do? I'd just turned 30, I was drowning in trauma, stuck in what Campbell would call the "Ordinary World" (though mine felt more like purgatory), and clearly, my strategy of "white-knuckle it through" wasn't working.

Classic "refusal of the call," eh? Part of me wanted transformation; part of me wanted to hide under the duvet forever. But eventually, desperation won out, and I found myself driving up a mountain, wondering what fresh hell I'd signed up for this time.

The retreat location itself was stunning—nestled among lush green mountains that reminded me of home in the UK but with an energy that felt... different. Alive. Like the land itself was watching. I felt it immediately when I arrived—this powerful frequency, like the mountain was vibrating at a pitch just beyond normal perception. It reminded me of Sedona's energy but older, deeper. More patient.

The program? Brutal. A week-long descent into truth. No gentle meditation circles here. We're talking intense men's councils where every mask got ripped away, physical challenges that pushed us past our breaking points, ceremonies that connected us to something primal. The structure was deliberate—a gradual alignment process that I only understood in retrospect. Within hours, my carefully maintained British emotional restraint was in tatters.

Day by day, we were being tuned like instruments. The vulnerable sharing in council created a connection between us. Facing our deepest fears together—both personal shadows and collective wounds—seemed to generate a particular frequency. With each breakthrough, each moment of authentic connection, each ceremony under the stars, we were unconsciously matching ourselves to the mountain's vibration.

The group sessions were savage in their honesty. Picture this: men from every walk of life, all of us raw and exposed, sharing traumas we'd never spoken aloud. My usual deflection tactics—humor, intellectualizing, that trusty British stiff upper lip—useless. But something magical happened in that brutal transparency. We weren't just processing individually; we were creating a collective field of transformation.

By mid-week, the synchronicities were off the charts. Dreams that multiple men shared. Insights that arose simultaneously in different conversations. Nature itself seemed to be participating—eagles circling during breakthrough moments, weather shifting with our emotional states. It was like we were gradually being woven into the mountain's consciousness.

The ceremonies deepened this connection. Ancient practices, like fire walking, that initially felt foreign began to feel right in our bones. We were accessing something cellular, something that knew these rhythms from long before our individual births. Light and dark, masculine and feminine, earth and sky—we were being initiated into polarities and finding the balance point between them.

Here's what I understand now that I couldn't grasp then: we were systematically creating the exact conditions we explored earlier in this chapter. A vast natural space? Check. Collective intention focused through ceremony? Check. Individual consciousness cracked open through intensive shadow work? Check. The gradual thinning of barriers between self and other, between human and nature, between ordinary and non-ordinary reality? Absolutely check.

By the final night, after a week of this intensity, something had fundamentally shifted. Those filters we talked about—the ones that normally keep our cellular intelligence and the collective unconscious at bay? They weren't just thin; they were gossamer. The boundary between my individual consciousness and the group's collective field had become porous. And perhaps most significantly, we'd spent seven days unconsciously tuning ourselves to match the mountain's frequency.

It's like the mountain had been waiting. Testing us. Seeing if we could drop our modern mental noise enough to hear its ancient song. And finally, on that last night, we were ready. Or rather, we were finally vibrating at the right frequency to receive what it had been broadcasting all along.

Lying in my tent, physically exhausted but energetically alive from the week's journey, I noticed the wind picking up. This wasn't your gentle mountain breeze—it built progressively into something that felt conscious, deliberate, personal. The sound morphed from a howl into something more unsettling: whispers circling my tent, footsteps crunching on ground that should've been empty, and underneath it all, a rhythmic chanting that made every hair on my body stand at attention.

Then—and I swear on everything I hold dear this actually happened— my tent started shaking violently, like a bunch of people were grabbing it from all sides, aggressively trying to tear it apart. Before I could even process what was happening, the entire bloody structure with me inside rose several feet into the air before crashing back down with a thud that rattled every bone in my body.

I'm not ashamed to admit I completely lost it. 'HELP! HELP!' I screamed, then as the terror really hit: 'What the FUCK is going on?! What the FUCK!' Eventually I heard tent zippers open and a voice nearby eventually called out, "Everything's okay, Lee... there's nobody there," clearly torn between concern for me and confusion at the scene.

When I finally found the balls to unzip the tent and look outside, what I found was more disturbing than any physical threat could've been: absolutely nothing. My tent sat exactly where I'd pitched it. The wind? Gone. Just perfect mountain stillness under a blanket of stars. No footprints. No disturbance. Nothing.

I spent the rest of that night wide awake, heart still racing, trying to process what had just happened. The physical sensations had been so real —the lifting, the wind, the voices. Yet there was absolutely no evidence. Just me and my apparently stationary tent under a calm mountain sky.

In the years since, I've turned this experience over in my mind count- less times.

Was someone playing an elaborate prank? Some twisted initiation? I spent hours convinced the other men were in on it, but their genuine panic suggested otherwise.

Considering everything we've explored in this chapter so far, what the hell do I make of this?

Was it a hallucination brought on by exhaustion and intensive psychological work? My brain creating something from nothing because it couldn't process the intensity of the week? And if so, why the chanting and drumming? Given the location—ancient Native American land— and the ceremonies we'd been doing all week, had my brain simply grabbed the most culturally appropriate soundtrack for a mystical experience?

Or was it my psyche, raw from trauma and a week of intensive work, simply staging its own intervention? The Trickster archetype Jung wrote about, finally the perfect moment to shatter my rigid worldview? After all the shadow work and vulnerability, maybe my unconscious needed to stage its own dramatic intervention?

Might it have been a collective psychological projection like Luke talked about? That we'd spent a week unconsciously creating the perfect conditions for something to appear? A group of men, barriers down, psyches cracked open, in a vast mountain space where consciousness has room to project? Maybe, just maybe, we'd accidentally created what physicists call "coherence"—individual waves aligning into something bigger?

Or—and this is where it gets proper weird—was it actually one of those interdimensional visitors he described? Some fourth-dimensional being having a laugh at my expense? A ghost? Some entity that could only break through because we'd spent a week accidentally creating the perfect conditions? A group of men, barriers down, psyches cracked open, in a vast mountain space where the veil was already thin?

Honestly? I lean toward this being the Trickster archetype from my own psyche making itself known in the most dramatic way possible. The psychological projection theory just makes the most sense to me. After months of trauma, a week of intensive work, in that charged mountain environment—the Trickster finally had the perfect opportunity to shatter my rigid worldview. My psyche staging a visceral demonstration that reality isn't as fixed as I thought.

Jung described the Trickster as the archetype that disrupts our neat categories precisely when we need it most. And there I was, literally lifted out of my grounded reality and dropped back into it. The perfect metaphor for what had been happening all week—being lifted out of ordinary consciousness and returned, changed.

But here's what really gets me: whether this was my personal unconscious projecting, some collective field we'd created, or something stranger still—it worked. Whatever lifted that tent lifted something in me too. Cracked open a door that's never quite closed since.

The week of ceremony and shadow work had thinned every barrier I had. Maybe thin enough that inner became outer for a moment? Maybe thin enough that the archetypal could manifest in ways that defied rational explanation? I don't know. But here's the thing—I'm at peace with not knowing. Well, mostly at peace. The unknown used to terrify me, but now I see it as territory to explore, an opportunity to grow within the mystery rather than solve it.

What I do know is this: after months trapped in very real human darkness, I needed something completely outside normal parameters to remind me that mystery still exists. That not everything can be explained, categorized, or controlled. Sometimes the best you can do is surrender to the experience and let it change you.

The trickster taught me that growth sometimes requires accepting that we don't have all the answers. That the universe—or our own psyche—might be far stranger than we imagine. Campbell's Hero's Journey suddenly made visceral sense: sometimes you need to be literally shaken out of ordinary reality to see how much bigger everything really is.

Whether that's terrifying or liberating probably depends on how tightly you're gripping your current worldview. Mine? Let's just say my grip has gotten a lot looser since that tent took flight. It's in navigating this liminal space, where our explanations falter and our certainties dissolve, that we're forced to grow.

The mystery itself becomes the teacher. And maybe that's the most essential part of the modern Hero's Journey—not conquering the unknown, but learning to dance with it.

In the following sections, we'll explore how humans have intentionally sought these consciousness-expanding experiences throughout history. But for now, I'll just say this: that night on the mountain showed me that our maps of reality might be kindergarten drawings compared to what's actually going on.

And honestly? I'm okay with that.

———

CHAPTER 7 SUMMARY

Okay, quick summary of Chapter 7's wild ride then: We dove into three possible explanations for weird experiences—hallucinations shaped by culture, psychological projections from the unconscious, or actual interdimensional visitors. Then came my tent levitation on that Appalachian mountain—because apparently the universe wasn't done messing with me. We explored how vast open spaces give consciousness room to project, and why the Trickster archetype might be the best explanation for reality occasionally going completely mental.

KEY LEARNINGS:

- Cultural beliefs shape how we interpret unexplainable experiences
- Jung's archetypes might actually show up in ways we can perceive
- Vast open spaces create conditions for consciousness to behave differently
- The Trickster disrupts our neat categories precisely when we need it most

KEY TAKEAWAYS:

- Your psyche might stage dramatic interventions when subtle hints don't work
- Group consciousness + sacred space + intense work = reality gets negotiable
- Cities constrain consciousness; wilderness lets it breathe
- Sometimes the best response is surrendering to the mystery

Reflective Question:
Where in your life might the Trickster be trying to shatter your rigid worldview through seemingly impossible experiences?

THE CONSCIOUSNESS HACKING TOOLKIT

Ancient Wisdom for Modern Seekers

So yeah, after getting lifted off the ground by unseen forces on a remote mountain, naturally, I started wondering—have humans always been this weird about consciousness? Turns out, yes. Absolutely yes.

Actually, every culture throughout history seems to have figured out their own ways to crack open ordinary awareness and peek behind the cosmic curtain. Whether it's through prayer, meditation, plant medicines, or spinning in circles until they fall over (looking at you, Sufi whirling dervishes), humans have been desperately trying to dial up the universe's customer service line since... well, forever.

And genuinely? After my own experiences, I get it. Once you've felt your tent levitate or had reality go all wobbly on you, suddenly those ancient practices don't seem quite so absurd.

But let me back up a bit. One of the most common ways cultures have tried to reach something beyond the usual mental fog of daily life is through rituals, ceremonies, and various practices that basically amount to 'let's see what happens if we do THIS.'

Prayer and chanting? Every tradition's got them. Turns out repetition does something interesting to the brain—like a key that eventually finds the right lock. Those Buddhist monks with their prayer beads aren't just keeping their hands busy. They're essentially hacking their own conscious-ness through repetition, creating what neuroscientists now recognize as altered brainwave states.

So what exactly have humans been doing to access these expanded states? Turns out, we've developed quite the toolkit over the millennia. From moving our bodies in specific ways to sitting still until our minds crack open, from creating beauty that bypasses rational thought to deliber-ately making ourselves uncomfortable (fasting and self-discipline), from building sacred spaces to paying attention to the weird films our uncon-scious plays while we sleep.

Think of these as different doors into the same room—that expanded space where ordinary consciousness gets a bit more... flexible. Some people respond to movement, others to stillness. Some need beauty, others need challenge. The ancients figured out that different tempera-ments need different keys, so they developed this whole range of practices.

And before you picture me floating cross-legged in some ashram (though you know I've tried that too), remember that I stumbled into most of these practices accidentally, usually while trying to make sense of what-ever weird experience had just warped my reality. So let's explore this consciousness-hacking toolkit together, starting with...

Another widespread practice involves what the fancy folks call "embodied practices"—yoga, tai chi, qigong. Basically, moving your body in specific ways to shift your consciousness. Sounds simple, right?

Wrong.

Now, I haven't done much of this myself. But someone I've been close to for years has had the most fascinating experience with this stuff.

When he meditates, his body just... moves. Automatically. Into these natural positions he's never learned or studied. The first time it happened, he thought he was having some kind of seizure. For years, he fought it—trying to stay still like meditation supposedly requires. But the movements kept happening, these flowing, almost dance-like positions that his body seemed to know without his mind's involvement.

It's like that Netflix show *The OA*—you know, where they do those movements that supposedly open portals to other dimensions? Except my mate isn't trying to jump dimensions (as far as I know). His body just knows these movements, performs them without his conscious direction, like there's some ancient choreography stored in his cells.

Eventually, he stopped fighting and started embracing it. Now he says it's like his body has its own wisdom, moving into exactly the positions needed to release whatever's stuck or process whatever's arising. No yoga teacher, no instruction manual—just his body doing its thing while his conscious mind watches in bewilderment.

But here's where it gets proper weird—he also does automatic writing. Just a normal bloke, right? One day he's messing around with a pen, letting his hand move without thinking, and suddenly he's writing stuff that makes him go "what the actual hell?" Messages, insights, sometimes in handwriting that doesn't even look like his own.

He showed me some of it once, and I'll be honest—it gave me chills. Not because it was spooky prophecies or anything, but because the wisdom in it was so clearly not coming from his conscious mind. Like his hand had become a direct line to something deeper, bypassing all the mental filters we usually operate through.

These practices combine physical postures, breathing techniques, and meditation to create what they call "alignment of body, mind, and spirit." I used to think this was just wellness-speak for "expensive stretching." But watching someone's body spontaneously move into complex positions during meditation, or seeing their hand write wisdom they didn't consciously know? That'll make you reconsider.

By bringing awareness to your body and breath, these practices quiet the mental chatter (you know, that voice that won't shut up about your to-do list) and create inner stillness. And in that stillness? That's where things get interesting. That's where you might accidentally access what Jung would call the deeper layers of consciousness—or where your body might just take over and show you it knows way more than your mind ever learned.

Pilgrimage to sacred sites has been a thing forever. People journey to these "power spots"—mountains, springs, ancient ruins—seeking transformative experiences. And after living in Sedona (remember my vortex adventures?), I can't entirely dismiss this as wishful thinking.

I mean, think about it—I've already told you how Sedona's energy literally had me vibrating like a tuning fork, seeing invisible children, and hearing angelic music. And Mexico? That's where I had my crown chakra explosion, dancing alone and crying with joy in ways that completely defied my British emotional programming. These weren't just nice vacation spots—something about these places cracked me open in ways that sitting in my London flat never could.

These places often have unique geological features, historical significance, or just that indefinable quality that makes your hair stand on end. Whether it's electromagnetic anomalies (Sedona actually has documented magnetic weirdness) or collective belief creating a morphic field (hey Sheldrake!), something happens at these sites that doesn't happen at your local Walmart. After experiencing firsthand how certain locations seem to amplify consciousness or thin the veil between ordinary and non-ordinary reality, I can't write off ancient traditions of sacred pilgrimage as primitive superstition. Maybe they knew something we've forgotten in our rush to pave over everything mystical.

Meditation—both solo and in groups—is probably the most accessible tool for consciousness expansion. No special rocks required, no exotic substances, just you and your mind having a little chat. Or rather, you watching your mind have a chat with itself while you try not to get involved.

When practiced collectively, meditation creates what they call a "field of shared intention." Like suddenly you're not just in your own head anymore, but swimming in some kind of collective consciousness soup. Delicious? Terrifying? Both?

Yeah, both.

This "field of shared intention" sounds suspiciously like what might have happened on that mountain in the Appalachians. Remember how I described the week-long process of gradually aligning ourselves through ceremony, shadow work, and vulnerability? How by the final night, it felt like we'd all been tuned to the same frequency?

Maybe these meditation practices are attempting something similar—that moment when individual consciousness start syncing up together, creating something bigger than the sum of its parts. What if on the mountain, we didn't just create a field of shared intention, but accidentally aligned ourselves with whatever ancient frequency that place was already broadcasting?

Like pendulums slowly synchronizing their swing. Maybe we spent a week unconsciously adjusting our rhythm until we swung in time with the mountain's, and then... well, then my tent decided to take flight. Could be that's what happens when human consciousness fields sync up with Earth consciousness fields—reality gets a bit negotiable.

Makes you wonder if all those meditation groups creating "fields of shared intention" might occasionally tap into something similar. Though hopefully with less tent-based aviation.

Music, dance, visual art, poetry—humans have always used creative expression to induce altered states. There's something about the creative process that bypasses the rational mind and taps directly into... whatever's underneath.

That mortifying dance session in Mexico I mentioned earlier is a good example of this. When I finally let go of trying to be cool (spoiler: I never was cool), something changed. The creative expression became a doorway to a state I'd never accessed before. Tears streaming down my face, dancing alone to house music, feeling more alive than I'd felt in years.

Mental? Yep. Transformative? 100%.

Some traditions take the "no pain, no gain" approach to consciousness —fasting, sensory deprivation, various forms of self-denial. The idea is that by temporarily depriving the body, you quiet the mind and create clarity.

I tried a float tank once (more on that later), and let me tell you—when you can't see, hear, or feel anything, your mind does some proper weird stuff. It's like it gets bored and decides to entertain itself by showing you those unknown parts of your psyche we keep talking about.

DREAMWORK: WHEN YOUR UNCONSCIOUS SLIDES INTO YOUR DMS

Dreamwork and dream incubation have been used across cultures as ways to connect with the unconscious mind and receive guidance from beyond ordinary reality. Setting intentions before sleep, paying attention to symbols and messages that arise—it's like leaving your psyche's inbox open for cosmic downloads while you snooze.

Every culture has these practices because dreams offer something our waking mind can't access. They're not just random neural firings (though yeah, sometimes they're definitely that). They can be bridges to deeper wisdom, showing us truths we're not ready to see with our eyes open.

I've had my share of dreams that felt more like transmissions than regular sleep cinema—messages that arrived with such force they fundamentally shifted how I understood myself and my place in the world.

Here's one that arrived during those raw weeks of integration after the mountain, when the individuation process was just beginning to show me all those unfamiliar aspects of myself:

I'm in my childhood home with my family, and I notice this silverback gorilla just... hanging around. Not full-sized, but clearly a silverback—that distinctive silver-grey fur across his back. Not threatening, not aggressive, just present. Watching me with these intense, knowing eyes.

Being back in my childhood home with this primal presence felt significant right away. Like my unconscious had chosen the perfect setting—the place where I first learned what safety meant, what family meant, what home meant.

As the dream progresses, he becomes increasingly focused on me. Eventually, he comes to sit above my bed like some kind of primate guardian angel. But it's not creepy—it's protective, almost tender.

Then he reaches out his arm, almost playfully, inviting connection. So dream-me responds, and we do that forearm grip—that warrior hand-shake where you clasp each other's forearms. The moment our arms connect, he tells me his name: "Sadique" and I feel this strong rapport. Like meeting someone who's known you since before you were born.

But then—and here's where it gets intense—Sadique places his hand on my chest and presses down. Hard. Not aggressive, but insistent, like he's trying to push something into me or wake something up that's been sleeping. The pressure was so real, so physical, it started pulling me out of the dream. Part of me wanted to surrender to it, part of me was terrified and fighting it.

The intensity overwhelmed me. I found myself pulling away, actually getting up and walking away from Sadique in the dream. I went looking for my mum and brother, needing... I don't know, permission? Reassurance? I asked them about the wisdom of befriending this creature, whether it was safe to engage with him so openly.

Their response? "He's 'Sadiqued' all of us."

Like this was some family initiation I was the last to receive. Like being "Sadiqued" was just a normal Tuesday thing in our household.

I woke up with my heart pounding, that chest pressure still lingering like a phantom touch. The name "Sadique" was burned into my brain—not just a word I'd heard, but a name I'd been given through touch, through connection, demanding investigation.

Unable to shake the dream, I did what any reasonable person would do —spent hours researching what the hell "Sadique" meant.

Plot twist: "Sadique" means "friend" in Swahili.

Swahili. The language from East Africa. The birthplace of humanity. The place where, evolutionarily speaking, we all come from.

My whole body went cold, then hot. You literally couldn't get more primal archetype than this! Remember Jung's collective unconscious? Those inherited patterns from our ancestral past? Well, here was my unconscious literally speaking to me in the language of humanity's birth-place, sending me a "friend" from the exact spot where Homo sapiens first emerged.

I mean, seriously? This wasn't just some random dream name my brain had conjured. This felt like something ancient in my psyche had intro-duced itself using the original human language. He'd literally told me he was "friend" in the tongue of our collective origins. It's like my uncon-scious went, "Right, Lee's been banging on about evolution and archetypes for chapters now—let's send him the most on-the-nose primal archetype possible: a silverback gorilla from humanity's cradle who wants to be mates."

What was I supposed to make of this? Was Sadique some kind of link to our primal origins? To the ancient wisdom and instinctual knowledge we supposedly carry in our DNA? That pressure on my chest—was it calling me to remember something? To reconnect with primal wisdom we've buried under centuries of civilization? Or was I just desperately trying to find meaning in random neural firings?

But it also felt intensely personal. Being in my childhood home, the fact that he'd "sadiqued" my whole family—this couldn't just be about broad evolutionary connections. This had to be about something specific to me, to whatever I needed to wake up to at that moment in my life. Right?

The dream stayed with me for weeks, and not because I couldn't figure it out. I knew exactly what had happened: I'd literally met my primal self. Not metaphorically, not symbolically—I'd had a direct encounter with the part of me that existed before civilization, before language, before all the layers of adapting and trauma and mask-wearing.

Look, I know by now you've probably noticed my pattern. Something weird happens, I immediately reach for Jung like he's my psychological comfort blanket. "Oh, that's clearly an archetype from the collective unconscious!" "Obviously this is shadow material!" "Classic anima projection!" I get it—I'm that guy who's read too much Jung and now sees individuation everywhere.

But come on—when a silverback gorilla shows up in your childhood home, grips your forearm warrior-style, tells you his name in Swahili (the language from humanity's birthplace), and then tries to initiate you with chest pressure... I mean, that's practically Jung bingo. All that was missing was a mandala and maybe some synchronicities involving the number four.

So yes, here I go again: this felt like a direct encounter with what Jung would call the "two-million-year-old human" within us—that primitive layer of the collective unconscious that contains our species' earliest patterns and instincts. Sadique wasn't just my personal primal self; he was tapping into that deeper reservoir of human experience we all carry.

And I'd run away from him.

It took me years to fully understand what had actually happened in that dream. But eventually, the penny did drop and here's the part that makes me simultaneously cringe and marvel at my unconscious mind's symbolic precision:

I'd literally run to my mum to ask permission to connect with my own masculine power.

Sit with that for a moment. A SILVERBACK GORILLA—the ultimate symbol of grounded, embodied masculine presence—who introduces himself as "Friend" in Swahili (the language from humanity's birthplace), offers me a warrior's forearm grip (classic masculine initiation ritual), tries to press ancient wisdom directly into my heart, and what do I do? I run to mummy asking if it's safe to be friends with him.

The layers of symbolism are almost too perfect: Here's masculine power so ancient it speaks Swahili, so primal it emerges from East Africa where humans first stood upright, so fundamental it literally means "friend" in our original tongue—and I need feminine permission to connect with it.

In my CHILDHOOD HOME. Where I first learned what masculine expression was "acceptable." Where those earliest patterns of "good boy" behavior were formed. Where I probably absorbed which parts of masculine energy were safe to express and which weren't.

You couldn't script it better. Here was my primal masculine self—the part that knows how to be powerful without apology, protective without being aggressive, embodied without intellectualizing everything—and I literally fled to the feminine for permission to connect with it.

Now, before you think I'm about to go all "alpha male" on you, let me be clear about what I mean by "masculine power." I'm not talking about domination, aggression, or any of that toxic nonsense. I'm talking about what Jung called integrated masculine energy—the ability to be grounded in your body, protective without being aggressive, assertive without being domineering, powerful without needing to prove it.

Think back to Jung's anima/animus concept from Chapter 4—those complementary energies we all carry regardless of gender. I'd done tons of work integrating my emotional, receptive side (what Jung called the anima), but here was Sadique representing something I'd been avoiding: grounded, solid presence that acts from its center without needing anyone's permission.

The irony is, I'd become so overidentified with my feminine aspects—the emotional sensitivity, the caretaking, the constant tuning in to others' needs—that my masculine energy had nowhere healthy to go. So it either hid completely or exploded in those aggressive outbursts I've mentioned.

A lion doesn't go around picking fights to demonstrate he's a lion. He just is. That's what Sadique was offering—not the need to justify anything, but the simple ability to BE powerful without apology or explosion.

This connects to every pattern I've explored in this book: the savior complex with women (being the "good boy" who rescues), the attraction to chaotic feminine energy, even my aggression challenges (untrained masculine energy exploding because it was never properly initiated or integrated).

Sadique wasn't trying to turn me into someone different. He was showing me what was missing. I'd been working on being more emotionally open (the feminine stuff) and more assertive and decisive (the masculine stuff). But what I hadn't realized was that even when I stood my ground, I was still in reactive mode—defending my position like I had to earn my right to have it.

It's the difference between a silverback who just sits where he sits versus one who's constantly ready to fight about it. True embodied presence doesn't rise to every challenge because it's not threatened by disagreement. But me? I was exhausting myself proving I deserved my seat at the table instead of just... sitting in it.

That recognition changed everything. These days, I catch myself looking for approval much less often—though when I do, at least I know what's happening. Old habits die hard, but they're less powerful once you can spot them. The defensive patterns still show up—someone challenges me and I still often feel that familiar surge, ready to justify and explain and win. But now I can feel Sadique's pressure on my chest, reminding me: mate, you don't need to defend your right to exist. You can engage with curiosity instead of combat. You can disagree without making it a duel. That's what he was trying to press into me—not the ability to fight better, but the security to not need to fight at all.

The fact that my family said "he's sadiqued all of us" suggests this integration is available to everyone—men and women alike. We all have aspects of primal wisdom, of embodied power, that we've learned to distrust or seek permission to express. How many of us, raised to be "good," to be safe, to not be "too much," are still waiting for someone else's approval to claim our full power?

That chest pressure Sadique offered? I think he was trying to press courage directly into my heart—the courage to be fully myself without apology, without permission, without constantly checking if it's okay. The courage to trust that primal wisdom that knows how to move through the world with both power and grace.

Right, so... that got a bit heavy, didn't it? From 'I had a dream about a gorilla' to 'I'm psychologically asking mummy for permission to be a man.' Bit of a journey there. If you need to take a break and stare at the wall for a while, I understand. I did the same thing when I first connected these dots.

But this is exactly why I believe dreams deserve their own deep dive, which we'll explore in 'Becoming a Modern Hero: A Practical Handbook for Living the Hero's Journey.' Because sometimes your unconscious serves up insights that would take years of therapy to reach—all wrapped up in the bizarre package of a silverback gorilla who speaks Swahili and wants to be mates.

Maybe that's why dreams remain one of humanity's most powerful tools for growth. They show us what we're not ready to see with our waking eyes. They offer initiations our conscious mind would reject. They patiently extend invitations to wholeness, waiting for the day we're finally ready to accept. The art of working with dreams as a practical tool for growth—learning to remember, interpret, and integrate their wisdom—is something we'll explore in depth in the companion guide to this journey.

Even now, I'm still learning from that dream. It showed me how often I look for permission, and even though I pulled away from Sadique, that reaction was exactly what I needed to see. Sometimes you have to catch yourself asking for approval before you can stop doing it. It's not about never wanting validation again—that's unrealistic. It's about noticing when you're doing it and having more choice about whether you really need it.

The question is: are you ready to accept the friendship of your own primal wisdom? Or are you still asking for permission?

THE LIONSGATE PORTAL: SYNCHRONICITY ON STEROIDS

So the Sadique dream, the tent levitation, those Sedona experiences—they weren't separate, isolated weirdnesses. They were all part of one long, strange integration that had been unfolding for years. That mountain retreat? It wasn't the main event—it was more like someone kicked open a door that's never properly closed since.

And sometimes—like what happened next—the universe apparently decides you need a concentrated dose of weird to really drive the point home...

The thing is, once you've cracked open like this, the universe seems to take notice. It's like you've been added to some universal mailing list for "people who need regular doses of weirdness to keep growing." And some-times—like what happened next—apparently you get enrolled in the accelerated program...

August rolled around, and with it came something called the "Lionsgate Portal"—this astrological alignment that happens every August 8th when the sun's in Leo and lines up with the star Sirius. The spiritual crowd goes a bit nuts for it, claiming it creates an "energetic gateway" for transformation.

Do I believe in astrological portals? Look, at this point, I can't rule anything out. What I will say is that I've learned to pay attention when synchronicities start stacking up, and during this particular period, they were coming at me like a bloody avalanche.

First, it was small things. Songs with specific lyrics would play at exactly the moment I needed to hear them. You know—thinking about a particular challenge and suddenly the radio's singing the answer. Conversations with strangers would eerily echo thoughts I'd had that morning. The usual stuff that makes you go "huh, weird" but could still be categorized as odd timing, maybe.

But then things really moved up a notch. I was driving down a beau-tiful backcountry road during a road trip, chatting with my dad on the phone (hands-free, before you judge). We're having a completely normal conversation about nothing in particular when out of nowhere, he says, "Don't get pulled over for driving too fast."

Completely random. We weren't even talking about driving or speed or anything remotely related.

I swear, no more than thirty seconds later, I heard the siren. In my rearview mirror, blue lights flashing. A cop pulled me over for—you guessed it—driving too fast.

I sat there on the side of the road, ticket in hand, proper freaked out. The precision of it. The timing. What were the odds? This wasn't just "oh, funny coincidence" territory anymore. This was "okay, wtf is going on" territory.

So a few days later, when my wife and I were on one of our early dates, casually strolling the city after coffee, and a little shop seemed to call out 'oi, come in here'—I didn't hesitate. After the cop incident, I'd learned to follow these nudges.

Inside, sitting there like it had been waiting specifically for me, was a journal with a Joseph Campbell quote on the cover: "Follow your bliss and the universe will open doors where there were only walls."

I just stood there, gobsmacked. Given everything we've explored about the Hero's Journey in this book, you won't be surprised that I'd been living and breathing Campbell's work. Re-reading passages, finding new layers of meaning after my recent experiences. But to have THAT specific quote appear right then... Given everything I'd been through—tent levitations, reality-bending mountain experiences, walls of 'what's possible' being shattered—here was Campbell basically winking at me from a shop shelf, saying 'See? Told you so.'

Follow your bliss and the universe will open doors where there were only walls. I'd followed my terror up that mountain, and the universe had responded by showing me doors I didn't even know existed. Doors to parts of myself I'd kept locked. Doors to realities I'd dismissed as impossible.

At this point, the universe wasn't being subtle; it was doing jazz hands while shouting *DO YOU GET IT NOW?*

Just hours later—and this is where it all came together—I got an unexpected call from my former partner—yes, from that difficult period I mentioned earlier. Now, in the past, this would've sent me spiraling. All those old patterns—defensiveness, emotional reactivity, maybe even some lingering attachment—would've kicked in like a broken jukebox playing the same awful song.

But something was different. Remember that dwarf in gold slippers from my dream? The guardian who'd ceremonially shown me out of her world? This call felt like the real-life version of that moment—a chance for actual closure.

Instead of getting pulled into our familiar dance of dysfunction, I found myself responding from this place of... clarity. Like I could see the whole pattern from above. I maintained my boundaries while still honoring what we'd shared. No drama, no getting hooked. Just clean, clear communication.

By the end of that call, I felt it—proper closure. Not the dramatic kind where someone storms off, but the quiet kind where you both acknowledge what was and peacefully let it go. The dwarf had shown me the door in my dream; this call let me close it gently behind me.

This was The Road Back in action—you know, that stage in the Hero's Journey where you get tested to see if your transformation actually stuck. The universe basically going, "Oh, you think you've changed? Let's see how you handle this blast from the past, shall we?" And for once, I actually passed the bloody test.

The real measure of any transformative experience isn't what happens in the safe container of a retreat or ceremony. It's how you respond when life throws your old triggers at you in the middle of a random Tuesday. Can you stay centered when your ex calls? Can you maintain your new awareness when your boss is being a right knob? That's where the rubber meets the road.

The escalation from random songs to my dad's prophetic warning to Campbell appearing to handling my ex with grace and finding closure—it felt like reality was building toward something. Like each synchronicity was preparing me for the next, bigger challenge.

At this point, I knew I was well and truly in the middle of some kind of synchronistic flow state. Synchronicities, coincidences, prophetic speeding tickets, emotional closure, Campbell quotes jumping off shelves—it was like something—my higher self, my unconscious, the universe, who the heck knows—had enrolled me in this mystical scavenger hunt, with that journal acting as my first proper clue. Every weird event seemed to lead to the next one, each more intense than the last.

Honestly? I was knackered. Being deep in your own personal integration work is exhausting, especially when reality keeps getting this wobbly. So when I remembered those float tanks I'd been meaning to try—you know, those sensory deprivation pods filled with salt water where you bob about in complete darkness—I thought, "Perfect. A break from all this mysticism. Just me, some salt water, and absolutely nothing happening for 90 minutes."

Just float there in silence. No synchronicities. No messages. No integration. Just... nothing.

Little did I bloody know...

The experience was strange from the moment I climbed in—naked, in the dark, trying not to splash the incredibly salty water that stings if it gets in your eyes. The water matched my skin temperature exactly—that weird sensation where you can't tell where you end and the water begins.

I pulled the lid closed above me, and suddenly I was in complete darkness. The kind that makes you wave your hand in front of your face just to check your eyes are actually open.

For the first twenty minutes, my brain threw its usual tantrum: *"Am I doing this right? Is this normal? Why can't I stop thinking about that mortifying dance in Mexico? Christ, this water is salty—"*

And then, as I settled into that strange, womb-like silence, something started happening. The mental chatter didn't stop exactly, but it became... distant. Like someone had turned the volume down on my internal monologue.

I began having this vivid vision of floating away from the Earth and into the stars. My sense of being "Lee" just started... dissolving. Instead, I was part of this vast web, connected to everything and nothing all at once. Terrifying and liberating in equal measure—like your ego is having a panic attack while your soul is having the best day ever.

But then—and this is the bit that really got me—as the drifting and dissolving intensified, I felt this powerful jolt in my back. Not a gentle tug, but a proper gravitational summons. Like the planet's molten core was personally calling me home through some kind of magnetic hotline.

The message was crystal clear: "You've had your transcendent adventure, mate. Time to bring it back down to Earth where it actually matters."

Classic Hero's Journey stuff—you can't just float about in the cosmos having mystical experiences. You've got to return to the ordinary world and actually use what you've learned.

This balance between expanded awareness and grounded presence— that's what the whole integration dance is about, eh? You need both. The cosmic perspective that shows you how everything's connected, and the earthly presence that helps you navigate everyday life without floating off into la-la land.

As I felt myself returning to earth, becoming aware of my body in the tank again, I had this distinct feeling that I wasn't alone. I sensed this... presence. Like meeting another consciousness that was just as surprised to find me as I was to find it. We shared this brief moment of mutual "what the hell?" before it dissolved back into the saltwater silence.

Was it another part of myself I'd never met? Some interdimensional tourist checking out the local float tanks? Given everything we've explored about Jung and consciousness projections, I'm betting on the first one.

I'd just gone from cosmic expansion to earthly grounding, literally integrating these opposite states of being. Maybe in that moment of balance, I finally had enough space to meet a part of myself that had been waiting in the wings. Not some external entity, but an internal one I'd never had the bandwidth to acknowledge before.

If that's what happened, then this wasn't just another weird float tank story. It was integration in real-time—that moment when a split-off part of the psyche finally gets welcomed back into conscious awareness. Jung would've had a field day with this one.

When I finally emerged from the tank, blinking in the sudden brightness, I felt... recalibrated. Like someone had hit the reset button on my nervous system while also downloading a software update I didn't know I needed.

A few days later, during one of my binaural beats meditation sessions (yes, I use audio shortcuts—sue me), a single word just... dropped in. Not like a normal thought that builds gradually. More like someone had placed a perfectly wrapped present in my mental inbox.

Phasm.

I'd never heard it before, so I looked it up. It comes from Greek— *phasma*—meaning apparition, phantom, or vision. Basically, something that appears between worlds.

The moment I read that definition, my whole body went "YES, THAT'S IT!"

How did a word I'd never consciously encountered perfectly describe experiences that have no recognized name in modern English? It's like my unconscious went rummaging through some deeper linguistic memory— that collective unconscious Jung kept banging on about—and pulled out exactly the right term.

The fact that ancient languages even had specific words for these liminal experiences tells us something. We modern folks struggle to describe these encounters, fumbling with phrases like "weird experience" or "mystical whatever." But somewhere in our collective linguistic history, humans found these experiences common enough to need precise vocabulary for them.

Remember Sadique introducing himself in Swahili, the language from humanity's birthplace? It's like there's this vast repository of human knowledge and experience that we can tap into when we need it most. The right word, the right symbol, the right understanding—just waiting in our shared psychic inheritance for the moment we're ready to receive it.

That single word perfectly captured everything I'd been experiencing. The Sadique dream? Phasm. The presence in the float tank? Phasm. Those moments when ordinary reality gets thin and something else peeks through? All phasms—glimpses of whatever exists in the spaces between our normal perception.

Consciousness had given me a linguistic container for experiences that previously had no name. A final gift to help me integrate everything that had just happened.

Whether you want to chalk this all up to astrological alignments, post-retreat brain changes, or just Lee finally losing the plot—honestly, it doesn't matter.

What matters is this: the integration journey doesn't end when you pack up your tent and drive home from the mountain. It continues to unfold in the most unexpected ways. Through synchronicities that feel too perfect to be random. Through old relationships that offer unexpected closure. Through moments in float tanks where you meet... whatever that was. Through words that arrive to name the unnameable.

The modern Hero's Journey isn't a one-and-done deal. It's this ongoing spiral of opening, integrating, and opening again. Each cycle takes you deeper, shows you more, cracks you open in new ways.

And if you're lucky, it gives you a word like "phasm" to help you make sense of it all. Because sometimes, being able to name the mystery is the first step to dancing with it.

PLANT MEDICINE

Right, I've been sitting here for the past twenty minutes trying to figure out how to write about ayahuasca without sounding like that guy at parties who won't shut up about his "journey to Peru that totally changed everything, man."

You know the type. Usually wearing hemp jewelry and smelling faintly of palo santo. Corners you by the kitchen and launches into a three-hour monologue about meeting his spirit animal (always a jaguar, for some reason) while you're just trying to find the crisps.

The thing is, plant medicines genuinely are one of humanity's oldest consciousness-hacking tools. But they've been so mythologized, commercialized, and Instagram-filtered that it's hard to talk about them without triggering everyone's eye-roll reflex. Including mine.

And yes, before you ask—I did eventually become one of those people who tried ayahuasca. Spoiler alert: there were no jaguars, but there was vomiting, existential terror, and a UFO sighting that I still can't explain. More on that palaver later. For now, let's ease into this topic with something less intense and start somewhere unexpected: with Santa Claus.

According to some historians and ethnomycologists (people who study fungi's influence on human societies), the legend of Santa Claus may be connected to the trippy traditions of shamans in the Siberian and Arctic regions. These shamans were known to bring Amanita muscaria mushrooms as gifts during the winter solstice. And by "gifts," we mean they'd drop off a basket of psychoactive mushrooms for the lucky recipient to enjoy (or not enjoy, depending on the dosage).

Amanita muscaria, also known as fly agaric, is a red mushroom with white flecks that grows in the Northern Hemisphere under conifers and birch trees. It has a symbiotic relationship with these trees, and it's been known to make people see things that aren't really there. That's why some people believe the placement of red and white presents under the Christmas tree, which resembles Amanita muscaria mushrooms, may be connected to this tradition.

Now, reindeer are common in Siberia and northern Europe, and they have a tendency to seek out these mushrooms. In fact, they're known to be quite fond of them. So it's no surprise that reindeer have become associated with shamans who used Amanita muscaria as part of their spiritual practices. In fact, it's been suggested that Siberian tribesmen who ingested fly agaric may have hallucinated that the grazing reindeer were flying, leading to the belief that Santa's reindeer could fly. (Well, that and the fact that they're apparently powered by magic.)

And let's not forget about Santa's iconic red suit with white spots. It's believed that shamans in Siberia used to dress in similar attire, which may have influenced the modern image of Santa Claus. Plus, the prevalence of mushroom-shaped ornaments in Christmas decorations... coincidence? Maybe. But it's a bloody good story, innit?

But wait, it gets weirder.

Some scientists have a theory that our ancestors may have had a little help from psychoactive plants and fungi in the whole "becoming human" department. It's called the "stoned ape" theory, and yes, before you ask, Joe Rogan has talked about it approximately 847 times on his podcast. (Drinking game idea: take a shot every time Rogan mentions DMT, chimps, or float tanks. Actually wait—that sounds like me.)

The theory, originally proposed by ethnobotanist Terence McKenna, suggests that early humans stumbling upon psilocybin mushrooms might have kickstarted our cognitive evolution. Picture this: our knuckle-dragging ancestors are foraging around, someone eats the wrong (or right?) mushroom, and suddenly they're having thoughts like "What if we could, like, control fire?" or "Dude, what if we made sounds that mean specific things?"

According to this theory, consuming these psychoactive substances may have helped early humans experience new and innovative thoughts, leading to the development of abstract concepts and advanced communication skills. Some believe these substances stimulated the growth of new neural connections, leading to increased intelligence and problem-solving abilities.

Now, it's important to note that the stoned ape theory is not scientifically accepted. Most anthropologists think it's absolute bollocks. But it does raise some interesting questions about the potential influence of psychoactive substances on human consciousness. Plus, it's a great story to break out when conversation gets dull. "Did you know we might all be here because a monkey got high?" Never fails.

Who knows, maybe our ancestors were just a bunch of stoned apes. But look at us now—we've got smartphones, anxiety disorders, and Joe Rogan podcasts. Progress!

The point is, humans have been using consciousness-altering plants for a very, very long time. Long before Silicon Valley discovered micro-dosing and wellness retreats started charging five grand for "plant medi-cine journeys," our ancestors were already deep in relationship with these substances. And crucially, they weren't using them recreationally—they were technologies for healing, divination, and connecting with whatever you want to call the bigger picture. The divine. The cosmos. The thing that makes you go "bloody hell" at 3 AM.

Now, I'm not saying you should go munching on red mushrooms hoping to see flying reindeer. Please don't. What I am saying is that plant medicines have shaped human culture in ways we're only beginning to understand. From the mysteries of Eleusis in ancient Greece (where participants drank a psychoactive brew called kykeon) to the peyote cere-monies of Native American churches, these substances have been gate-ways to experiences that defy ordinary description.

The science behind it is actually fascinating. Take ayahuasca, for instance—that Amazonian brew I mentioned earlier. It's made from two plants: the Banisteriopsis caapi vine and the leaves of the Psychotria viridis shrub. Here's the mental bit: neither plant does much on its own. But together? They create a biochemical key that unlocks parts of consciousness we normally can't access.

The vine contains MAO inhibitors that allow the DMT in the leaves to become orally active. Without getting too technical, it's like one plant says "here's the door to expanded consciousness" and the other says "and here's how to open it." The fact that Indigenous peoples figured this out among the 80,000+ plant species in the Amazon? That's not random experimenta-tion. That's sophisticated botanical knowledge that makes our modern pharmacology look like child's play.

Interestingly—some researchers reckon these plant medicines might be working through a tiny pine cone-shaped gland in the middle of your brain. The pineal gland, which Descartes called the "seat of the soul" (apparently even 17th-century philosophers were having mystical moments).

Remember when we explored the third eye chakra back in Part 1? That indigo energy center between your eyebrows that governs intuition and inner knowing? Well, turns out that's roughly where your pineal gland sits. Ancient traditions called it the "third eye" for millennia—from Egyptian depictions of Horus to Hindu and Buddhist imagery—without having a clue about the anatomy. Makes you wonder if they were onto something through pure intuitive wisdom that we're only now catching up to through neuroscience.

This little gland produces melatonin for sleep, but check this out: it might also naturally produce small amounts of DMT. Yes, the same DMT that's in ayahuasca. Some researchers think plant medicines work by flooding this system, basically turning your third eye from a peephole into a bloody panoramic window.

But here's what really gets me: these aren't just chemical interactions. In traditional contexts, plant medicines are used within elaborate ceremonial frameworks—songs, prayers, dietary restrictions, community support. It's technology, yes, but technology wrapped in wisdom traditions that recognize you're not just messing with brain chemistry. You're potentially opening doors to experiences that can fundamentally reorganize how you see yourself and reality.

Which is exactly why the modern commercialization of these medicines makes me nervous. You've got "shamans" who did a two-week training course administering powerful psychoactives to people who've done zero preparation beyond reading a Vice article. It's like giving someone the keys to a Formula One car when they've never driven a stick. Sure, something will happen. It might even be profound. But it might also send you straight into a wall.

The Indigenous peoples who've worked with these plants for millennia approach them with the kind of respect you'd give to a wise but potentially dangerous teacher. There are protocols. Preparations. Integration practices. Because they understand something the modern world is still catching up to: consciousness is vast, mysterious, and not to be fucked with lightly.

Look, I'm not here to convince you to try plant medicines. That's between you, your conscience, and preferably some very experienced practitioners if you do decide to explore. What I am saying is that these substances represent one of humanity's oldest tools for exploring consciousness—predating meditation, breathwork, and definitely predating float tanks.

They've shown up in our myths (hello, Santa), our religions (early Christianity may have involved psychoactive sacraments), and our ongoing quest to understand what the hell consciousness actually is. They're not magic bullets. They're not shortcuts to enlightenment. But they are powerful tools that, when used with genuine respect and guidance, can show us aspects of ourselves and reality that our ordinary awareness simply can't access.

And sometimes—though this is definitely not guaranteed and please don't quote me on this—they might even show you a UFO. But that's a story I'll save for another time!

For now, just know that humanity's relationship with consciousness-expanding plants is ancient, complex, and ongoing. Whether we're talking about Siberian shamans feeding mushrooms to reindeer or modern researchers using psilocybin to treat depression, we're participating in a conversation that's been happening since before we had words for it.

The question isn't whether these tools are valid—thousands of years of human experience suggests they are. The question is whether we can approach them with the wisdom, respect, and integration support they require. Because unlike a float tank or a meditation cushion, once these doors open, they don't always close quite the same way again.

Even Jung, who spent his career mapping the unconscious, was pretty cautious about these shortcuts to the psyche. After researchers started sending him reports about LSD in the 1950s, he admitted these substances might give people a glimpse of the unconscious realms he'd been exploring through dreams and active imagination. But—and this is classic Jung—he worried that without doing the actual psychological work first, people might get the cosmic download without the integration manual.

His concern? That you'd see the destination without learning how to get there on your own. Like being helicoptered to the top of Everest—sure, you've seen the view, but you haven't developed the strength to climb back up when life inevitably drops you at base camp again.

And honestly? I agree. Which brings us back to why these medicines demand such respect. They're not just showing you pretty colors or spiritual Instagram moments. They're potentially opening the same doors Jung spent decades teaching people to approach carefully through dreams, symbols, and shadow work. The Indigenous peoples who've worked with these plants for millennia understood this—that's why they wrapped them in ceremony, preparation, and integration practices that would make Jung's analytical sessions look brief by comparison.

The question isn't whether these tools can open doors—clearly they can. The question is whether we're prepared for what's on the other side. Because unlike a meditation cushion or a dream journal, once these particular doors open, they don't always close quite the same way again.

So yeah, if you're feeling called to explore—do your homework first. Find guides who understand both the medicines and the integration. And definitely, definitely don't start with the red mushrooms. Even Santa had to work up to that.

SWEAT LODGES & TRADITIONAL CEREMONIES

So, we've gone from Santa's mushroom-munching reindeer to the possibility that we're all here because a monkey ate the wrong fungi. But plant medicines aren't the only ancient technologies for expanding consciousness. Sometimes, instead of ingesting something to alter your state, you can just... cook yourself into a different dimension.

Now, before I go any further, let me be clear: I may have joked about cooking yourself into a different dimension but sweat lodge ceremonies are sacred practices that deserve real respect. They're not wellness trends or TikTok experiences. They're powerful, time-tested practices that Indigenous cultures have refined over millennia. So when a friend who'd been deep in men's work for years invited me to participate in one, I approached it with equal parts awe and terror.

The ceremony would be led by someone who'd been correctly trained by a Lakota elder—not some weekend warrior who'd watched a YouTube video, but someone who'd spent years learning the traditional ways directly from Indigenous knowledge keepers. This mattered. A lot.

These dome-shaped structures create a womb-like environment where participants work with elemental forces through heated stones, water, and ritual. And the use of heat for spiritual purification shows up everywhere —Native American sweat lodges, Finnish saunas, Russian banyas, Japanese onsens. It's like humans worldwide independently figured out that extreme heat does something intense to consciousness.

In these sacred spaces, all the elements come together: earth (the stones), fire (heating them), water (creating steam), and air (what you're desperately trying to breathe). Many traditions believe this combination creates the perfect conditions for connecting with higher consciousness. And after what I experienced, I'm not about to argue.

The invitation came with a bonus—the outdoor intensive also included a fire walk ceremony. Because apparently, one potentially terrifying fire-based ritual wasn't enough for one weekend.

The day began with something called a spirit walk—basically wandering alone through the wilderness with instructions to shut up and pay attention. Walk in silence, remain present, let nature teach you. What followed was hours of me stumbling about in the woods, trying to look spiritual while mostly hoping I wasn't lost.

For the first hour, my brain threw an absolute tantrum about having nothing to do. But by late afternoon, the mental chatter finally quieted down, and I gradually fell into this calm state of heightened awareness. Which was probably good preparation for what came next.

Crawling into that small, dark dome was like voluntarily entering Dante's personal sauna. The heat hit immediately—not your gentle spa experience, but an aggressive wall of intense heat. Packed in with a group of other men, all of us naked and vulnerable, trying to breathe in what felt like liquid air.

My back screamed. My lungs protested. The steam pressed down from all sides like the atmosphere was trying to flatten me into submission. Every instinct said "get out now." But something else within me said "stay."

So I stayed. And as I sat there, sweat literally streaming off me in rivers, heart hammering like it was planning an escape, something cracked open. The physical discomfort became a doorway. Instead of fighting the heat, I started working with it. Or maybe it started working with me.

Then the visions began. And no, I hadn't taken anything—this was all courtesy of extreme heat and whatever happens when you push your body and consciousness past its comfort zone.

First came these mesmerizing red swirls of light, dancing behind my eyelids like a 1990's screensaver. The patterns seemed to pull me, inviting me into... somewhere. My rational mind tried to grab hold, to categorize what was happening—"just heat hallucinations, Lee"—but the experience was already beyond that kind of analysis. Then the swirls slowly began to morph into a massive wolf—deep red fur, eyes like burning coals, radiating this presence that was as terrifying as it was hypnotic. It called me forward, though where exactly a heat-induced vision-wolf wants you to go is anyone's guess.

A few moments later, the whole vision shifted again. The wolf and the swirls were swallowed by this incredible, supreme white light. Not gentle meditation light—this was old-as-dirt, primal, absolute light that seemed to come from the source itself. The only reasonable response was complete surrender. I felt this overwhelming need to drop to my knees and bow down before it, like meeting something so fundamentally powerful that your ego has no choice but to yield.

As that supreme light absorbed me, thousands upon thousands of our ancestors suddenly flashed before me in rapid succession. Like someone was scrolling backwards through humanity's photo album at warp speed. Medieval knights, Roman soldiers, Greek philosophers, Viking warriors, ancient Chinese dynasties—faces, bodies, lives from every era imaginable, all of them experiencing this same light, this same overwhelming presence.

The visions accelerated until suddenly I slammed into what felt like ancient Egypt. Thousands of people gathered near the pyramids, all of them on their knees, heads bowed, bodies trembling before this supreme light that had appeared in their sky. Not some gentle spiritual moment—this was raw, primal awe. The kind that drops you to the ground because standing simply isn't an option anymore.

Then I wasn't watching anymore. I WAS one of them. My knees hit the sand, my forehead touched the earth, my entire body filled with recognition of something so fundamentally powerful that my modern mind just... switched off. This ancestor I'd become didn't need to understand the light intellectually. They KNEW it in their bones, their blood, their breath. A knowing that bypassed thought entirely—the kind of bone-deep recognition we modern humans have completely forgotten.

The feeling was this impossible mix of terror, desire, respect, and something that can only be described as a full-body "hallelujah." Not the

Sunday school version—more like every cell simultaneously recognizing what it's part of and being completely humbled by it.

The vision gradually faded, returning me to the pressing heat of the lodge, my body drenched in sweat, and disoriented from what I'd just experienced.

When the sweat lodge door was finally opened and we crawled out, gasping for air, everything seemed alive with meaning. The campfire's crackling sounded like conversation. The moonlight looked conscious. Even the watermelon the elders offered tasted like earth's way of saying "welcome back."

Sitting by that fire afterward, watching the watermelon juice drip down my chin, I couldn't help but think about how many people never get to experience this. Not because they wouldn't want to, but because we've systematically dismantled the very structures that once made these transformative experiences accessible to everyone.

That experience left me legitimately humbled by forces way bigger than anything I'd imagined. The visions, the connection to something primal, that encounter with the supreme light—they left marks on my psyche that haven't faded. They taught me about respect, balance, and recognizing our connection to something greater than ourselves. Even if that connection sometimes comes through heat-induced wolf hallucinations.

These ceremonies work because they bypass our mental defenses through physical intensity. You can't think your way out of that heat. You can't intellectualize visions of cosmic light. You either surrender or suffer —and sometimes the suffering IS the surrender.

As we've become more focused on material success and less connected to spiritual traditions, we've lost something vital. These rituals and ceremonies that once marked every major life transition—puberty, adulthood, marriage, death—have been replaced by... what exactly? A piss-up at the pub for your 18th? A gender reveal party that sets fire to half of California?

This isn't just some nostalgic "things were better in the old days" rant. Studies show that losing these rituals correlates directly with rising anxiety, depression, and isolation—we're literally making ourselves sick by disconnecting from practices that helped humans navigate life for millennia.

Think about it—historically, every major life transition had a rite of passage. You weren't just expected to figure out adulthood on your own; the community guided you through it with ceremony and wisdom. Now we wonder why young people feel lost and disconnected, why mental health issues are skyrocketing. Could be because we've stripped away the very structures that helped humans make sense of existence.

But here's the hopeful bit: these practices are coming back. More people are seeking out sweat lodges, plant medicines, meditation retreats —not as trendy wellness experiences but as genuine attempts to reconnect with something we've lost. The challenge is doing it authentically, with wholehearted respect for the traditions we're drawing from, rather than creating some watered-down version for Instagram.

My sweat lodge experience showed me what we're missing. Not just the visions or the heat or the ceremony itself, but the container it created for real change. The way ancient wisdom held space for my modern consciousness to expand. These aren't outdated primitive practices— they're technologies for human development that we abandoned at our own peril.

As we stumble forward trying to make sense of an increasingly mental world, perhaps the answer isn't always in the next app or life hack. Maybe sometimes it's in returning to practices that have worked for thousands of years. Not to live in the past, but to bring forward the wisdom we need for the present.

And hey, if you do seek out one of these experiences, do your home-work. Find someone who learned from actual Indigenous elders, not some bloke who bought some sage on Amazon and did a weekend course in Malibu. When we approach these practices with respect—letting tradi-tions that go back thousands of years guide us—we can really open ourselves to transformation that our normal consciousness simply can't access.

Just maybe pack extra water. Take my word for it.

———

CHAPTER 8 SUMMARY

So Chapter 8 was basically a tour through humanity's consciousness-hacking toolkit—from prayer and meditation to sweat lodges and float tanks. I shared my Sadique dream (meeting my primal masculine in the form of a Swahili-speaking gorilla), the Lionsgate Portal synchronicity cascade, and that mind-bending sweat lodge where reality basically said 'watch this' and showed off. Turns out we've been trying to dial up the universe's customer service line since forever.

KEY LEARNINGS:

- Ancient practices aren't outdated—they're technologies for consciousness expansion
- Dreams can deliver insights that would take years of therapy to reach
- Synchronicities often escalate during periods of intense integration
- Group consciousness events can create impossible alignments

KEY TAKEAWAYS:

- The word "Phasm" exists for experiences between worlds—finally, a label!
- Your unconscious speaks multiple languages, including ones you don't consciously know
- Flow state might be our most accessible gateway to expanded consciousness
- Plant medicines are powerful but require serious respect and preparation

Reflective Question: What consciousness-expanding practice keeps calling to you that you've been too scared or skeptical to try?

"We shall not cease from exploration, and the end of all our exploring will be to arrive where we started and know the place for the first time."

— T.S. Eliot

MODERN GATEWAYS TO EXPANDED CONSCIOUSNESS

You know that feeling when you're at a concert and everyone starts swaying to the same rhythm? That moment when thousands of strangers somehow sync up without anyone orchestrating it? Well, that's just scratching the surface of what can happen when groups of people come together with focused intention.

Throughout Part 2, we've been exploring different ways people try to crack open ordinary consciousness—from float tanks to sweat lodges to interdimensional tent flights (yeah, that happened). But what's been gnawing at me is this: the wildest experiences I've had weren't solo—they happened in groups, all of us aligned, energetically speaking.

And no, nobody made me wear robes or drink anything weird. That time!

GROUP CONSCIOUSNESS EVENTS: TAPPING INTO THE POWER OF COLLECTIVE INTENTION

Group consciousness events come in all flavors. You've got your mass meditations where thousands of people sit together, breathing in sync, focusing on peace or healing or whatever the intention might be. Sounds a bit woo-woo? Maybe. But there's something undeniably powerful about that many hearts and minds aligned. Remember how I described that week on the mountain in Appalachia, where we gradually synced up through ceremony and shadow work? That's exactly what I'm talking about.

Then there's group visualization workshops—everyone closing their eyes and imagining the same outcome. It's like a massive psychic art class where everyone's painting the same mental picture, hoping their collective imagination might give reality a nudge.

Different traditions have their own versions of healing circles. People gather, maybe chanting, maybe drumming, maybe just holding space while looking slightly uncomfortable (that'd be me). The focus is on healing—sometimes for someone specific, sometimes for the world, sometimes just... healing in general. The energy in these circles can get intense. I've been in ones where the air felt so thick with whatever we were generating, you could practically swim through it.

And of course, every culture has its community rituals. Harvest festivals, coming-of-age ceremonies, your nan's Sunday roast. They're not just about marking time—they're about creating shared meaning, shared experience. Even if you're not particularly religious or spiritual, you've probably felt it singing carols at Christmas or counting down to midnight on New Year's Eve. There's something that happens when humans do things together, in sync, with purpose.

I've been fortunate enough to participate in several healing circles over the years as part of my own ongoing journey. These gatherings—whether in the mountains, by the ocean, or deep in the forest—have become essential moments of leeway on my journey. Each one different, yet all sharing that quality of creating containers where the impossible becomes... well, still impossible but somehow happening anyway.

In these circles, I've seen collective intention do things that would make a physicist weep. When a group commits to dropping their armor and focusing their energy on mutual support, something definitely happens in the space. You can feel it—like the emotional equivalent of static electricity before a storm. It's that same energy I felt building all week on the mountain before my tent went airborne—that sense of reality getting... negotiable. Through meditation, ceremony, and the kind of vulnerable sharing that would normally have me running for the exits, these groups create conditions where healing seems to accelerate.

But one evening stands out as the moment my rational brain finally threw in the towel and admitted defeat...

I found myself in a tipi with 10 other men after a week-long intensive. We were about to participate in something called a Giveaway Ceremony.

The concept was simple enough: we'd each brought something meaningful from home to give away. Not expensive—meaningful. The kind of thing that carries weight in your life, that has a story. We'd place them anonymously in the center, then take turns choosing gifts. When your gift got picked, you'd reveal yourself and share why you were letting it go.

Our leader explained that this was about energy exchange, the blurring of giver and receiver, creating space by releasing what we're attached to. But there was something in how he said it, in how the tipi felt, that made me pay closer attention. This wasn't going to be just another exercise.

The leader went first, reaching into the pile and selecting a hand-carved wooden octopus sculpture. One of the participants had made it thirty years ago. Interesting synchronicity—the leader had been practicing a fluid movement technique all week that resembled something octopus-like. We exchanged knowing glances. A nice coincidence to start with.

The second person unwrapped a compass. The giver had carried it through a divorce, using it as a reminder to find his true north. The receiver? Going through his own divorce, had literally been journaling about feeling lost that very morning.

A few more exchanges happened—some with little threads of meaning, others just random. But there was this building sense in the tipi that something was happening. Maybe it was just the week of intensive work making us all hyper-aware. Maybe we were reading meaning into normal coincidences.

Then came the drums. One guy unwrapped a bongo. The giver stood up, getting visibly emotional as he explained: this drum had been gifted to him at his very first men's retreat fifteen years ago. It had become part of his family's life—his daughters played it during bedtime rituals, used it for their own ceremonies, treated it like a beloved family member. When he'd packed it for this retreat, they'd wept. They'd even written the drum a goodbye letter, thanking it for all the years of rhythm and comfort it had provided.

But he knew it was time. The drum carried the weight of who he'd been back then—old patterns, old wounds he'd been working to release. Passing it on was part of his own letting go.

After that emotional closure, when it was his turn to pick his gift, my whole body tensed. I knew—somehow just knew—what was about to happen.

He unwrapped another bongo drum.

The tipi went silent except for this collective intake of breath. Another drum. Hand-crafted. Over thirty years old. Never played. Made by another group member as a gift for his father that never got given.

The new drum's owner explained he'd handmade it thirty years ago as a gift for his father, but somehow never gave it to him. It had sat unplayed all these years, waiting.

Two men, two drums, two stories of things held too long, meeting in this impossible moment.

The rest of the ceremony continued with similar impossible alignments. Each exchange seemed to carry its own perfect logic, as if some invisible thread connected giver to receiver in ways none of us could have planned.

That night, lying in my sleeping bag, I couldn't shake this feeling of being watched. Not by a person—by reality itself. Like I'd seen the man behind the curtain, except the man was some kind of interdimensional stage manager who found human confusion amusing.

Whatever happened in that tipi—whether it was collective unconscious shenanigans, morphic field resonance, or just reality pulling my leg—it worked. People left transformed. Old patterns got released. New connections formed through impossible coincidences.

These group consciousness experiences keep teaching me the same lesson: when enough people gather with genuine intention, pointed toward transformation, reality gets... flexible. The usual rules seem to soften. Synchronicities stack up like a rigged deck of cards, except no one's doing the rigging—at least not anyone with a physical body.

The skeptic in me still searches for the trick, some psychological explanation to file this under. But sitting in that tipi, watching impossible meetings unfold one after another, I had to accept that some experiences refuse to fit in neat boxes. They just are.

Starting to notice a pattern yet?

FLOW STATE: GATEWAY TO THE INFINITE?

Have you ever been so completely absorbed in something that time seemed to vanish? Maybe you were playing music, lost in a creative project, or having a conversation that felt particularly meaningful. We call this flow state, and most people think of it as peak performance—when you're fully present, energized but calm, challenged but capable. But what if that's just the surface? What if flow is actually our awareness temporarily breaking free of its usual boundaries, becoming a conduit for something far larger than ourselves?

By now, we've covered a fair amount of ground in this chapter—sacred ceremonies, liminal spaces, inner initiations, and more than a few WTF moments that probably still echo in the background. From those early Sedona experiences to the Lionsgate Portal synchronicities, from the float tank to the sweat lodge visions, from plant medicine ceremonies to that impossible Giveaway Ceremony—what connects all these experiences isn't just that they're weird or consciousness-expanding. It's that they all involve dropping into a particular state of being where the usual rules don't just bend—they dissolve entirely.

Think back to when I described the so-called Lionsgate Portal period—synchronicities were hitting me like waves. Or in the sweat lodge when those visions completely took me over. Or sitting in that tipi watching impossible alignments unfold between the men and their gifts. There's a common thread in all my experiences—moments when I got so absorbed, so aligned, that I became a channel for something larger than myself.

Psychologist Mihaly Csikszentmihalyi (try saying that three times fast) described flow state as "a state of optimal experience characterized by total absorption in the present moment, a sense of effortless action, and a strong sense of fulfillment and purpose."

But here's how that feels in everyday experience: it's when you're so into what you're doing that everything else fades away. You're not thinking about your to-do list, what you'll have for dinner, or that embarrassing thing you said five years ago. You're just... there. Completely present. And somehow, you're performing at your absolute best without even trying.

The brilliant thing about flow is that it doesn't belong to any one specific field or activity. You might find it while surfing a wave, writing a poem, having a heart-to-heart with a friend, solving a tricky problem at work, or even doing the dishes—seriously, some people find flow in the most mundane tasks.

Elite athletes know this space intimately. Tom Brady has talked about those moments in games where everything slows down and he can see the entire field with perfect clarity. LeBron James describes entering "the zone" where the basket looks twice its normal size. Lionel Messi (and yes, even Cristiano Ronaldo, for my fellow futbol fans) speak about moments where their bodies move without conscious thought, where the perfect play unfolds through them rather than from them.

Writers describe it too—that state where the words write themselves, where hours pass in what feels like minutes. Musicians talk about becoming one with their instrument. The music plays itself through them.

There's something fascinating about deep conversations when we're truly in flow. Most of us have experienced this—moments where insights emerge that surprise even us, where we're clearly not drawing from our usual storehouse of knowledge but tapping into something larger. It's as if wisdom flows through the conversation itself rather than from any individual participant.

When we're truly present with someone, information seems to pass through us rather than from us. The right words arrive unbidden by conscious thought, and perspectives emerge that feel fresh and insightful, even to ourselves. We become less deliberate authors and more conduits—a common enough miracle that perhaps marks a subtle crossing of a threshold on our own Hero's Journey.

This resonates deeply with Alan Watts' wisdom. He often suggested that when we cease to interfere with our own minds—when we create that vital "leeway" for the unknown to enter—and become truly receptive, we tap into what he described as a deeper, spontaneous intelligence. (Okay, he didn't actually reference this book when he said "leeway," but the principle fits perfectly with what we're exploring here!)

Now, this might sound like Jung's collective unconscious stuff, but

Watts was pointing at something even simpler—what he called the "Way" or "Tao" of the universe. He wasn't talking about some psychological storage unit we inherit. For Watts, it was the natural flow of how everything works. The basic intelligence built into reality itself. His whole thing was about "getting out of our own way"—stop interfering and let this natural wisdom do its thing through us.

You see this happen in healing circles and deep conversations all the time. It starts with actually listening—like, really listening—and letting whatever bubbles up from your gut just sit there, even when it feels uncomfortable, so you can actually let what's being said land. What then surfaces often feels raw and authentic, a form of guidance stemming from the heart. Maybe it's from the heart, maybe it's that bigger wisdom Watts talked about. But when it happens, you know it. It's like touching something larger than yourself.

For those of us on a growth journey, flow takes on even more significance. When we enter flow during our practices—whether that's meditation, prayer, or dancing around the living room like nobody's watching—we open ourselves to something larger. The boundaries between "me" and "everything else" start to blur in the most beautiful way.

This is why so many of the practices I've talked about in this chapter aim to help us access flow. They create the conditions for us to drop our armor, quiet the mental chatter, and show up completely present.

During a period when I felt particularly connected and in a flow state, I started having what I can only describe as "downloads"—sudden transmissions of insight or imagery that would arrive out of nowhere. Usually while I was sleeping, meditating, or just staring off into space like a weirdo.

One evening, after listening to some music and doing some journaling, I fell into a meditation. That's when something bizarre happened. I found myself mentally transported back to those trippy red rocks of Sedona.

At first, I was just there in the landscape, taking it all in. But then my attention became laser-focused. In my mind's eye, I started zeroing in on the horizontal rings of sandstone and limestone in these formations—you know, those distinct bands that record millions of years of geological time.

Then something extraordinary happened. My perspective changed—as if I was lifted into a bird's-eye view, looking down into the very heart of the rock formation. From this elevated viewpoint, I could see the rings continuing inward. And that's when they started moving, coming alive, morphing into a spiral pattern. The ancient bands spiraled deeper and deeper into the rock, creating an endless inward pathway.

I know how this sounds. Trust me, I was thinking the same thing: "Lee, mate, you're properly losing the plot now, pal." Honestly? It scared the shit out of me. Here I was, a grown man, having visions of spirals in rocks like I'd lost my marbles completely.

But instead of fading away, the vision only got stronger. I found myself following this spiral with my mind's eye, tracing it inward through what felt like millions of years of accumulated history—not just geological time, but something that seemed to carry the weight of all experience, all memory, spiraling deeper like rings in some ancient tree of existence. Each ring felt alive with information, as if dense with collective memory.

And then I hit it—the center of the spiral. The endpoint. It felt like an absolute threshold I simply couldn't cross.

But despite that sense of completion, a stronger sense inside me felt like there was more. Pulling me in, like one of those classic hypnotic spirals. I wanted to continue, but my inner vision reached its limit.

That's when an understanding hit me: the spiral didn't end there. It continued, but beyond what I could follow. Imagine following a spiral that keeps going smaller and smaller until your eyes simply can't track it anymore, even though you know it continues. The spiral was still there, still spiraling inward from that center point, but my mind's eye simply couldn't follow it and see it any further. I was restricted by the limitations of my sight.

But it wasn't just about seeing.

Imagine trying to follow that same spiral with your entire physical form—like reaching a point in a maze where the path continues but you're too big to squeeze through. Like that scene in Willy Wonka where the corridor keeps getting smaller and smaller—you can see the hallway continues stretching ahead, but your body simply can't fit through to follow where it goes. You're standing at this threshold, knowing there's more to explore, but your physical size is the only thing stopping you. If I could somehow be smaller, exist differently, I could keep going into whatever lay beyond. I was literally seeing the edge of what my three-dimensional body and brain could process.

The message was crystal clear—just because I couldn't physically continue didn't mean consciousness itself couldn't. My psyche was showing me something fundamental: our bodies have limits, but awareness itself might not. Our bodies, our brains, our sensory equipment—they're all bound by dimensional limitations. But consciousness? Consciousness might operate beyond those boundaries entirely.

Look, I know how heavy and weird this all sounds. I'm also not suggesting there are actual infinity spirals carved into Sedona's rocks. As we've learned by now, the psyche and subconscious can communicate in mysterious ways. Maybe Sedona was simply the perfect metaphor my subconscious chose—a landscape dramatic enough to get my attention and deliver a message about consciousness and dimensional boundaries? Who knows.

But here's the thing—Sedona wouldn't leave me alone. And after its most recent appearance I found myself tumbling down a bit of a research rabbit hole. And that's when I stumbled across something that made me sit up straight: Sedona actually has documented magnetic anomalies.

The iron oxide that gives those red rocks their otherworldly color? It creates measurable variations in Earth's magnetic field. Real variations. Detectable with actual scientific instruments. The United States Geological Survey (USGS) has documented these anomalies, and research published in scientific journals confirms their existence. Not massive, but they're there.

Which got my mind spinning (never a good sign, that): But what if these magnetic field anomalies affect consciousness in ways we're only beginning to understand? What if they create conditions where the boundaries between dimensions become... thinner?

Everything around us—your morning cuppa tea, the air you're breathing, even you—is made of matter. And all matter is composed of tiny particles like electrons, protons, and neutrons. In our everyday world, these particles behave predictably. Kick a football across a field and it eventually stops rolling because it loses energy through friction. Similarly, electrons and other particles bump into things, lose energy, and come to rest. It's why your car coasts to a stop when you lift off the gas.

Now here's where I leave science behind and go full speculation: But what if Sedona's magnetic fields could interact with charged particles, fundamentally altering their behavior? Imagine those particles doing something that defies common sense—like a football that never stops rolling or a stirred cup of tea that keeps swirling forever without additional input. Instead of gradually losing steam like everything else, these particles would somehow keep moving forever, constantly re-energized by the magnetic fields themselves.

This would—in theory—create a continuous, self-sustaining flow of particles that defies our normal understanding of energy in the physical world. And here's where it gets really wild: What if enough particles caught in this never-ending dance, moving in perfect harmony, could create an energy pattern so intense it actually wears through the fabric of reality itself?

Picture rubbing the same spot on fabric until you create a hole—except the "other side" might be an entirely different dimension.

I know I might be sounding like a complete crackpot here, and I've just committed about seventeen physics crimes in two paragraphs.

But here's what's fascinating—while my portal theory is pure speculation, the science behind magnetic fields affecting consciousness? That's actually real. Research shows geomagnetic variations can affect brain activity, especially in regions linked to altered consciousness. Studies suggest locations with unique magnetic properties correlate with increased reports of heightened experiences.

But the most mind-blowing confirmation was still to come. Years later, I stumbled across something called the Planck scale while researching physics.

Basically, scientists have discovered there's a smallest possible size in the universe. It's unimaginably tiny—like comparing a grain of sand to the entire planet Earth, except even smaller. It's nature's pixel size—the smallest 'dot' in reality's resolution.

At this incredibly tiny scale, something amazing happens: the laws of physics, space and time themselves completely break down. Think of it like zooming into a digital photo until you can see the individual pixels— except when you get to the 'pixels' of reality itself, they start behaving in impossible ways. Now this concept is more mind-bending than trying to explain cricket to an American, but stick with me, I'll try my best.

Remember Ant-Man shrinking down in the movies? At normal size, he can't walk through walls. But shrink small enough, and suddenly he can slip between the spaces in the wall that were always there but too small to see.

That's exactly what my vision had shown me! I hit what felt like a solid wall at the center of the spiral—but the spiral didn't actually stop there. It kept going into spaces too small for my normal perspective and physical body to follow.

Physics was basically confirming what my vision had shown me: what looks like a dead end might just be a doorway you're too big to see. My consciousness somehow knew what scientists are just discovering: what looks like a dead end from our perspective might have secret passages that are only visible from a completely different scale.

It was like my vision had given me a glimpse of reality's hidden architecture—the secret doors that only open when you're looking from the right dimensional angle.

Now, I'm not suggesting ancient civilizations like the Mayans or Anasazi disappeared through magical dimensional gateways. But what if a 'portal' isn't what we typically imagine? What if it's simply a place or moment where perception shifts and awareness opens to new possibilities—where you gain access to new vantage points that were always there but previously invisible?

Maybe these civilizations didn't vanish mysteriously at all. What if they achieved such expanded awareness that they could foresee natural disasters, societal collapse, or simply received insight that they wouldn't thrive in their current circumstances anymore? Through their own version of 'portal experiences'—moments of expanded consciousness—they gained the perspective to see beyond immediate limitations and make decisions others couldn't even imagine. When you can perceive reality from multiple vantage points, conscious migration to entirely new territories or ways of living becomes not just possible, but obvious.

And what of the infinity spiral? Well, the infinity symbol itself appears across countless cultures and civilizations throughout history—from ancient Celtic knots to Hindu concepts of eternal cycles, from Tibetan endless knots to Native American medicine wheels. This isn't just coincidence. Humans have been seeing these spiral, infinite patterns for millennia, suggesting this insight about consciousness and dimensional boundaries isn't unique to my Sedona vision but something our species has been accessing across time and geography.

So what does all this mean for your own journey? Well, if humans have been accessing these consciousness-expanding insights for millennia, and if physics confirms these dimensional thresholds actually exist, then maybe these experiences aren't rare mystical events but natural capacities we can all develop.

I've come to realize that the Hero's Journey itself isn't just a circle as it's often depicted—it's an infinity spiral. Think about it: when we complete one cycle of departure, initiation, and return, we never actually return to the same place we started. We arrive back with new wisdom, expanded perspective, and different capabilities. We're essentially operating at a new 'dimensional level' of understanding.

Each time we go through the cycle, we're spiraling upward to a new layer of awareness. What looks like an endpoint in our journey—that moment of 'return'—is actually a threshold into the next spiral of growth.

Maybe the modern hero isn't someone seeking one epic quest and retirement. Maybe it's someone who recognizes that each apparent 'arrival' is just the beginning of the next spiral. We don't graduate from growth—we spiral deeper into it.

These modern heroes don't get stuck thinking they've 'arrived' somewhere final. They see the infinity spiral for what it is—an endless invitation to keep growing, keep expanding, keep following the spiral where bodies can't go but consciousness can.

And maybe that's where flow state becomes the gateway. Remember how this whole journey started—I was in a connected flow state when I received that download about the spiral. Perhaps flow isn't just about peak performance or feeling good. Maybe it's actually our most accessible doorway to these expanded states of consciousness.

When we're truly in flow—whether we're creating, problem-solving, or deeply connecting with someone—we might be touching the same dimensional thresholds that physics describes at the Planck scale. We temporarily step beyond our usual boundaries and touch perspectives that were always there but usually hidden.

So those moments when you lose track of time, when insights arrive without effort, when you feel connected to something larger—maybe you're not just having a nice experience. Maybe you're actually practicing dimensional navigation. Maybe you're learning to follow the spiral where consciousness can go but bodies cannot.

The question isn't whether these expanded states exist—physics and human history both suggest they do. The question is: what would change in your life if you started treating every moment of flow not as lucky accident, but as evidence of your consciousness touching something infinite? What would you do differently if you knew that every time you lose yourself in the work, you're actually finding yourself in something larger?

———

CHAPTER 9 SUMMARY

Chapter 9 revealed how group consciousness events tap into collective intention, creating conditions where impossible becomes possible. We explored flow state as a gateway to the infinite, discovered that Sedona's spiral vision connected to actual physics (the Planck scale), and realized the Hero's Journey is actually an infinity spiral—we never arrive, we just spiral deeper. Also, apparently reality has dimensional thresholds we can't physically cross but consciousness can.

KEY LEARNINGS:

- When groups align with genuine intention, reality gets flexible
- Flow state isn't just peak performance—it's dimensional navigation practice
- The infinity spiral appears across all cultures because it's basically true
- Physics confirms what mystics knew: reality has secret passages at tiny scales

KEY TAKEAWAYS:

- Collective consciousness is real and measurably affects outcomes
- Your consciousness can go places your body cannot
- Each Hero's Journey completion is just the beginning of the next spiral
- Sacred sites often have measurable magnetic anomalies—coincidence? Probably not

Reflective Question: If you knew every moment of flow was actually practicing dimensional navigation, how would you approach your creative work differently?

"There is another world, but it is in this one."

– Paul Éluard

Chapter Ten

THE DANCE OF EGO AND SOUL

Integration for the Modern Hero

S o here we are then, approaching the end of Part 2. And I can't help
but keep thinking about that forest clearing I mentioned way back at
the beginning—you know, that moment when you stumble through all the
darkness and suddenly find a patch of light where you can actually catch
your breath. We've ventured through many shadowed paths together,
exploring the ego's quirks and corners, the challenges of authentic connection, and the mysterious territories of consciousness and growth.

THE JOURNEY THROUGH MYSTERY

What a ride it's been, eh? We've traveled from invisible children playing in
my Sedona bedroom to tent levitation in Appalachia—basically a crash
course in "when reality decides to show you who's boss." We've explored
consciousness as humanity's oldest mystery, diving into everything from
ancient shamans painting cave walls to modern float tanks where you
meet... well, whatever the hell that was.

If your head's spinning a bit, that's normal. We've gone from Jacques
Vallée suggesting faeries and aliens might be the same interdimensional
phenomenon to discovering that your cells might actually be smarter than
you think. We've explored why vast open spaces give consciousness room

to breathe and project archetypal material you can't access in cities, and witnessed how the Lionsgate Portal turned reality into a synchronicity cascade—prophetic speeding tickets, Campbell quotes materializing on shelves, and closure arriving exactly when needed.

Then there was that Giveaway Ceremony where impossible alignments unfolded like some cosmic joke, the sweat lodge visions of supreme white light connecting me to thousands of ancestors, and float tank encounters with mysterious "presences" that felt more like meeting lost parts of myself. We discovered that flow state isn't just peak performance but potentially our most accessible gateway to dimensional navigation, and that the word "Phasm"—ancient Greek for apparitions between worlds— gives us language for experiences that have no modern name.

Most importantly, we've seen how consciousness isn't trapped in individual brains but part of a vast, interconnected web where inner work transforms outer reality. The universe has been showing us that quantum entanglement isn't just physics—it's a template for conscious relationship where two whole individuals support each other's highest expression.

Now comes the crucial question: How do we actually integrate all this weirdness into a life that works? How do we bridge the gap between extraordinary consciousness experiences and ordinary daily existence?

Looking at your own journey so far, where do you sense your ego and soul are most out of alignment?

In these pages, I've tried to be what I promised at the outset—not a guru or sage, but a fellow traveler, still failing, still learning, still navigating my own Hero's Journey while offering what insights I've gathered along the way. I've shared stories from the boxing rings of the Australian Outback to the boardrooms of Silicon Valley, each illustrating different aspects of the modern hero's path.

The answer lies in understanding what I've come to see as the most essential dynamic of human existence: the relationship between ego and soul.

UNIVERSAL PRINCIPLES REVISITED: THE COSMIC CONTEXT OF PERSONAL GROWTH

Before we dive into this crucial relationship, let's step back and remember where we began. In Chapter 2, we discovered that growth isn't just a human obsession—it's the operating system of the universe itself. From the explosive inception of the cosmos during the Big Bang, everything has been in a constant state of expansion, adaptation, and evolution.

We explored how this universal drive manifests through a fundamental principle: maintaining internal stability while adapting to external circumstances. This principle emerges at every level of existence—from atoms forming stable bonds while remaining responsive to environmental changes, to ecosystems maintaining balance while evolving, to human consciousness seeking balance while growing.

The same pattern appears in every framework we've explored:

- **Campbell's Hero's Journey:** Departing the known, take a bit of a beating through trials, returning transformed but stable
- **Maslow's Hierarchy:** Meeting basic stability needs while reaching toward growth
- **Jung's Individuation:** Bring your shadow into the light while keeping your ego functional
- **Barrett's Consciousness Levels:** Establishing security while evolving toward service and helping people
- **The Chakra System:** Grounding in lower centers while opening to higher awareness

Every single one of these frameworks point to the same essential truth: growth requires both roots and branches, both foundation and aspiration, both stability and change.

But what does this look like in the lived experience of being human? How do we actually navigate this dance between stability and growth in our daily lives?

The answer lies in understanding the most personal expression of this universal principle: the relationship between ego and soul.

THE EGO-SOUL DYNAMIC: A NEW LANGUAGE FOR ANCIENT WISDOM

Along our journey, we've bumped into this dynamic wearing different costumes. Jung described it as the relationship between the ego and the Self. Maslow explored it through deficiency needs versus growth needs. Eastern traditions speak of it as the relationship between personality and essence. But I've found that the simple terms "ego" and "soul" cut through all the academic jargon and actually help us understand this fundamental aspect of human experience.

Let me be clear about what I mean by these terms, because they've been muddied by both new-age spirituality and pop psychology.

The Ego isn't the enemy—it's the part of our consciousness that maintains our sense of identity and navigates the external world. It typically emerges around age two as a necessary adaptation to living in physical reality. The ego is driven by needs for survival, safety, security, and control. It's the voice that says "I am Lee," that remembers our history, that plans for the future, that protects us from harm.

As spiritual teacher Eckhart Tolle notes, "The ego is a false sense of self, a nonstop stream of mind chatter, a voice in the head that pretends to be you." But I'd refine this: the ego isn't false—it's partial. It's a necessary but limited aspect of who we are.

The Soul represents our most authentic essence—call it our immortal core if you like or our connection to universal consciousness. The soul yearns for growth, connection, self-expression, and contributing to something greater than itself. It's the source of our creativity, intuition, and higher purpose. The poet Rumi really nailed it when he beautifully said,

"The soul has been given its own ears to hear things the mind does not understand."

— RUMI

The soul tends to operate from love, abundance, and unity. It sees beyond the ego's concerns about survival and control to recognize our fundamental connection with all life.

Think of this as a field guide for recognizing which aspect is driving your experience in any given moment. Remember, neither is inherently good or bad—they're just different operating systems with different purposes.

EGO LOVE	SOUL LOVE
MIND	HEART
SECURITY	CREATIVITY
KNOWING	EXPERIENCING
SELFISHNESS	CONTRIBUTION
REACTIVE	RESPONSIVE
SCARCITY	ABUNDANCE
JUDGEMENT	DISCERNMENT
WITHOLDING	OPENNESS
SEPARATION	UNITY
DOING	BEING
CRITICISM	GRATITUDE
PAST / FUTURE	PRESENCE
RESENTMENT	FORGIVENESS
BLAME	UNDERSTANDING
CONTROLLING	FREEING
HURTFUL	HEALING
COMPETITIVE	COOPERATIVE
DENIAL	ACCOUNTABILITY
AVOIDING	ENGAGING
HIDE	SEEK
ME	WE

Figure 8.1: Ego Love vs. Soul Love.

As we can see from Figure 8.1, the ego operates from a place of mind-centered analysis, constantly seeking security and the comfort of knowing. It's inherently selfish in its orientation, reacting to circumstances from a place of perceived scarcity. The ego loves to condemn what it doesn't understand, withholding its gifts until conditions feel safe. It experiences life through separation, always doing rather than just being, criticizing rather than appreciating. The ego lives oriented toward past regrets or future anxieties, holding onto resentment and blame, desperately trying to control outcomes. When the ego dominates our relationships, it can create competition and games, preferring to hide rather than engage authentically.

The soul, by contrast, often speaks through the heart's wisdom, expressing itself through creativity and direct experience. It naturally moves toward contribution, responding rather than reacting, operating from a foundation of abundance. The soul exercises good judgement without condemnation, remaining open and seeing unity where the ego sees separation. It often dwells in *being* rather than constant *doing*, expressing gratitude naturally and staying present-oriented. The soul can forgive more easily, takes responsibility without blame, and frees rather than controls. When the soul guides our relationships, it creates cooperation and win-win integrity, choosing engagement over avoidance, embracing "we" over "me."

Both aspects serve essential functions in our human experience, but the art lies in learning when each is appropriate and making sure they work together rather than against each other.

Here's what I believe is crucial to understand: this isn't about the soul being "good" and the ego being "bad." Both are essential aspects of human existence. The ego provides the stability and structure we need to function in physical reality. The soul provides the growth and meaning that make life worth living.

The challenge—and the art—lies in getting them to dance together rather than fight each other.

In the early stages of human development, the ego needs to dominate as we focus on meeting basic needs and establishing our place in the world. This is healthy and appropriate. A two-year-old needs a strong ego to navigate the complexities of physical and social reality.

But as we mature, especially after our basic needs are reasonably secure, the soul begins to call more loudly. This is when we start feeling that familiar restlessness—that sense that "there must be more than this." It's the soul's desire for expression, connection, and contribution beginning to emerge.

The problems can arise when either aspect dominates completely:

- **When the ego dominates:** We can become trapped in survival mode even when we're safe, driven by fear and scarcity, constantly defending and controlling, disconnected from meaning and joy.
- **When we try to bypass the ego:** We might become ungrounded, impractical, unable to function effectively in the world, often spiritually inflated and disconnected from reality.

Integration occurs when we learn to honor both aspects—providing the ego with enough security and recognition to relax its defensive stance, while creating space for the soul's desires for growth, creativity, and service.

THE TREE OF LIFE: EGO AND SOUL IN PERFECT BALANCE

Throughout this journey, we've returned repeatedly to the Tree of Life as our guiding metaphor. Now we can see its meaning: the ego and soul in dynamic balance.

The roots of the tree represent the ego—descending into the dark earth, creating stability, drawing nutrients, anchoring the entire structure. Without strong roots, the tree cannot survive storms or reach its full height.

The branches and leaves represent the soul—reaching toward light, expressing beauty, bearing fruit, contributing oxygen to the world. Without healthy branches, the tree cannot fulfill its purpose or continue its species.

Just as a tree needs both strong roots and flourishing branches to thrive, we need both a stable ego and an expressed soul to achieve true wholeness. Neither can exist successfully without the other.

This pulls together everything we've been exploring:

- **Jung's individuation:** The ego (roots) has to be strong enough to handle meeting the unconscious (soil), so the Self (full tree) can emerge

- **Maslow's hierarchy:** Basic needs (root system) have to be met before growth needs (branches) can be fully expressed
- **Campbell's Hero's Journey:** The hero must be grounded in their ordinary world (roots) before they can venture into the unknown and return with gifts (fruit)
- **The chakra system:** Lower chakras (root system) provide the foundation for higher chakras (crown/branches) to open

When ego and soul are working in harmony, we can experience what Jung called "the privilege of a lifetime"—becoming who we truly are. We might feel grounded yet aspiring, secure yet growing, individual yet connected.

As we achieve greater harmony between ego and soul, something beautiful often begins to emerge: a natural desire to serve something greater than ourselves. This isn't forced altruism or spiritual obligation—it's the organic result of feeling secure in who we are (ego) while connected to the larger web of existence (soul).

The journey of human emergence can naturally lead us to this place where our own growth and fulfillment become inextricably linked to the well-being of others and the planet as a whole. When we've done the work of integration, service doesn't feel like sacrifice—it can feel like the most natural expression of who we've become.

As beautiful as this integration journey has been to explore together, we find ourselves at a unique moment in human history where this work has never been more critical. We're living through what many call a "meaning crisis"—rising rates of anxiety, depression, and isolation despite unprecedented material prosperity. We're facing challenges that require not just individual healing but collective wisdom: climate change, social division, and the breakdown of traditional meaning-making structures.

The Hero's Journey was never meant to be a private affair. Campbell understood that the hero returns with gifts that serve the community. In our hyperconnected yet strangely disconnected world, we bloody well need people who've done the inner work of integration—people who are able to respond rather than react, who can operate from abundance rather than scarcity, who are able to see connection rather than separation.

This isn't spiritual bypassing or naive optimism. It's recognizing that the external challenges we face are reflections of internal imbalances blown up big. A world where ego dominates without soul guidance can create the very problems we're now confronting. But a world where more people achieve ego-soul integration? That could become a world capable of conscious evolution.

Our personal journey of becoming whole isn't selfish—it's the most generous gift we can offer a world in need of conscious leadership at every level.

Which brings us to the practical question: How do we actually do this work? How do we move from understanding these concepts to living them in our daily lives? How do we create the leeway—the shelter, space, and support—necessary for our emergence?

These are the questions I'll explore in depth in *Becoming a Modern Hero: A Practical Handbook for Living the Hero's Journey.* But before we close this journey together, I want to share how this ego-soul integration actually manifested in my own life. Because while the practical tools and exercises await you in the companion guide, sometimes the most powerful teaching comes through witnessing transformation in action.

LOVE AND QUANTUM ENTANGLEMENT: WHEN INNER WORK TRANSFORMS OUTER REALITY

What is love? Ah, the age-old question that has puzzled philosophers, poets, psychologists, and even '90s Eurodance singer Haddaway. While his catchy refrain of "What is love? Baby, don't hurt me" may have ruled the dance floors, it hardly scratches the surface of what I'm about to share with you.

This story begins at the end of that long, difficult integration period I've been describing throughout this book. After years of inner work— therapy, retreats, shadow integration, consciousness exploration—I found myself in a completely different relationship with love and partnership than I'd ever experienced before.

My parents had set the bar pretty high for love. Together since they were thirteen, they made love look effortless. To me, that relationship became the gold standard—but unconsciously, I began holding their dynamic as the only valid model for love.

For years, I chased that ideal, guided by comfort, safety, and a romantic notion of what love should look like. But as we explored in my dream about the witchy women and the alien being, I was unconsciously seeking the maternal in the romantic, trying to heal childhood wounds through adult relationships.

This pattern led to a series of relationships that followed a familiar script: intense attraction to emotionally complex women, followed by my unconscious casting myself as the rescuer or stabilizer. I thought I was being loving, but I was actually being driven by unmet needs and unconscious projections.

After the serious inner work—particularly that dream where the alien being gave me the pearl of wisdom about the difference between maternal and romantic love—something fundamental shifted in my psyche. I was finally free to recognize a completely different kind of partnership.

Picture this: fresh off a period of intense self-discovery, I find myself sitting across from my future wife, a molecular biologist, at a cozy café. The date seemed to be teetering on the edge of disaster, thanks to my tendency for discussing matters that most people reserve for late-night philosophy classes—or at least until after a few dates.

You know you've veered off the typical first-date script when you find yourself diving headlong into theories about the nature of love. In a fit of total enthusiasm, I launched into a soliloquy that would make a Hallmark card writer blush.

"So, what do you think about love?" she asked, with that direct curiosity I'd learn was characteristic of her scientific mind.

Channeling my inner philosopher, I responded: "Imagine two particles. Each has its own vibrational frequency, and sometimes they meet other particles that resonate in a complementary way. They don't become one; instead, they dance around each other, creating a vortex of energy—the force we call love. External forces can distance these particles, but they remain connected, always able to support and elevate each other's existence. When they're in sync, the universe rewards them with synchronicities."

I won't lie; my first-date sermon on love was more than a bit over the top. My poetic waxing could've been an episode right out of "When Spirituality Goes Cheesy." As I went on about particles and vibrations, my future wife cut through the philosophical fog with a simple question, asked with deadpan precision: "So, you're talking about science?"

Let's pause for a moment to appreciate the irony. Here I was, fresh off a transformative journey filled with therapy, ceremonies, and lots of soul-searching. I had just laid bare my most esoteric views on love, hoping for a love-struck nod or an impressed sigh. Instead, she took my abstract, intuitive understanding and tied it neatly to a scientific principle known as quantum entanglement.

My wife eloquently explained that quantum entanglement is a phenomenon where particles become so deeply connected that their properties are intertwined, no matter the distance separating them. Change the state of one particle, and the other reacts instantaneously. Ring a bell?

My whole spiel about particles vibrating and dancing around each other in a "vortex of love" was less mystical revelation and more Physics 101, according to my brilliant future wife.

This was a humbling moment for me, but also an eye-opening one. I had no idea I'd stumbled into scientific territory; this understanding had emerged purely from intuition and inner work. My wife's explanation didn't debunk my thoughts; it validated them. It also gave us a shared language for discussing a subject that is often divisive and misunderstood.

I realized that the language of science can bridge gaps and bring a balanced, inclusive understanding that doesn't get stuck in either pure spirituality or hard science.

The Science of Love: Quantum Entanglement in Relationship

Here's where quantum physics gets interesting—and how it connects to conscious love. The concept of quantum entanglement is fascinatingly complex yet remarkably intuitive when you break it down.

In essence, when two particles are entangled, a change in the state of one particle is immediately reflected in its partner, regardless of the distance between them. Einstein famously dubbed this "spooky action at a distance," and I can't help but think of it as an eloquent metaphor for the bonds that form in conscious relationship.

Here's a simple way to picture this: imagine you and your partner each have a coin that's been 'entangled.' No matter how far apart you are—

whether you're in London and they're in Tokyo—when you flip your coin and it lands heads, their coin instantly lands tails. Not because of any signal traveling between the coins, but because they're fundamentally connected at a level that goes beyond physical space.

In relationship terms, this might look like thinking about your partner just as they're thinking about you, or both of you independently deciding to call each other at the same moment. It's those uncanny synchronicities that happen when two people are deeply connected—not coincidence, but evidence of genuine entanglement at the level of consciousness.

Imagine you and your partner as these entangled particles. You could be continents apart, both navigating the ups and downs of your individual Hero's Journeys, yet the connection remains. It's as if there's an invisible thread that links your consciousness, a thread that isn't bound by the laws of time and space.

But here's where quantum physics offers another mind-boggling insight. In the famous double-slit experiment, particles behave differently when they're being observed versus when they're not. When you're not observing which path the particle takes, it behaves as if it goes through both paths simultaneously. But the moment you observe it, the particle "chooses" a specific path. It's like the universe's version of "a watched pot never boils"—except here, the watching actually changes what happens.

How does this relate to conscious love? Think of observation as attention and intention. When you focus on your partner—really focus, not just casually observe—you might influence their reality, bringing out certain aspects of them. And when they focus on you with love and presence, the same thing can happen. Just like in the quantum world, conscious attention seems to influence reality.

This understanding transformed how I approached relationship. Instead of seeking someone to complete me or heal my wounds, I was now looking for what I call "quantum entanglement"—a connection where two whole individuals support each other's highest expression while maintaining their unique vibrations.

What made this relationship different from all my previous patterns was that it wasn't based on projection. I wasn't unconsciously casting my partner in the role of the nurturing mother figure. She wasn't looking to me to rescue her or provide something she couldn't provide for herself.

Instead, we met each other as conscious individuals who had each done significant inner work. My ego was secure enough not to need constant validation or control. My soul was expressed enough to offer genuine gifts rather than seeking to take or fix.

Similarly, she approached the relationship from her own integrated place—scientifically grounded yet spiritually curious, intellectually rigorous yet emotionally open.

As Carl Jung observed, "The meeting of two personalities is like the contact of two chemical substances: if there is any reaction, both are transformed." But what Jung was pointing to is exactly what can happen in this entangled state—two distinct entities that can become mysteriously connected while maintaining their individual properties.

This love story represents more than just personal happiness—it demonstrates how inner work can translate into transformed outer reality. Every framework we've explored, every consciousness experience we've discussed, every piece of shadow work and ego integration—it all culminated in this capacity for conscious relationship.

The dream about the witchy women and the alien being had cleared the psychological space for this new type of love to enter my life. The consciousness explorations had shown me that reality is far more interconnected than our isolated egos assume. The ego-soul integration work had created the internal stability necessary to meet another person without neediness or projection.

This wasn't just a relationship—it was proof that the Hero's Journey works. That consciousness exploration can lead to practical transformation. That all this inner work can bear fruit in the outer world.

I'm incredibly grateful for the balanced perspective my wife and I have cultivated together. I admire how she appreciates the poetic beauty in scientific phenomena, while I find powerful intuitive truths reflected in rigorous science. Her scientific insights merge seamlessly with my intuitive understanding, enriching our discussions on everything from cellular biology to the nature of consciousness.

This synergy isn't just a happy coincidence; it's evidence that different worldviews can not only coexist but also evolve together, guiding us both toward a more nuanced and complete understanding of existence.

When you understand that love can operate like entangled particles, you see why maintaining individual journeys within relationship is so crucial. You don't merge into one blended mass; you dance around each other in complementary orbits. And just like entangled particles, your individual actions have ripple effects, strengthening or weakening the field between you.

Whether you're in a committed relationship or still seeking partnership, getting your head around quantum entanglement can enrich your understanding of conscious love. It can help you navigate the complexities of human connection with a sense of wonder and scientific curiosity, rather than unrealistic expectations or unconscious projections.

THE PERFECT INTEGRATION

When I think about this experience now, I see how perfectly it illustrates the entire journey we've been exploring throughout this book. Without the shadow work, I might never have recognized my unconscious maternal projections. Without the consciousness exploration, I might not have understood the interconnected nature of reality. Without the ego-soul integration, I might have approached this relationship from old patterns of neediness or control.

Each step in the Hero's Journey had prepared me for this moment of transformation—this integration of intuition and science, of spiritual understanding and practical application, of inner work bearing fruit in outer relationship.

The universe seems to operate on the principle that when we do our inner work authentically, external reality reorganizes itself to match our new level of consciousness. What we call "synchronicity" might simply be this entangled dance between inner and outer reality becoming visible.

"How terrible to think of not being
the hero of one's own life;
this is the role for which each of us is cast,
no matter how unsuccessfully we play it.
And if the part seems too big,
if we picture the hero as being indeed "more than
life sized",
it is because our daily life has dwindled,
become less than real,
and only pygmy proportions seem natural to us."

- Dorothea Dooling

PART TWO CONCLUSION

The Spiral Continues

So here I am, looking back at this wild, impossible journey, and what strikes me isn't how far I've come—it's that I'm still traveling. The Hero's Journey doesn't end with enlightenment or a perfect relationship or some final achievement. It spirals. Each completion and entry of the center point opens up a new spiral and dimension of being. Each mastery becomes tomorrow's apprenticeship.

That love I found—built on mutual respect rather than desperate projection? It wasn't the destination. It became the launchpad for conscious fatherhood, for deeper work, for challenges I couldn't have imagined when I was a young lad prize fighting his way through the Australian outback. Like life, every punch in that boxing ring was scripture. Every knockdown, resurrection. That tent wasn't teaching me to fight; it was teaching me that the thing trying to break you is actually trying to wake you.

This is what everything in Part 2 keeps circling back to: consciousness isn't individual. It's not locked in our heads. Every impossible encounter, every weird experience, every synchronicity that defied explanation—they're all glimpses of the same truth. We're not separate beings struggling alone. We're nodes in something vast, each of us a unique expression of universal consciousness having a temporary human experience.

Writing these final words, I keep returning to that sailor's wisdom about leeway—the protected space where winds calm and waters settle, where you can finally breathe and recalibrate. But leeway isn't a place you arrive at. It's what makes the voyage possible. Everything we've explored—from shadow work to consciousness expansion, from ego transcendence to soul alignment—has been about creating this essential space. Space to breathe, to grow, to become who we truly are beneath all the programming and conditioning.

The three elements of leeway we discussed at the beginning of the book—shelter, space, and support—take on greater meaning now:

1. **Shelter:** The safe containers created through therapy, retreats, and conscious community where we can drop our masks and do authentic inner work.
2. **Space:** The psychological and spiritual room we create by releasing limiting beliefs, integrating shadow material, and opening to expanded consciousness.
3. **Support:** The allies we find on the journey—mentors, fellow travelers, and ultimately the conscious partnerships that emerge when we're ready to love from wholeness rather than neediness.

With these three elements in place, we can better navigate storms, explore any territory, become who we're meant to be. That's leeway.

The beautiful paradox? You can't wait until you're ready to create it. You start where you are, with what you have. A single conscious breath. One honest conversation. The smallest step toward what feels real.

A mentor of mine, Michael Mervosh, whose guidance through the Hero's Journey Foundation has shaped not just my understanding but my entire approach to life, puts it this way:

"Honor where you've been - accept where you now are - and prepare yourself to step differently into your future. Be the hero of your own life."

This isn't about becoming someone new. It's about finally being who you've always been underneath the armor. Honor the wounds that taught you. Accept this moment as your starting point. Step forward knowing you're writing your own story now.

And as you take that step, you learn to trust the process. Trust that your psyche knows how to grow. Trust that the universe is conspiring to help you become who you're meant to be. Trust that every challenge is also an opportunity, every breakdown is also a breakthrough, every ending is also a beginning.

Never forget that same force that spent 13.8 billion years turning stardust into consciousness is working through you right now. Every star that formed, every atom that bonded, every creature that learned to cooperate, all of it prepared the universe for your unique contribution.

That contribution? It's not your achievements or accomplishments. It's you, whole, integrated, awake.

Carl Jung understood:

> *"The privilege of a lifetime is to become who you truly are."*

But I've come to understand something more:

> *The true gift isn't finding your self; it's recognizing that you were always your self, and you were never really lost. The journey itself was the transformation.*

You're not reading these words by accident.

That restless hunger we talked about at the beginning?

It's not a problem.

It's the universe calling you home to yourself.

You've already opened the door.

Come, come, whoever you are.

ALSO BY LEE MALCHER

Becoming A Modern Hero - The Practical Handbook (2025)

You've opened the door. Now here's how to walk through it.

Where *LeeWay* revealed the path, *Becoming a Modern Hero* provides the practical tools for your own journey. This companion handbook transforms philosophy into daily practice through shadow work exercises that actually work, integration practices for impossible experiences, navigation tools for each stage of the spiral, and real-world applications for everything you've just discovered.

The journey from knowing to living begins here.

Maskup: The Modern Hero's Guide to Hustle and Harmony (2026)

You've done the inner work. Your boss still sucks. Or do they?

The third book in the Modern Hero series explores the messy reality after transformation: how to stay true to yourself while keeping your job. Because morning meditations get interrupted by Slack notifications, and your authentic self still needs to pay rent.

Learn the Mask Up Method—how to consciously wear the professional mask without becoming it. Strategic authenticity for emerged beings with material needs.

For everyone trying to honor their soul while hitting their KPIs. Because enlightenment doesn't pay the bills.

ABOUT THE AUTHOR

Lee Malcher is a writer and modern myth-maker exploring what it really means to grow, transform, and emerge as who you're meant to be. His work lives at the intersection of psychology, spirituality, and raw human experience—where ancient wisdom meets modern struggle.

Before writing *Leeway: Emerging Through the Modern Hero's Journey*, Lee spent years tracing the arc of transformation through his own life: from prize-fighting in Australian carnival tents to corporate boardrooms and sacred ceremonies in the mountains. His writing blends memoir, myth, and meaning into stories that speak to anyone standing at the crossroads of change.

He walks in two worlds: by day he's a business consultant helping brands grow, while by night he guides individuals through their own heroic emergence. The common thread? Real growth—personal or professional—requires facing what's hidden, embracing what's been rejected, and having the courage to become authentic.

Lee lives in San Diego with his wife—a molecular biologist who keeps him grounded—and their children, who remind him daily that presence matters more than enlightenment. When he's not writing over at modernherocollective.com or growing brands, you'll find him walking the California coastline or playing soccer with friends and his kids.

SUGGESTED READING

This book sits at the intersection of mythology, depth psychology, and the science of consciousness. If you're a Modern Hero ready for the next spiral, maybe start here.

I. THE HERO'S JOURNEY & PSYCHOLOGICAL FRAMEWORKS (STRUCTURE & SELF)

- **The Hero with a Thousand Faces** (Joseph Campbell). The definitive monomyth map; language for transformation.
- **Pathways to Bliss: Mythology and Personal Transformation** (Joseph Campbell). How to apply myth directly to modern life.
- **The Power of Myth** (Joseph Campbell & Bill Moyers). Accessible conversations on archetypes and meaning.
- **Man and His Symbols** (Carl Jung). Clear intro to Ego, Shadow, Anima/Animus, and the Self.
- **Finding Meaning in the Second Half of Life** (James Hollis). A sober guide to individuation through mid-life changes.
- **Motivation and Personality** (Abraham Maslow). Foundations for needs, safety, and self-actualization.

- **The Road Less Traveled** (M. Scott Peck). Discipline, love, and reality as paths to maturity.
- **Flow: The Psychology of Optimal Experience** (Mihaly Csikszentmihalyi). The classic on flow states and deep engagement.
- **The Hero's Mythic Adventure: Walking in Two Worlds, Becoming the Bridge** (Michael Mervosh). A straightforward incorporation of the Hero's Journey myth.

II. GLOBAL CONTEXT & EVOLUTIONARY CONSCIOUSNESS (THE BIG PICTURE)

- **Sapiens: A Brief History of Humankind** (Yuval Noah Harari). How shared myths shape human emergence and power.
- **Soul-Centred Living: From Survival to Service** (Richard Barrett). A practical map for aligning needs with purpose.
- **Sophie's World** (Jostein Gaarder). A story-led primer on Western philosophy to place myth and self-inquiry in context.

III. CONSCIOUSNESS, FOLKLORE & SCIENCE (EDGES & SPECULATION)

- **Passport to Magonia: On UFOs, Folklore, and Parallel Worlds** (Jacques Vallée). Faeries, UFOs, and the same phenomenon in different costumes.
- **Abduction: Human Encounters with Aliens** (John E. Mack). Psychiatrist's study of abduction narratives and psychological impact.
- **The Threat** (David M. Jacobs). A controversial researcher's thesis on abductions and programmatic patterns.
- **Science Set Free** (*aka* **The Science Delusion***)* (Rupert Sheldrake). Nine "dogmas" of science re-examined; morphic resonance/memory of nature.

- **Food of the Gods** (Terence McKenna). Psychedelics, culture, and the "stoned ape" hypothesis.
- **True Hallucinations** (Terence McKenna). A firsthand mythopoetic expedition into psyche and symbol.
- **The Mind in the Cave: Consciousness and the Origins of Art** (David Lewis-Williams). Cave art as visions from altered states.
- **The Fairy-Faith in Celtic Countries** (W.Y. Evans-Wentz). Ethnographic accounts of seership and the otherworld.
- **An Outline of Esoteric Science** (Rudolf Steiner). A core map of Steiner's supersensible worldview.
- **The Secret Commonwealth of Elves, Fauns and Fairies** (Robert Kirk). A 17th-century minister's account of faerie beings "like us, but without bodies."
- **Flatland: A Romance of Many Dimensions** (Edwin A. Abbott). A parable on perception limits and paradigm shifts— 2D minds meeting 3D reality.
- **Sphereland: A Fantasy About Curved Spaces and an Expanding Universe** (Dionys Burger). Extends *Flatland*— curved space, relativity, and "seeing more" made intuitive.

IV. MYTHOPOETIC, INTEGRATION & EMBODIMENT (PRACTICAL NEXT STEPS)

- **The Book of Awakening** (Mark Nepo). Daily presence practices to stay with the work.
- **Iron John: A Book About Men** (Robert Bly). Masculine initiation and integrated strength.
- **Fate & Destiny: The Two Agreements of the Soul** (Michael Meade). Mythic framing for calling and destiny

V. PHILOSOPHICAL & SPIRITUAL WISDOM

- **The Essential Rumi** (trans. Coleman Barks, Rumi). Poems on soul, intuition, love—"ears the mind can't hear with."

- **Thus Spoke Zarathustra** (Friedrich Nietzsche). Root/branch wisdom on becoming and growth; fierce self-overcoming.
- **The Wisdom of Insecurity** (Alan Watts). Presence, spontaneity, and trusting the Way.
- **The Republic** (Plato). Allegory of the Cave and the education of perception.

VI. POETRY FOR THE ROAD (SHORT DOSES, BIG EFFECT)

- **The Three Marriages** (David Whyte). Poetic, practical reflections on work, self, and relationship.
- **River Flow** (David Whyte). Selected poems to move from concept to felt truth.
- **The House of Belonging** (David Whyte). Poems for belonging, courage, and return.

VII. MEDITATION (KEEP IT SIMPLE, DAILY)

- **Practicing Mindfulness: 75 Essential Meditations** (Matthew Sockolov). Straightforward, doable daily practices.

RESOURCES

HERO'S JOURNEY—COMMUNITY

- **Hero's Journey Foundation.** Wilderness intensives (men's & women's), 16-week web-courses, Soul Tavern weekends, and more. Visit: herosjourneyfoundation.org
- **Joseph Campbell Foundation.** Official hub for Campbell's work: MythBlast, podcasts, events, and archives—anchor for ongoing study. Visit: jcf.org
- **C.G. Jung Institute of San Francisco.** Public programs and analyst training; doorway into living Jungian community. Visit: junginstitute.org
- **Jung Society of Washington (James Hollis).** Hollis teaches live/recorded Zoom series here. Visit: jung.org

PODCASTS & LONGFORM DIALOGUES (GATEWAYS TO THE WORK)

- **This Jungian Life (Lisa Marchiano, Deborah Stewart, Joseph Lee).** Weekly depth-psych conversations + listener dream analysis; 25M+ downloads. Also offers Dream School if you want a structured practice. Visit: thisjungianlife.com

- **The Power of Myth (Audio Series) (Campbell/Moyers).** The core myth conversation in its most accessible form. Visit: pbs.org/show/joseph-campbell-and-power-myth/

www.ingramcontent.com/pod-product-compliance
Lightning Source LLC
Chambersburg PA
CBHW051607120626
46551CB00014B/1707